safirka

safirka

An American Envoy

Peter Bridges

The Kent State University Press
Kent, Ohio, and London

© 2000 by The Kent State University Press, Kent, Ohio 44242
All rights reserved
Library of Congress Catalog Card Number 99-055501
ISBN 0-87338-658-2
Manufactured in the United States of America

06 05 04 03 02 01 00   5 4 3 2 1

Portions of this work appeared in slightly different form in *Diplomacy & Statecraft* (9:2, July 1998), *Michigan Quarterly Review* (37:1, Winter 1998), and the *Virginia Quarterly Review* (73:3, Summer 1997; 76:1, Winter 2000).

The lines by Andrew Marvell are from "Upon Appleton House," reprinted in *Andrew Marvell: Selected Poems*, ed. Fred Marnau (London: Grey Walls Press, 1948).

Library of Congress Cataloging-in-Publication Data
Bridges, Peter, 1932–
    Safirka: an American envoy / Peter Bridges.
        p.   cm.
    Includes bibliographical references and index.
    ISBN 0-87338-658-2 (cloth: alk. paper)
    1. Bridges, Peter, 1932– 2. Ambassadors—United States—Biography.
    3. Ambassadors—Somalia—Biography. 4. United States—Foreign relations—
    Somalia. 5. Somalia—Foreign relations—United States. 6. Somalia—Politics and
    government—1960–1991. I. Title.

E840.8.B75 A3 2000
327.73'0092—dc21
[B]   99-055501

British Library Cataloging-in-Publication are available.

This book is dedicated to my fellow travelers
Mary Jane, David, Elizabeth, Mary, and Andrew.

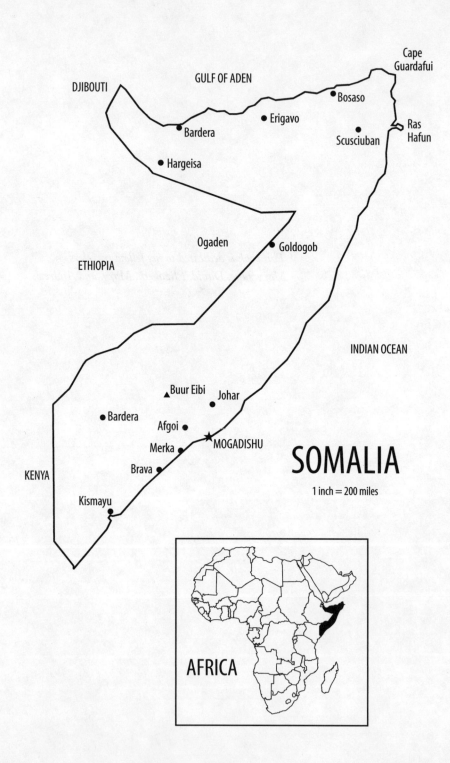

Cape
Guardafui

DJIBOUTI

GULF OF ADEN

Bosaso

Erigavo

Ras
Hafun

Bardera

Scusciuban

Hargeisa

Ogaden

Goldogob

ETHIOPIA

INDIAN OCEAN

Buur Eibi
Johar

Bardera

Afgoi

MOGADISHU

Merka

SOMALIA

KENYA

Brava

1 inch = 200 miles

Kismayu

AFRICA

Why should, of all things, man, unrul'd,
Such unproportioned dwellings build?
The beasts are by their denns exprest,
And birds contrive an equal nest;
The low-roof'd tortoises do dwell
In cases fit of tortoise-shell:
No creature loves an empty space;
Their bodies measure out their place.
But he, superfluously spread,
Demands more room alive than dead.

—Andrew Marvell

contents

introduction

In spite of the tragic recent history of Somalia, there is a dearth of books about that country and its people. The horrors of the Somali civil war were extensively covered, at least as long as they continued, by world media. The massive intervention by the United States and by the United Nations in the early 1990s has been described in several published works. But what happened before that in Somalia? What comes next in a Somalia that heads the list of failed states? The country has fallen out of the headlines, but its millions of likable and intelligent humans still want—and deserve—a decent place in the world. Can they have any hope of this in a region still prey to strife and famine?

This book recounts my experiences as a career officer of the American Foreign Service, as ambassador to Somalia in 1984–86 and during the years before I went to Africa. Our Foreign Service includes many experienced Africanists, but I was not one of these; I was experienced in diplomacy, but before I went to Mogadishu I had traveled only briefly in Africa. What follows, then, does not claim to be the commentary of a lifelong expert on Africa but simply an objective account by a man who came to love Somalia, but not its dictatorial president; who studied carefully that country's long and fascinating past and its appalling present; who did what he thought right both for American interests and for Somalia, sometimes on instructions from Washington and sometimes without them.

I have tried to avoid a dry, diplomatic account. I want to convey to readers what it is like to spend three decades in the Foreign Service: what it is like to be a young vice consul in Panama, a political officer in Moscow, a senior officer in Washington, an ambassador in Africa. It is not just what you tell the country's president but what you think to yourself; it is not just what you report to Washington but what your senses tell you as you run along a Somali beach at glorious dawn—or when you see emaciated infants dying in a dusty refugee camp. This ambassador got out of Somalia before its final collapse, but as long as he lives the tragedy and beauty of that country will stay with him, and so will the question whether America might have pursued a better policy in Somalia and elsewhere in postcolonial Africa. The horrors of Somalia's civil war and the problems of America's African policy are the subjects, almost inevitably, of the concluding part of this book.

There is a Somali proverb that goes, *Run iyo ilkaba waa la caddeeyaa*. In English, that would be "Both truth and teeth get polished." Readers may decide for themselves whether polishing was applied to the facts that follow.

one

The Interesting Possibility

It was May in Rome, a pleasant season. I sat in my office in the Palazzo Margherita, an oversized, high-ceilinged room that had once been a queen mother's bedroom. I wished that it were Sunday and that my wife and I were making our way toward the top of some mountain in the Apennines, Monte Semprevisa, perhaps, or Monte Gennaro. The intercom buzzed, and my secretary—that marvelous lady from Boston, Maria Lo Conte—said that I had a call from Robert Oakley in Washington. Bob Oakley was our ambassador to Somalia; he was in Washington, I knew, for a few days' consultation. We had agreed by cable that on his way eastward back to Mogadishu he would stop in Rome for lunch with people from the Italian foreign ministry. We and the Italians both had major interests in Somalia. Our interest was largely strategic, a result of the Cold War. Theirs was in good part historical; much of Somalia had been an Italian colony. We were both major donors of aid to Somalia, and we often compared notes on aid and other questions. I had done so as a political officer in the Rome embassy in the late 1960s, and I did so now as the number-two in that embassy, together with Bob Oakley whenever he passed through Rome.

Oakley was calling to say that he was going to be a few days late leaving Washington. He wondered if I could put off for a week the date for our luncheon—and of course I could. Oakley went on to say that he would soon be leaving his post. He was being transferred back to Washington, where he was to head the State Department's Office for Combating Terrorism. "A big, hard job," I said; "congratulations. Who's going to replace you in Somalia?"

"I don't think they've given that any thought yet," he said. "Why, would you be interested?"

My question had come from simple curiosity, and I had not expected his question in return. I thought for a minute. "Yes," I said, "I'd be interested."

"Good," said Oakley. "Let me just tell a couple of people here. See you soon."

He hung up, and after a bit Maria came in and found me staring out the window. "Spring fever, Peter?" she asked. Not quite. What had I put myself in for?

The year was 1984, and my wife and I had been in Rome—our second time there—for two and a half years. I was the deputy chief of mission ("DCM" in Foreign Service lingo) in the big Rome embassy, with the diplomatic title of "minister." It was the biggest overseas job, and the most interesting, that I had had in twenty-seven years as a Foreign Service officer. An American television network had recently made a film, called *The Deputy*, that was supposed to be about the DCM in Rome. I laughed when I saw it. It showed correctly that we had a magnificent embassy—before the United States bought it (for a bargain price), our office building had been the palace of Italy's Queen Mother, Margherita. But the TV film did not begin to convey what the DCM did to earn his pay.

In Rome I was the deputy and executive officer to an ambassador named Maxwell Rabb, a Ronald Reagan political appointee, a New York lawyer with long experience who had been secretary to the cabinet under President Dwight Eisenhower. Max Rabb was a canny man who knew the elemental rule of politics: do someone a favor and he will owe you one. Indeed, the better I got to know him, the more it struck me that this had been the heart of his clearly very successful law practice. His string of friends and personal acquaintances seemed to include most of the influential people in the United States, and many of those in Italy.

The ambassador left to me the management of our oversized embassy —which included representatives of twenty federal agencies besides the State Department—and he also left me room to act as a senior American representative in Italy. The two of us, the other embassy officers, and our seven consuls general in other Italian cities had a wide range of personal contacts in government, politics, business, journalism, academia, and the arts. We sometimes suggested gently to Washington that ours was the best embassy in Europe and that Italy, in part thanks to our efforts, was our best ally. Sometimes, we sensed, Washington agreed.

Rome diplomatic life was not all roses. I am not just talking about hard work. Around October 1981, the time that I arrived in Rome as DCM, the Red Brigade terrorists decided to target Americans for the first time

—although we did not know that. The Red Brigades had been born of the Italian student rebellion at the end of the 1960s. The 1970s had been for Italy the *anni di piombo*—years of lead: almost fifteen thousand acts of political violence had occurred, and more than four hundred people had been murdered by terrorists of both Left and Right. As a chronicler of the Red Brigades wrote later, Italy's political violence was the most serious of any advanced country, other than the crazed nationalism in Northern Ireland and Spain.[1] It had reached perhaps its worst point in 1978, when the Red Brigades captured and then killed former prime minister Aldo Moro. By 1981, violence was declining; the Italian police were making inroads on the *brigatisti*, who had never found popular support. Perhaps, Red Brigade leaders now decided, an anti-NATO campaign would prove more popular.

On the evening of December 17, 1981, my wife and I were sitting in bed, reading, in our Rome apartment. The telephone rang. It was Sergio Berlinguer, the diplomatic adviser to the prime minister. "Peter," he said, "the Red Brigades have kidnapped an American general. You had better send someone down to our crisis center at Palazzo Chigi."

The kidnapped officer was James Dozier, a brigadier general stationed at a NATO command in Verona; I had met him at an embassy meeting only days earlier. In ensuing weeks we worked closely with the Italians on the case. The official responsible for terrorism questions in the Pentagon phoned to tell me that we needed to bring a lot of U.S. personnel into Italy; the Italians, who had not one but two competing police forces (the Polizia Nazionale and the Carabinieri), obviously were incapable of finding and rescuing our man. I said that there were six or eight police forces in the District of Columbia, the last time I had counted, and that the Italians had much more antiterrorism experience than we did. Still, a month after General Dozier was kidnapped, the embassy agreed to have a small Delta Force unit come to Rome. They were trim and impressive men, but none spoke Italian or knew Italy. The Italians pointed them to a town in Tuscany where they could check out a lead. Some time later I took a phone call from the police station in Padua. A strong voice said, "Hi! This is Jim Dozier." The Italians had learned that Dozier was being held in an apartment in Padua, and an Italian team had stormed the apartment and freed him without loss of life.

But we remained under a terrorist threat. In May 1984 I lost a good friend and onetime Foreign Service colleague, Ray Hunt, head of the Sinai

---

1. Robert C. Meade Jr., *Red Brigades: The Story of Italian Terrorism* (New York: St. Martin's, 1990), p. xxi.

peacekeeping force; he was gunned down on his way home from his Rome headquarters. He was the third friend of mine killed by terrorists. Frank Meloy, whom I had worked for during my earlier tour in Rome when he had the same job I had now, had been assassinated in Beirut in 1976 soon after arriving there as our ambassador. Spike Dubs, with whom I had worked years earlier in Moscow, had been killed in 1978 while serving as our ambassador in Afghanistan. More American ambassadors had died violent deaths since World War II than generals and admirals of all our military services.

One could not let this affect one's work. I ran several miles a day, varying my routes as best I could. When I ran around Piazza Navona at midday in my shorts and T-shirt, I did not suppose anyone knew that the runner was the minister of the American embassy. Although I had an armored vehicle, I had no bodyguard. If the Red Brigades should ever interest themselves in me, they would find me a good target. It was not a subject I brooded over.

I did sometimes wish inwardly that the increased terrorist threat might reduce the flow of visitors to the embassy from Washington; hundreds came each year, causing us a tremendous workload. But we could not in good conscience warn off visitors; terrorists usually targeted not people on brief visits but individuals whose abodes and travel routes they could study for some time. Top Washington figures were of course targets at any time, but these VIPs came with good protection. So our visitors kept coming—officials from various federal agencies, many members of Congress, President Reagan in 1982, Vice President George Bush the following year.

My first view of George Bush in Rome had come over a dozen years earlier, just after he had been named our ambassador to the United Nations. The new ambassador had made a trip to major Western European capitals, including Rome, to consult with our allies on questions of mutual interest in the UN, the Middle East above all. I was serving in Rome as a midlevel political officer. Our ambassador, Graham Martin, told us at the morning staff meeting that Ambassador Bush would make himself available that afternoon for an informal session with interested embassy officers. About a dozen of us showed up, and we stood in a semicircle as Mr. Martin introduced Mr. Bush. Ambassador Martin asked if our guest wanted to make some comments before we got to questions and answers. George Bush replied that he was happy to be here, that he had been honored when President Richard Nixon had asked him to take on this new responsibility—and that we might not like it, but that at the UN he was going to be a fierce defender of American interests and American ideals. My friend and fellow political officer Charlie Stout was standing just opposite me; as Mr. Bush continued, Charlie and I looked at each other, incredulous. We might not like it? We Foreign Service officers, who had taken an oath to defend the Constitution? Who *was* this bird?

To put the best possible face on it, Mr. Bush was no doubt on edge: we were professional diplomats, and he was new to the diplomacy game. But his comment was inexcusable, and I do not suppose any of us ever forgot it. Certainly I did not.

When in 1983 George Bush visited Rome again, as vice president, it was after many weeks of detailed preparations. As DCM I had responsibility in the embassy for making sure all went well and for coordinating embassy efforts with those of the many Secret Service and White House people who had come to Rome in advance to work on the visit. It had been agreed that among the vice president's Rome meetings would be a call on the president of the Senate, Amintore Fanfani, a former prime minister and one of the founders of the Christian Democratic party, with which we were always on close terms. Bush had a pleasant meeting with Fanfani. Early the next morning, there were four people in the ambassador's office: Ambassador Rabb, Vice President Bush, a White House staffer, and me. The ambassador told the vice president that the president of the lower house of Parliament, the Chamber of Deputies, had sent word that the vice president having called on her opposite number in the Senate, she expected Mr. Bush to call on her. Her name was Nilde Jotti, and she was a Communist. The vice president went nearly through the ceiling, which was a high one. If he did not rave, he certainly ranted. We had sabotaged him, we had gotten him into a trap—and what would the president say? What would the president say?

We told him that we did not think his call on Madame Jotti would have any consequences; we had had contacts with the Italian Communist party for a number of years. After some minutes the vice president calmed a little and agreed to go see the lady. The call resulted in modest coverage and, as I recall, no comment in the Italian press.

But now the question was Somalia, and me. I had served on several continents but never in Africa. Did that matter? The Somalis did not like to be lumped in with other Africans, and although they belonged to the Organization of African Unity, they were also in the Arab League. Every group of Somali clans claimed an Arab ancestor who had come across the water to the Horn of Africa with the new Islamic faith.

I had followed Somali affairs off and on for many years, and I knew a fair amount about Somalia and its relations with the outside world. Italian was still a useful language there, and my Italian was fluent. I had served in the Soviet Union and in Moscow's Communist satellite Czechoslovakia; the president of Somalia had for years been one of Moscow's closest African allies. More important, as regarded my chances of getting the assignment to Mogadishu, was the fact that none of the senior Africanists in our service seemed interested in going there.

My own dream when I reached Rome in 1981 had been to become ambassador to Czechoslovakia whenever the time came for me to leave Rome, which I assumed would be when Max Rabb did. I had, in my view at least, good credentials for the top Prague job. But my friend Bill Luers (who would later, in retirement, become the president of the Metropolitan Museum of Art) had gone to Prague as ambassador at the end of 1983 and would presumably be there at least three years. That was longer than I could expect to stay in Rome; in 1984 I was already well into my third year there. Nor did it look like there would be any other ambassadorial opening soon in Central or Eastern Europe. I assumed Mr. Reagan would continue to fill all the posts in Western Europe with political appointees, and he might well send one to Prague.[2]

I did not want to go on forever being a number-two—better, to paraphrase Caesar, to be first in a small place in Africa than second in Rome. Nor was Somalia small, though it was terribly poor. As the spring progressed in Rome, I kept thinking about what might be in store for me. I thought that perhaps I had been pointing toward Somalia for many years.

---

2. As in fact he did, when he sent Julian Niemczyk to Prague in 1986. Niemczyk was followed in 1989 by that famous former child star Shirley Temple Black.

two

Scholar, Soldier, Someday Diplomat

When I was an undergraduate at Dartmouth College, I planned to go on and earn a doctorate at Columbia University, marry some rich and beautiful girl, and teach Russian in some pleasant New England college. The Korean War was ending. I was confident that our military draft system would also end soon.

By the time I began my second year of graduate work at Columbia, I could not abide the thought of spending more than two years in New York. The city was too big and noisy, even for a Chicagoan like me. My main subject of study was Soviet literature, but nothing of interest was being written, or at least published, in the Soviet Union. Yet my professor, Ernest Simmons, insisted that those of us who entered his department in odd-numbered years (and I had entered in 1953) should concentrate on the Soviet period, while the fortunate ones entering in even years could study Leskov, Afanasy Fyet, and the creation of *byliny*. Besides all this, I was in love and wanted to get married, to a beautiful girl as planned, though not a rich one. I had a generous Ford Foundation scholarship, and it would pay me more if I was married, but I wanted to support my intended wife—although she was doing quite well on her own. Her name was Mary Jane Lee. Like me she had grown up in Chicago, but we had met at Columbia, where she was the first woman Standard and Poor Fellow in Columbia's Graduate School of Business. I was wondering what alternative I might find to academia when I saw at the university employment office a poster urging students to take the examinations for the Foreign Service. The Foreign Service would certainly mean travel, and next to teaching I wanted to travel.

My urge to travel stemmed, I always thought, from my father, Charles Scott Bridges, born in 1903 as the twelfth child of a farmer in Gloucester County, Virginia. Our ancestors had been there a long time—my ancestor

7

Simon Stubblefield received a land grant in Gloucester in 1688—but in 1912 my grandfather had had a stroke, sold the farm, and moved to Norfolk with his family. At nineteen my father signed on a tramp steamer as apprentice seaman and first saw the Caribbean and the Mediterranean. On his return he spent a year at the University of Virginia, but he wanted an international career. By his early twenties he was working out of New Orleans, selling Libby's canned goods in Central and South America; then he was transferred to company headquarters in Chicago. For years, while my mother and my sisters, Shirley Bartow and Mary Elizabeth, and I stayed home, Gov—short for Governor—roamed the world for the company's export department. The year I finished college, he became president of Libby, McNeill & Libby.

My mother, Shirley Amelie Devlin, was a New Orleanian whose paternal grandfather, born in County Donegal, had ended up on the Atchafalaya River, where he married into a Louisiana French family. Her other grandfather, born in the north of England, had immigrated to New Orleans and married a lady whose father had been mortally wounded at the battle of Shiloh in 1862. My immediate background, then, was all southern—I was born in New Orleans in 1932—but I grew up on Chicago's South Side and later in a Chicago suburb, Hinsdale. Nor did I ever think of a career in the South.[1]

In 1954 I took the Foreign Service written examination, a three-day ordeal, and somewhat to my surprise I passed it. Next step was the oral exam, for which I went to Washington in May 1955. Four stern examiners at the State Department subjected me to hard questions. One of the men kept asking me what I knew about Africa, specifically about Liberia; what would I think about assignment to a post like Monrovia? I said it would no doubt be interesting. He said he had just returned from Liberia, and it had been awful; what would I say now? My throat went totally dry, but I took a drink of water and told my questioner I supposed I could do at least as well in Liberia as he had. And I passed the exam. Then I walked in bliss down Constitution Avenue and strolled under the big trees on the Capitol grounds, thinking, "I shall be a servant of the Nation."

1. For good or bad, Southerners can have long memories. My great-great-grandfather Louis Amedée Roussel, who spoke only French until he was sent upriver to school in St. Louis, liked to tell grandchildren that one of our female ancestors was the most beautiful dancer at the court of le Roi d'Angouleme—Francis I of France, who died in 1547. My family sometimes names children Bartow; my great-grandfather Dr. Thomas Jefferson Hughes was the first to do so, because he admired Col. Francis Bartow, who fell at First Manassas commanding a Georgia brigade.

But the first service coming was the military kind. The draft had not ended. The army wanted me, and I was too myopic for officer training school. My love and I got married in June, as soon as I got my M.A., and we went on a honeymoon paid for by most of my savings. Then I said goodbye to her and, together with two dozen other young men, boarded a sleeping car at Union Station in Chicago for an overnight train trip. My sleep ended suddenly before dawn the next morning with a sergeant shouting at us to get out of our berths. We new privates had reached our new home, Fort Leonard Wood in Missouri.

I spent the next eight weeks in basic training. The only really bad part was the lack of sleep. The order for lights out came after ten in the evening, and the platoon sergeant woke us every morning before five. Then we did calisthenics under the oak trees and ran to the mess hall, where, after chin-ups on the bars, we stood outside waiting to be admitted to the home of scrambled dried eggs and bitter coffee. As we waited, dawn came to Missouri, and a pale green lit the castles of the sky. I looked at the delicate clouds and thought of my young wife, far away in Chicago.

But for the time being, life was six-mile forced marches through the oak woods with heavy packs and rifles and sitting in a hot building listening to a lecture on machine guns (*"On your feet, men!* Two of you was sleeping!"*), and firing the M-1 rifle on ranges that were a long, dusty march from anywhere. Our company commander was a fine black captain not long back from Korea. He found that we had some amateur musicians among us, and the first sergeant rustled up a couple of drums and horns; now when we marched we had march music, and we sang. It was the way things ought to be. We got tough, and we felt like soldiers.

We were Company B, all recruits whose last names began with B. My immediate bunk mates were Prince Bentley, Bob Branham, and Ellis Brown. Bentley and Brown were black Southerners, Branham and I white Midwesterners. I had until now lived in a white world. I had had no black high-school classmates. Our Dartmouth class of seven hundred had four black members, and none was a close friend of mine. After the first few days, we four bunk mates began to get on well; after two weeks we were comrades.

Meanwhile, we were told that anyone with proficiency in a foreign language could take a language exam. I took the Russian and Spanish exams and scored high in both. A personnel clerk called me in and told me that without doubt I would be sent to an intelligence unit in Germany, to make use of my Russian. That sounded fine to me. Meanwhile, the clerk continued, I had to have eight weeks' more training to be qualified for overseas duty. It would make no sense to give me expensive training; in my case, the added eight weeks were a formality. So I ended up in the combat engineer course, along with the least-bright privates of Fort Leonard Wood—the ones not smart enough to qualify for tractor-scraper school. We learned how to fill sandbags, how to drive nails into boards, how to read a compass and a map (our most intellectual exercise, and a puzzling one for many of the boys), and how to build pontoon bridges and Bailey bridges. Bridge building was hard work but satisfying, when we watched our final product carry trucks across the Big Piney River.

Two other men besides myself in the new company could claim a higher education. Both had been sent to fill sandbags for the same reason that I had: they spoke a foreign language and were destined for intelligence work. One was a young lawyer from Milwaukee, the other a singer who had come home from the Berlin Opera in order to get drafted. Bentley, Branham, and Bosworth were still my buddies, no doubt about that, but with the lawyer and the bass-baritone I formed a small circle of, well, intellectuals. We might be muddy privates, but we had gone to college.

Soon the small circle of intellectuals made friends with one of the training noncoms. At training sites, the circle's members had observed, the noncoms carried clipboards. Ostensibly these were used to hold pads on which to record things, but our analysis was that the clipboards mainly served as symbols of authority. One day, when our company was to build a bridge, our noncom friend issued a clipboard to each of the three of us. And it worked! Suddenly we were staff, not just recruits. We stood by busily recording things on our clipboards while our comrades lugged heavy pieces of Bailey bridge to the river's edge. Our act worked well for most of our remaining weeks, and we saved ourselves a lot of lugging, although occasionally some sergeant would remember that we too were privates. Aleksandr Solzhenitsyn wrote later of labor-camp inmates who saved themselves from literally killing jobs with a Russian version of this same technique. But ours was an independent, Western invention.

One cold day in January, the training finally ended. That evening our company was divided without forewarning into two halves—one bound for Korea and one for Europe. I was for Europe. We the Europe-bound boarded an eastbound troop train next morning, and twenty-four hours later we were at Fort Dix in New Jersey, to be sorted out and consigned to troopships. At Fort Dix the personnel people fed each man's name into a computer. The computer considered what it had been told about me and produced a card saying I had been assigned as engineer-helper to CO A 97 ENGR BN (CONS) APO 122 TOUL FRA. France? An engineer battalion? Where was the promised intelligence unit in Germany? I managed to get hold of a personnel clerk, who consulted the computer. The computer knew I had completed combat engineer training; it knew nothing of any expertise in Russian. But, I asked, can't this be changed? After all, I have a master's degree in Soviet studies. No, said the clerk, it cannot be changed now. But when you get to the other side, just talk to your personnel officer; he'll fix things up. Sure he will.

That evening they graciously gave us an hour off to telephone our families. I ran the half-mile to the telephone center, stood in line for forty minutes, and finally, when the hour was almost over, I got my wife on the line in Chicago. "Quick, get the atlas! I'm being sent to T-o-u-l in France. It must be Toulouse, but see if there's a place called Toul in France."

Pause. "Yeah. Yes, there is."

"Mary Jane, *where is it?*"

"About an inch and a half east of Paris."

"*What?* Look at the scale!"

"Oh, maybe it's a hundred miles. I bet you'll like it. I love you. I'll come join you as soon as I can."

The next day was the 22d of January, and we sailed out of Brooklyn on a gray, mild afternoon, bound for unknown Europe. Our bunks were in the hold, in tiers of six. I stayed on deck as much as I could. It was a crummy troopship, but we were on a voyage, and it might lead to adventure—goodbye, finally, to that shabby camp in Missouri. I watched the waves and thought deep thoughts about the little ship and myself and our places in time and space. On the third day my metaphysics became pure nausea, from the smell of brass polish that I was sent to apply to fittings in the head every morning after scrambled eggs. The troop lounge reeked of smoke. The sleeping compartments stunk of sweat. Even on deck the sea air was fouled by what the ventilation exhausts brought up from the bilges.

But on the eighth morning, I saw a lighthouse amid the waters and then the green, low Scilly Isles. On the ninth morning, coming on deck before dawn, I saw the lights of Dover Harbor. On the tenth morning, we sailed up the Weser to dock at Bremerhaven and watched its snowy piers and Germans all day from the deck. Finally, at 6 P.M., we boarded a troop train at dockside and went off into Europe: Bremen, Osnabrück, Munster, Essen, Duisburg. I lay in the top bunk of a six-man compartment and peered out at the dim night landscape of Saxony and Westphalia and at the rebuilt cities. At dawn I went to stand in the corridor and pulled down the window. We were riding through the cool, early morning Mosel valley. The train stopped for a while across the river from a hilly town, and in the still dawn a church bell began ringing slowly, and another church began to answer, with a lighter bell.

All was fresh and fascinating. I had no thought for now of being in the cloddish army, a private en route to an unknown battalion. I was abroad, for the first time in my life, a traveler in a new country, with new discoveries every minute: new kinds of power lines, new trees, new shapes for farms, an unknown style of railroad station, a different architecture entirely, new people, strange shapes even in the clouds.

By early afternoon we had reached the army's Engineer Depot outside Toul, which I had never heard of until two weeks earlier but had been a capital of the Celts and the seat of Joan of Arc's bishop. At six the next morning, my duffel bag and I were in the rear of a truck headed up to Verdun to report in at 97th Engineer headquarters. Our battalion headquarters was in the Caserne Maginot, in a long, four-story, brick and sandstone building. The personnel officer made clear that the 97th had no need of my Russian. He needed a clerk. I would stay in Verdun and peck at a typewriter, not go back to Toul and work a shovel.

André Maginot, the creator of the Maginot Line, had once served as a corporal in our barracks. To come to Verdun as a soldier in 1956 was to come late to a cold, old cauldron, an ancient charnel house. Just east of here on the battleground stood the Ossuaire, with the bones of a quarter-million men slaughtered there in the First World War. The signs at the edge of unkempt woods still warned *Danger de mort*, and from time to time a walker would be blown up by an old shell. I was glad I had not been at Verdun in 1916.

When spring came my wife arrived, and we moved into a garret, bought a little car, and began to investigate Europe. We had no idea where the future would take us. As we spent our weekends busily touring Paris and Domremy and Luxembourg and Vittel and Trier, I hoped that somehow in the future for us there might be more of Europe. I was confident that I would serve in Moscow; Latin America might make sense, too, and perhaps someday Africa, where my father had traveled when I was small.

three

From Foggy Bottom to the Isthmus

It was June 1959, a hot summer in Washington. I was completing my first two years in the State Department and waiting to learn what would be our first post abroad. I came home one evening to our little Virginia apartment, which lacked air conditioning, and my suffering wife said, "I don't care where they send us, just so it's not the tropics!" Two evenings later I came home with our assignment: Panama. Well, we decided, it could hardly be worse than this. We outfitted ourselves for the tropics as best we could afford. In my case this meant buying one more forty-dollar, lightweight Haspel suit to add to the two I had, plus new swimming trunks. And there we were on an October day with our two small children, David and Elizabeth, heading south in a DC-7 to the tropics, which we imagined would prove less exotic and more Americanized than what we had seen of Europe.

We arrived at Panama's Tocumen Airport at six that evening, the hot sun almost down and the runway still wet from rain. At planeside we were met by my new chief, the first secretary and head of the embassy's political section, and his powdered and padded wife. As we drove away from the airport toward Panama City, the tropical night suddenly came down. The countryside was utterly black, with only an occasional candle or lantern visible in a roadside hut, and the warm, humid air was full of exotic smells. It all excited me. But what my new chief and his wife were telling us was that we would be able to shop at the commissary and PX in the Canal Zone; that there were two military swimming pools we could use in the Zone; that we would want to join the Fort Amador officers' club. That was not the stuff of adventure, not what my wife and I wanted to hear on our first night at our new post in the tropics. I wondered what the future would bring.

Until we could find a permanent place to live, we were to stay at the Tivoli Guest House. This was a big old wooden hotel with a long veranda on the Canal Zone side of Fourth of July Avenue, which formed the border between the Zone and the Republic of Panama. The Tivoli was a vestige of the days before World War I when the Americans were building the Canal and President Theodore Roosevelt told the world, "I took Panama." We settled into two high-ceilinged rooms. At the rear of the hotel was a quiet, cool courtyard shaded by a great corotu tree. It was the kind of place we had hoped to find in the tropics, and no less pleasant for being a remnant of a semicolonial past.

I had been assigned to Panama as third secretary of embassy and vice consul, with responsibilities as a political officer, the most junior of three such positions in the embassy. I was not well prepared to take on my new responsibilities. Two years earlier, our small class of new Foreign Service officers had taken a three-month orientation course at the Foreign Service Institute. We had toured the various State Department bureaus and several other federal agencies claiming an interest in foreign affairs. We had been told a little about protocol, and two entertaining gentlemen from the U.S. Information Agency had impressed on us how different foreign cultures and foreign usages might be from our own. A personnel lady had explained the pension system, which interested us little at this stage in our careers. We had also received instructions on how to prepare travel vouchers. But no one had impressed on us that what the president and secretary of state needed from our service was succinct reporting on the world and effective representation of American views and policies to other governments. Nor did our course teach us anything about international law, though few of us had studied law before entering the service. Nor were we taught anything about diplomatic practice, beyond an hour or two of instruction in preparing diplomatic notes.

Fortunately, my first two years in the service had been spent in the bowels of the Department, as the most junior of five officers on the Soviet desk. I had at least learned how the Department functioned and had come to realize that lengthy despatches from posts abroad were not going to reach the eyes of an overbusy under or assistant secretary, while a terse, timely cable might. In the weeks before we left Washington, I had also read all I could about Panama and our position there. Our embassy was in the republic, but the republic was cut in two by the Canal Zone, a belt of land ten miles wide, five miles on either side of the Panama Canal, that the United

States held, by treaty with Panama, in perpetuity. The Canal and the Zone were administered by the Panama Canal Company, a corporation with a single stockholder, the secretary of the army. The governor of the Canal Zone was always a major general in the Army Corps of Engineers. We paid Panama not quite two million dollars a year for our position on the isthmus. That was all we said we could afford; but we had not raised tolls since the Canal was opened in 1914; low tolls benefited transcanal traffic between the Atlantic and Pacific coasts of the United States. It seemed that the relationship between Panama and ourselves was at best tense. In the past, it had erupted into violence more than once.

It was seven o'clock on a Thursday morning when I first walked into the American embassy on the sea front, a few hundred feet from the monument where Vasco Nuñez de Balboa stands looking proudly out at his great discovery (discovery for Europeans, that is), the Pacific Ocean. The instruction of the junior political officer began. My boss, the first secretary, explained what I already knew, that there were normally three officers in our section but for now there were just the two of us. So what was I supposed to do? Reporting and representation, the boss explained briefly. He and his wife were planning a reception for my wife and me the following week to introduce us to a number of influential people. I thanked him. Meanwhile, he said, today was a weaker day. At least that was what it sounded like in his Louisiana accent, but I knew that he meant Weeka. In those days before optical character readers and computers made it possible to send cables faster than we could write or read them, embassies sent the Department weekly summaries and assessments of the local political scene by diplomatic pouch. This was the Weeka, and of course it was supplemented by cables on urgent matters and by longer despatches reporting on various subjects in detail.

My boss said he would show me how he composed his, or rather our, Weeka. I could start helping the following week. It began with scissors.

There were four or five American intelligence agencies, civilian and military, operating on the Isthmus of Panama. Each sent a lot of reports to Washington on recent and potential Panama events, and they sent our embassy copies of most of these. My chief found it convenient to snip pieces from the various reports as they came in during the week. Then, on Weeka day, he would combine these snippets, using Scotch tape, with little paragraphs he pounded out with two fingers on his typewriter. Thus was the Weeka constructed. By late morning there were four or five pages of it, which the master let his apprentice read. What the master had typed

largely summarized the reporting in Panama's numerous and generally un-
reliable newspapers. My chief had very little of his own to contribute. He
handed the mess to our stenographer to type in final form as a dispatch to
the Department and invited me to join him for a sandwich in the embassy
snack bar. Next day, he said, he would introduce me to an informal Friday
luncheon group that included some of the embassy's most reliable contacts.

The luncheon group turned out to be a pleasant one—Panamanians,
Americans, and the counselor of the Peruvian embassy. The luncheon conversation ran free after a couple of rounds of pisco sours. My boss casually—
or rather, I thought, attempting to sound casual—asked the others what was
really going to happen on November 4, the national holiday. We were appre-
hensive about November 4 that year, because Aquilino Boyd and Ernesto
Castillero Pimentel were threatening to raise the Panamanian flag in the Canal
Zone, where our Canal Company insisted that only Old Glory could fly.

Castillero was a small, hunchbacked professor who was a fierce nationalist. Boyd, who owed his surname to an Irish grandfather and was still in
his thirties, had already been foreign minister. Our ambassador, a career
officer named Julian Harrington, had looked on Boyd as a sort of protegé
when the latter was minister. Now, though, with the flag-raising business,
Harrington had ended the relationship.

The November 4 celebrations were to include a morning parade in the
old quarter of Panama City, which the president of the republic, together
with foreign ambassadors, would review from the balcony of his palace.
Neither my boss's "reliable contacts" nor the combined powers of our intelligence agencies could forecast just what Boyd and Castillero would do
on the 4th or whether serious trouble would result. The day before, I told
my boss I would walk down to see the parade. He was planning a day in the
Zone and did not demur. As I walked toward the palace, I had the impression that I was the only gringo in the crowd of darker-skinned people. I
found a place on the sidewalk near the cathedral and was watching Guardia
Nacional units with a good band march by when a well-dressed woman
came up to me and said in Spanish that I seemed to be a North American.
She told me quickly, quietly, that this was no place for me; I should leave
before there was trouble. I decided to take her advice.

As I neared Fourth of July Avenue, with the modern building of Panama's National Assembly on my right, I saw in front of me several groups of
mainly dark-skinned, barefoot boys from the nearby slums, a type known
pejoratively as *cocos pelados*, or "peeled coconuts," to well-to-do Panamanians.

The *cocos pelados* were throwing rocks at a line of Canal Zone police in gas masks who were facing them along the avenue. Behind the boys, closer to me, a group of six or eight lighter-skinned, better-dressed men was egging them on: "Hurrah, boys, give it to the Yankee imperialists!" It was my first look at elemental Panama politics. The trouble was, I was on the wrong side of the line. Eventually there came a lull, and I made my way across the street. A few minutes later I found a taxi to take me to the embassy. It was closed for the holiday, and the only people inside were a marine guard and our deputy chief of mission, John Shillock. The DCM had decided trouble was likely, and so he had come down to the embassy rather than accompany Ambassador Harrington to the president's palace.

I had just finished telling Mr. Shillock what I had seen downtown when, looking out the window, we saw Aquilino Boyd walking along the sidewalk below. As usual there was a Guardia Nacional car with two agents parked nearby—but now we saw the car drive off. John Shillock, a veteran of thirty years in Latin America, said, "I think I know what's going to happen now." He phoned down to the marine that we could expect some visitors outside and that he should in any event keep the door locked and barred and stay at his post.

Several minutes later a group of fifty or sixty *cocos pelados* came walking up Avenida Balboa. They walked across the embassy lawn to our flagpole, pulled down our flag, and tore it up, with appropriate shouts about Yankee imperialism. I had expected to see Aquilino Boyd egg them on, but he kept a distance, perhaps discomfited by seeing the deputy to his onetime friend the ambassador staring down at him. Eventually the barefoot patriots departed, and so did Boyd. As I was helping John Shillock write a reporting cable to the department, the executive secretary of the Canal Zone government, Paul Runnestrand, phoned with more news. A couple of hours earlier, Boyd and Castillero had led an automobile caravan into the Zone, stopping every so often to plant small Panamanian flags by the roadside and running into trouble at every stop with the Zone police, who pulled up the flags. I was not attracted by either side of this affair. Planting little flags in the Canal Zone seemed childish; pulling down and tearing up our flag I thought atrocious. But neither did I see much virtue in the Canal Company's insistence that only the American flag could fly in the Zone—an insistence based on a provision in the Treaty of 1903 that the United States should enjoy all the rights in the Canal Zone that it would possess were it sovereign there. The Panamanians, of course, said that this language meant we were *not* sovereign there.

This argument had gone on for over four decades; now it grew sharper. There was no more stone throwing after the 4th, but it appeared that every Panamanian without exception backed Boyd's and Castillero's doings and agreed that Panama's flag must fly—along with ours, most agreed—in the Zone. Only a dreamer could have imagined that a time would come when only Panama's flag would fly there—when indeed there would be no more Canal Zone.

The next several months were a time of stiff relations between the two republics, but my wife and I, who had rented a hillside apartment with a view over the sea, found it easy to make friends in Panama. I wanted to get to know a broad range of Panamanians, but the friendliest were those from the upper classes, whose nationalism was coupled with a strong desire that we see them as our country's best Panamanian friends and allies. These people, known by the lower classes as *rabiblancos*, or white-tails, sent their children to colleges in Texas and Louisiana; their wives went shopping in Miami; the men had their annual checkups at the Ochsner Clinic in New Orleans. Nor were they averse to marrying off children to Americans; if chaos ever came to the isthmus, one could hope to get the family to the North through such a *yanqui* connection. I met a lot of such people, but I rejected from the start the idea that these well-to-do Arosemenas and Arias were the only Panamanians we should deal with—the only Panamanians whose interests mattered.

I developed a short list of relatively honest, well-regarded Panamanians who were something other than *rabiblancos* and whom I wanted to befriend. One was a young university professor, said to be the most popular and principled man at his institution. We met and found that we did not agree on much but that we could discuss frankly the many problems between our two countries, all of them relating to the Canal. When national elections were held, the professor's small party joined with others in a coalition that obtained a majority of seats in the National Assembly. Rumor had it that my friend would become vice minister of education; instead he became collector of customs at Tocumen Airport. I suspected, but had no proof, that he had taken the customs job because it would provide illicit income. He and his wife had lately had my wife and me to dinner, and now we offered dinner to them on his birthday, inviting also several of his friends. After dinner the men sat on our balcony and made me a proposal: the United States should quietly finance an apartment complex for them. We were, after all, friends; what were friends for? The evening left me wondering where I should find an honest man in Panama.

In fact, I knew such a person, though I did not much like him. He was Carlos Garay, the desk officer for United States affairs in the foreign ministry. His father had been one of Panama's first foreign ministers. Carlos Garay knew every detail of the vexed relationship between our two countries, beginning with Panama's declaration of independence from Colombia in 1903 and the first treaty between us, signed for Panama by a Frenchman, Philippe Bunau-Varilla—who all Panamanians agreed had signed away more Panamanian rights than any Panamanian would have done. It seemed to me that we had more problems, big and little, with Panama than we did with perhaps any other country, including the Soviet Union.

To Carlos Garay it was all a catalog of wrong deeds by the Colossus of the North. Garay and his ministry protested our selling postage stamps in the Canal Zone, robbing the republic of revenue; protested our permitting Chinese truck farmers to grow and sell produce in the Zone, taking business from Panama City shopkeepers; protested our establishment of a federal district court in the Zone, run by my friend Judge Guthrie Crowe; protested our continued operation across the isthmus of a railroad that competed with Panamanian bus companies. In the Panamanian view, none of these activities was sanctioned by any of the bilateral treaties, and they each harmed Panamanian interests. I did not like Garay's hard and bitter way, but we maintained a polite relationship. And although I did not say so to Garay, I thought that the United States could easily change several practices that damaged our relations.

The most important of these was the Canal Company's method of hiring at the professional level. They would not hire Panamanians for responsible positions, on grounds of national security. But even if one thought this reasonable, and I did not, there was the additional fact that the company hired Americans locally where possible. This policy had resulted in the creation of a colony of Zonians, people whose families had lived in the Canal Zone for two and often three generations. They held American passports, but many or most of them visited the United States only when they were forced periodically to take home leave. Nor were they all North American in origin; many had Panamanian mothers or grandmothers. But they hated the Panamanians of the republic; their fatherland was the Zone, the ten-mile-wide strip between the seas. Although few of these people ever went to Washington, they had found their voice in the Congress, among members easily swayed by arguments that a change in hiring practices would weaken security. The Zonians also disliked our embassy. We did not, admittedly, always stand up for them. We were more concerned about overall American interests.

Fidel Castro had come to power in Cuba some months before I reached Panama, and there was a certain amount of pro-Fidel feeling in Panama, as elsewhere in Latin America. It had one pitiful result. A group of students in Santiago, the capital of Panama's Veraguas Province, decided to emulate Fidel, took whatever rifles and shotguns they could find in town, and went up into the low sierra, from which they sent a manifesto down to Santiago proclaiming revolution and calling on the peasants and townspeople to join them. Two companies of the Guardia Nacional, Panama's combined military and police force, were sent into the sierra, where they found and soon killed all the young men. Years later, I recalled these senseless killings when a similar slaughter occurred in Somalia.

I traveled when I could to Veraguas and other parts of the Interior, the area between the Zone and the Costa Rican border that the Pan-American Highway made relatively accessible, although much of the highway was still unpaved. I liked to travel to the Interior with two Spanish-speaking military veterinary officers who made up the U.S. Army Mission to Panama. It was the only effective aid element we had in Panama. (Our embassy contained a large element from the U.S. Agency for International Development, whose members clearly accomplished little; many of them did not even speak Spanish. This, too, I recalled later in Somalia, when I took over an embassy that contained an oversized AID mission.) Their mission dated from World War II, when their predecessors had inspected Panamanian beef to be consumed by our hundred thousand servicemen occupying the isthmus. My two friends knew every rancher up and down the country, and they ran an artificial-insemination program, injecting into Panama's small native cattle strains of the disease- and heat-resistant Santa Gertrudis breed, developed in Texas. By 1960 Panama, which had been importing beef, had started to export it.

Panama was a continuing series of interesting if modest adventures. My Russian was fluent, and I spent a day in the Canal on the bridge of a Soviet freighter bound for Vladivostok with a cargo of Cuban sugar, serving as interpreter between the ship's captain and the Canal pilot. I became interested in the Cuna Indians, an admirable nation who inhabit the San Blas Islands along Panama's Caribbean coast and also the valleys of the Bayano and Chucunaque Rivers, which flow through Darien into the Pacific. I spent several weekends in San Blas villages, chartering a small plane to fly to landing strips along the coast that our military had built during World War II. Another weekend I traveled with a young Canadian missionary in a long, slim *piragua* made from a single tree trunk and powered by an outboard motor, traveling up the Bayano to primitive Cuna villages little touched by the outside world. The results in terms of reporting to Washington may have been meager, but I came to know Panama better than most foreign diplomats did, and I came to realize that one could not learn everything about a country by sitting in its capital.

After some months I was happy to say goodbye to my chief the first secretary, who was transferred to South America. He was replaced by Edward Clark, an energetic man who had served in Panama before and now renewed his friendships with many leading Panamanians, including the president of the republic. The vacant number-two position in our section was filled by Neil McManus, a hardworking and good-natured Irish-American who ended his career a decade later as our consul general at Belfast. Most importantly, Ambassador Harrington went into retirement and was replaced by a Republican political appointee named Joseph Farland, who had made a name for himself as ambassador to the Dominican Republic by standing up to the Dominican dictator, Rafael Trujillo. Joe Farland and his wife Virginia got off a Panama Line ship in Cristobal Harbor and were met by his new staff and by a large and friendly crowd of Panamanians. Many of the latter were carrying signs that, instead of expressing anti-gringo sentiments, said, "Yankee Stay Here! Don't Go Home!"

What the signs meant was that the State Department had decided for reasons of economy to close the American consulate in Colon. Cristobal and Colon (which in English would be Christopher and Columbus) were twin cities at the Caribbean end of the Canal. Cristobal, in the Canal Zone, was the deep-sea port; Colon, a larger place just over the border in the republic, could handle only shallow-draft coastal shipping but had once been prosperous. The opening of the railway from Colon to Panama City in 1853 had made the trans-Isthmian route the fastest way from the eastern United States to booming California, but that had lasted only until 1869, when the first transcontinental railway was completed in the United States. Later, the construction of the Canal and then military and civilian projects during World War II—including work on a never-finished third set of canal locks—had brought prosperity back to Colon. For decades, cruise ships had stopped regularly for a day at Cristobal so their passengers could tour and shop in Colon. But after 1945, Canal employment had dropped sharply and the cruise ships had stopped coming. Colon had opened a new free trade zone, but in most of the city, which received an average 140 inches of rain a year, the mold was literally growing up the walls. Now, the Panamanians complained, the American government was going to show it thought that Colon was finished, by closing the consulate it had opened there even before the railroad was built.

In succeeding weeks we heard intimations that there might be anti–United States demonstrations again this year on November 4—not over the flag issue but because we were closing our Colon consulate. My new ambassador made clear to Washington that he did not think that was a good reason to have demonstrations: we should keep the consulate open. Sorry, said the State Department, but we have transferred the consul and vice consul, and there are no replacements—but if you think it important, we do not mind if you send an embassy staff member to Colon to maintain an official presence.

The next week I began commuting across a continent, perhaps the only member of the American Foreign Service ever to do so. The Panama Railroad train left Panama City at 7 A.M., four old coaches and a diesel locomotive, and after a pleasant hour's trip through the forest and along Gatun Lake, I would reach Colon. There Victor Lambert, the consulate's only remaining Panamanian employee, would meet me in the consulate Ford, and we would drive to the consulate and raise the flag. Our premises consisted of two buildings that had once been the residences of senior army officers, with an acre of gardens bordered by a former sixteen-inch gun emplacement. The gun emplacement was now inhabited by large parasol ants that periodically invaded the garden and were in turn attacked by Victor with chlordane.

I enjoyed having my own post, although it was a little one, as a vice consul aged twenty-eight. I traveled up and down the Caribbean coast of the republic and made friends with Colon's business and political leaders, including José Dominador Bazan, a *colonense* who was second vice president of the republic. Most evenings I took the train home, but occasionally my wife would leave our children with the maid in Panama City and join me for an evening in Colon. Soon the November holidays came. Colon celebrated both the 4th, the national holiday, and the 5th, which was Colon Day. Our third child, Mary, was soon to be born, so I left my family at home in Panama City and moved into my consulate for three days. The holidays would be special this year. The Canal Company had softened its stand on flags and had agreed that on the 5th, after a ceremony at Colon's city hall, Colon's officialdom could march into the Canal Zone behind the Panamanian flag.

On the 4th I wore my best Haspel suit to an official reception and luncheon in Colon. But formal dress in Panama was a white suit, and that was indicated for the 5th. Soon after we had come to Panama, my wife found me some good linen, I found a Hindu tailor, and for forty dollars the tailor made me a handsome white suit. I wore it once, the maid had washed it and it shrank a little; I wore it again, and the maid washed it and put it away. White-suit occasions were not frequent.

On the morning of the 5th, I woke up early in Colon, had coffee and a mango, shaved, showered, and put on my white suit. Incredibly, awfully, it had shrunk again, and drastically, at its last washing. The jacket sleeves ended unacceptably far above my wrists, the trousers above my ankles. I was due at City Hall at 10 A.M., and the invitation said "white suit." The second vice president would be there; everyone who counted would be there. The Cuban consul would certainly be wearing his white suit; all the consuls would. I found that by pulling the trousers down below my waist I could almost achieve a respectable trouser length. If I kept my arms somewhat retracted in the sleeves, I would not look exactly like a teenager who had sprouted out of his clothes. I dressed and drove to City Hall.

I made a quick entrance on arriving—the second vice president inquired politely if I had hurt my shoulder, when I tried to retract my arm after shaking his hand—and took my seat with the other consuls. After lengthy oratory we went down to the street. The notables began arranging themselves for the march, behind the Colon firemen's band and the honor guard with the flag. I stood on the curb watching. The second vice president came over to me and said, "But you're going with us!"

"No, Vice President, this is your day."

"But you are; we would feel insulted if our friend the vice consul didn't come. This is a historic occasion!"

"Yes, but it's your occasion, not mine."

"Bridges, you wouldn't want to insult us?"

"No, Vice President, I'll come."

The band began to play a march. Maneuvering the waist of my trousers down below my navel again, I joined the other white-suited gentlemen. The vice president was on my right, the provincial governor on my left. Off we stepped. The Cuban consul was in the row just behind me, and I wondered if I heard him say something about gringo tailors. That no longer bothered me. What bothered me now was what the Canal Company people, a jingoistic lot, would say if they saw the American vice consul marching into the Canal Zone behind the flag of Panama. We rounded the corner of

Front Street, and the Zone was just ahead of us. Standing on the corner was the head of the Atlantic Division of the Canal Company, looking straight at me. I winked at him as we passed. He did not wink back.

An hour later I got back to the consulate and quickly phoned Ambassador Farland to tell him, before Tom Caldwell could, about my forced march. Well, he said, Caldwell had already phoned him, pretty angry, but he had told Caldwell that he shouldn't be upset; sometimes in diplomacy people might be forced to do things that others might find funny. I sat looking at my white trouser cuffs up near my knees and thought, "funny" is the word.

Soon after Colon Day the Department decided to keep my consulate open. A permanent vice consul was sent to replace me, and I returned to the embassy to issue visas. It would be almost another quarter-century before I had a post of my own again, in Somalia.

One day six months later, I walked up the street to the DCM's house. In the North it was spring. Here, it was the usual blazing Panama noon. Big-winged buzzards were circling in a column of air, and a thunderhead was building its dazzling throne in blue sky. John Shillock had invited me and four other embassy officers to lunch to meet an officer named Ellsworth from the State Department's personnel bureau, who was visiting the half-dozen embassies between Guatemala and Panama. Ellsworth shook my hand and said, "Bridges? You made it to Class Six in good time; congratulations." The promotion list had come out the previous month. I was in fact pleased that I had been promoted from Class Seven to Class Six in two years, faster than most of my contemporaries. Now I was eligible for the army's Detachment R in Oberammergau. This was a school for military officers bound for service behind the Iron Curtain; two Foreign Service officers were sent each year before assignment to Moscow. Competition for Detachment R assignments was intense among would-be Russian hands in our service. I thanked Ellsworth for his congratulations and said that if he had a minute after lunch, I wanted to talk to him about where I might go next, when I left Panama in another year.

"Ah, I need to bring you up to date. You're leaving here this year, not next. We want to send you to Detachment R. I assume with your background that would be acceptable to you."

"Yes, of course. But just when do you mean?"

"Well, it's May 10th. The course begins in August. I think you should plan to leave here in about six weeks."

The rest of the day seemed a kind of dream. At five, as usual, Mary Jane came by the embassy with our three small children in our aging Austin, and we drove out to the beach at Fort Amador. I dived into the salt sea, washing off cares and sweat, and came back to my wife where she sat on the sand with David, Lizzie, and Mary. The sun had gone down behind the wooded hill, and the air felt almost cool. I said, "I have some news to tell you."

four

The Moscow Hand

Our nine months in Bavaria were in part an Alpine vacation, in part a brief tour in the army, and in good part a chapter from some Nabokov novel. My family and I were assigned an apartment in a housing complex for American army officers outside Garmisch, near the base of the 1,900-meter-high Kramerspitze. The first Sunday we were there, my wife asked me to watch the children while she took a walk. Four hours later she returned with a wild and happy look; she had taken the path to the top of the mountain, seeing several chamois on the way, and from the peak had looked out over all the Bavarian Alps. We began a strenuous series of weekend hikes. The following spring I successfully walked David, just five years old, a thousand vertical meters to the top of the Wank, the mountain next to Partenkirchen. But it was not all vacation. Each weekday morning at seven, an army bus would pick up us students and take us ten miles up to Detachment R, located in a former Wehrmacht garrison on the edge of Oberammergau.

The detachment commandant was an American colonel, his deputy was a major, and there were several staff noncoms. We students numbered less than fifty, mostly army officers spending two years at Detachment R after a year of Russian-language study and a year in the Russian Institute at Columbia University, where I had done my own graduate work. Most of the army officers would go on from Oberammergau to become military attachés at Moscow or to join the American liaison mission with the Group of Soviet Forces in East Germany. Either job was tough, especially the one in East Germany. The four-power agreements for the occupation of defeated Germany in 1945 had specified that each of the four occupying powers—the United States, Britain, France, and the Soviet Union—could send liaison missions to the others' occupying forces. The Soviet missions to the

Peter and Mary Jane
Bridges hiking in
the Bavarian Alps,
October 1961.

three Western armies concentrated not on liaison but on obtaining intelligence about their hosts' weaponry and preparedness; the Western missions in East Germany did the same. Sometimes the Soviets and East Germans used rough techniques to keep the American, British, or French officers from getting close to their missile emplacements or armored units.

We students included also two marine officers, a navy lieutenant commander, a dozen civilian analysts from the National Security Agency in Washington—and two Foreign Service officers, Robert German and me. The FSOs sent to Detachment R had to be already proficient in Russian, and we went there for just nine months, to be followed by a two-year tour in Moscow.

It was the staff of instructors that provided the Nabokov-like quality. They taught in Russian, and they *were* Russian, except for a pleasant gentleman named Ozolins, who had been a Latvian diplomat until Stalin occupied his country, and a Chechen writer named Avtorkhanov, who had been a Soviet professor—and both of these spoke perfect Russian. As for the Russians, they ran the gamut from two former KGB officers who had defected to the West to an ethnic Russian who had lived in Poland until World War II and a former Soviet economist who had skipped from East to West Berlin before the Wall was built.[1] In general, most of the Russians despised one another; they all hated one of the ex-KGB colonels. Several times I heard it told how five years earlier, in 1956, the staff had been watching on German television the Soviet tanks entering Budapest

1. The KGB officers actually came from the MVD, predecessor to the KGB.

to crush the Hungarian revolution. The KGB veteran had looked around at the others and commented, almost with satisfaction, "What remains is only a technical question."

The other KGB veteran had a gold watch inscribed to him by Lavrenti Beria, Stalin's police chief; he had defected after Beria was executed in 1953 soon after Stalin died. He had been at Detachment R for five or six years, but he still, for most of us, seemed to personify the Stalinist system. One evening after a few drinks he told Rick Agather, one of our army captains, that he thought that by now he understood the American military pretty well. There was just one question that continued to bother him: what did our chaplains really do?

The Soviet press would occasionally make mention of Detachment R as the American spy school at Oberammergau, but it was not that. To be sure, our military officers would be assigned to gather information on the Soviet military, and the two of us from the State Department would no doubt be assigned in Moscow to report on what was going on in the Soviet Union. But we would do this openly; we were not being taught clandestine work. What we were being taught at Oberammergau was to perfect ourselves in the Russian language, to comprehend the intricacies and absurdities of the Soviet economic system, and to master the Soviet geographic, ethnographic, and climatic map; we were also taught a lot about the Soviet military and police system.

When spring came in 1962, our deputy commandant (Bill Thoma), the eleven army officers who were completing their second year at Detachment R, Bob German, and I left Bavaria for a four-week trip in a little German touring bus through Eastern Europe and the Soviet Union. The Communist authorities raised no obstacles to our trip, except for the Czechoslovaks, who would not let us visit major cities, so we had a pleasant drive from Budapest to Cracow through green Slovakia. We had several hours free one afternoon in Warsaw, and I went down to our embassy to see my friend Jack Scanlan, who had earlier spent two years in Moscow.[2] I asked him what it was like to work in Moscow. "Well," said Jack, "one day you will be sitting there reading *Pravda*, trying to figure out whether anything it says corresponds to reality, and you will ask yourself just what in hell you are doing in Moscow—and then it will come to you that you are representing one of the world's two superpowers in the capital of the other superpower, and you

2. Scanlan would end his diplomatic career as ambassador to Yugoslavia, 1985–89.

will realize that no matter how hard it is, the job is well worth it." I hoped he was right as regarded this last.

The next day our little Setra bus crossed the Soviet border at Brest, and we continued east toward Moscow through bleak woods, the unkempt fields of collective farms, and the Pripet Marshes, where we just missed a moose that ran in front of our bus. In the following two weeks, we saw Moscow, Leningrad, several smaller cities, and a couple of thousand kilometers of countryside. I had been studying Russia and Russian since I was nineteen, and Moscow and Leningrad looked as I had expected they would. But the villages were worse than I had expected, miserable settlements of log houses where the only handsome structures, the Orthodox churches, had long since been converted into warehouses. As I stood one day in a village street near Moscow, a huge military jet lumbered over, taking off from some nearby airfield. There was a striking contrast between that modernity in the air and the squalidness below. How could a country of muddy villages produce such a great plane? The obvious answer was that the Soviet police machine took what it needed for the military and left little for the populace. Eventually this machine would prove incapable of keeping up with the West. But on that day in May 1962, neither I nor anyone else on our bus, nor indeed anyone in either the Western or the Eastern world, could foresee the collapse of the Soviet system.

We had been pestering the Intourist guide who accompanied us from Brest onward to show us a collective farm. On our last afternoon in the Soviet Union, we visited a huge collective farm outside Kishinev, the capital of Soviet Moldavia. The collective farm included several thousand acres of vineyards and a cool winery. There young ladies in white aprons invited us to sample the local products, seven kinds of wine plus a cognac. They poured our glasses full, but we noticed that our Soviet hosts were not drinking. Clearly they intended to get us drunk. We insisted that they drink with us, and so we all got drunk together. The next day at the Romanian border, the Soviet border guards held us up for four hours while they went through every bit of our baggage. That, considering the ninety-degree heat and our hangovers, was the only really cruel treatment we received on the trip.

When I visited Russia on the little bus it was May, with blue skies and things in bloom; after I returned to Garmisch, my family and I had fine outings in the Bavarian mountains before home leave in America. Eventually September came. My wife and I and our three children got off a Finnair flight in Moscow on a gray, cold, rainy day. As we drove down

Leningradskoye Shosse into central Moscow, I wondered if I had made a horrid mistake in bringing my family to this grim place. My spirits lifted a little when my wife declared herself satisfied with our embassy apartment, and we began to make friends in our embassy and elsewhere in the foreign community. But there was little satisfaction in my job.

For at least the first year in Moscow, I was to be the assistant general services officer, with the possibility (but no promise) of becoming a political officer in my second year. The assistant GSO supervised the embassy motor pool, our Soviet workmen and charwomen, our supply link with West Germany and Finland, and other housekeeping and maintenance, all of this under the watchful eye of the senior GSO, James B. Moran, an experienced administrative officer. I had no experience in admin work and not much interest. In later years, a bureaucratic State Department would proclaim that all main lines of Foreign Service work—administrative, consular, economic, and political—were of equal value; a number of senior admin officers with little direct experience in conducting our foreign relations would be made ambassadors.[3] But to me, in Moscow and later, those who maintained an embassy's premises and kept its vehicles running were doing work that was necessary but amounted to a support function—support for our service's most vital work, which was to maintain the relationship between our government and another and to keep Washington supplied with the reports and analysis that our policy makers needed to execute effective foreign policy. That was the kind of work I wanted to do, not ordering furniture and forms.

In odd hours when the embassy house seemed in order and during evenings before going to bed, I read all the Soviet literary journals I could find. Soon after we reached Moscow an astounding thing happened. The journal *Novyi mir*, whose editor was the solid ex-Stalinist Aleksandr Tvardovsky, published a stark account of a *gulag* prisoner named Ivan Denisovich, written by an unknown author named Aleksandr Solzhenitsyn. In this and other ways we could see a degree of thaw on the Soviet literary scene, which had been so frozen when I was a Columbia student.

One of the other interesting journals was *Inostrannaya literatura* (Foreign literature), in which one could find occasional penetrating and informative pieces on Western authors. I found several articles by someone named R. Orlova on contemporary American writing to be especially frank and objective. Soon I got to know Raisa Orlova, and later I got to know her husband,

---

3. Jim Moran himself would become ambassador to the Seychelles in 1987. To be clear, he served there very ably.

a specialist on German literature named Lev Kopelev. They would sometimes come to dinner with my wife and me; they talked of having us out to
their dacha but were afraid to do so. Each couple enjoyed the other's company, and we discussed each other's country and literature frankly, but the
Kopelevs talked relatively little about themselves. I knew that they were
Jewish and that Kopelev had been an army officer in World War II and had
then been arrested and sent to a labor camp for eight years. What they never
told us, and what I never learned until I had left the Soviet Union, was that
Kopelev had a fellow prisoner named Solzhenitsyn—and that it was Kopelev
who first took Solzhenitsyn's "Ivan Denisovich" to Tvardovsky and urged
him to publish it in *Novyi mir*.

In two years in Moscow I got to know a number of writers and artists.
Some were Stalinist types; some were decidedly not. I befriended the most
popular younger Soviet writer, Vasily Aksyonov. His father, a member of
the Central Committee of the Communist Party, had been executed during
Stalin's purges of the 1930s, after which young Vasily was taken from his
mother, Evgeniya Ginzburg, and she was sent to the gulag.[4] Often on Saturday mornings my wife and I would meet Andrei Amalrik, an aspiring
writer lately expelled from Moscow State University, who would take us to
visit dissident artists like Oskar and Valentina Rabin, who refused to obey
the dicta of socialist realism and painted what they liked.

In December 1962 Nikita Khrushchev was taken to see an exhibition of
modern Soviet art that, although it included some unorthodox works, had
opened at the Manezh exhibition hall just off Red Square. The great leader
exploded, saying that these paintings reminded him of droppings from a
donkey's tail. The result was a halt in the thaw. Direct retribution fell only on
Valentina Rabina's father, Evgeny Kropovnitsky, who was expelled from the
Union of Soviet Artists. But Kropovnitsky, the Rabins, and their artist friends
kept selling to foreigners—and to a group of top Soviet scientists who were
de facto patrons of these brave people. Several months after the Manege and
other official exhibit halls were closed to the unorthodox artists, I visited an
exhibition of their work in a key Soviet physics institute on Lenin Hills.

The KGB under Khrushchev might not be quite as awful as it had been
in Stalin's day, but the pressures of the Soviet police state were everywhere
felt. Our telephones were tapped, and our walls were full of microphones
(an American team pulled one out of my office wall, but we did not even

4. Her account of this was smuggled out and published in Italy (*Viaggio nella vertigine*
[Milano: Arnoldo Mondadori Editore,1967]) and later in the United States.

look for the ones in our apartments); we were followed by KGB agents, and we could not travel more than forty kilometers from Red Square without the concurrence of the Soviet foreign ministry. At each of the two entrances to our embassy on Chaikovsky Street, where we both lived and worked, stood two burly Soviet policemen, who denied entrance to anyone whom they did not identify as American or who could not show reason to enter. When my wife and I invited Raisa Orlova and Lev Kopelev to dinner, the invitations had to be sent through the Union of Soviet Writers, and our guests had to show the invitations to the cops at our gate.

Living in Moscow taught me to be extremely discreet. In later years one of my Africanist colleagues suggested that I was cold toward Africans—I had said that I knew few Somalis I felt I could trust completely. The fact was that I found most Somalis quite likable; but they lived in a police state, and I knew full well (and our intelligence confirmed this) that they were compelled to report to the authorities on their contacts with me.

In Moscow, I could never be sure of the true sentiments of the intellectuals I knew. It was possible that, beyond being forced to report on Westerners, some of them had been recruited to serve as professional police agents; this happened even to leading members of the Russian Orthodox clergy. Some of my intellectual friends eventually proved their sentiments by emigrating (or being forced to emigrate) to the West. Orlova and Kopelev ended up in West Germany, where he won Germany's top literary prize. Aksyonov came to America, where we had lunch soon after his arrival; today he teaches in Virginia. Young Amalrik was exiled to Siberia after I left Moscow, but he and his wife Gyuzel later left the Soviet Union, and they spent a New Year's Eve with us in Virginia before his untimely death in a road accident in Spain.[5] I never asked any of these people if they had been forced to report on me. Orlova admitted later in her memoirs[6] that she had kept the KGB informed of her contacts with Westerners. I want to believe that she had stopped doing so by the time we met.

After spending a year without distinction in General Services, I was happily transferred to the embassy's political section, to become one of three officers reporting on Soviet domestic matters. My main fields of interest were the intellectual scene, Soviet nationalities problems, and religion. The job taught me to be assiduous in seeking information. I learned what I could

5. Amalrik had made his name in the West with his works *Will the Soviet Union Survive until 1984?* and *Involuntary Journey to Siberia.*

6. Published by Random House, New York, in 1983.

from my Soviet acquaintances, which was not often much, and exchanged information with diplomats from other embassies, who were usually less well informed than I was. I read all the Soviet newspapers and journals I could. *Pravda* and *Izvestiya* might reflect Soviet reality only dimly, but intellectual journals sometimes told more, and sometimes one could glean things from the provincial press. We were not permitted to subscribe to provincial newspapers, but I got a reader's card at Lenin Library and read them there. And I traveled, all I could.

More than a third of the Soviet Union was officially closed to foreigners, and we had to apply to the foreign ministry to visit even the areas that were supposedly open. I was turned down about half the time, but still I averaged a trip or more per month. My favorite traveling companions were two Australian diplomats. Bill Morrison, with whom I spent a memorable ten days in Siberia, later abandoned diplomacy for politics and served as Australia's defense minister.[7] Gregory Clark, with whom I toured the western Ukraine, left diplomacy for academia and later became president of Tama University, founded in Tokyo in 1988. Clark and I both spoke good Russian, and when we traveled we saw no need to advertise ourselves as Westerners. One day in Chernovtsy a buxom blonde Ukrainian waitress said, as she gave us our bill for lunch, that she was hoping to exchange her apartment for one in our capital. Greg and I looked at each other. Our capital? Did she mean Canberra or Washington? Obviously neither. Tell us, we said, just where do you think we're from? Oh, come on, she said, I know you're from Riga. We smiled and paid.

My best trip was with John and Elaine Steinbeck in the autumn of 1963. Steinbeck had been urged by the State Department to spend a month touring the Soviet Union and meeting with Soviet writers. He agreed to do so on condition that the embassy provide him a Russian-speaking escort and that a younger American writer—Edward Albee—come along. The job of accompanying Steinbeck fell to me, while my colleague Bill Luers would travel with Albee, who reached Moscow two weeks after Steinbeck. For some reason it was not Luers but I who accompanied Edward Albee to a meeting at the Union of Soviet Writers, a couple of days after Albee had reached Moscow, to discuss his Soviet itinerary. We sat down around a table

7. See the author's "May Days in Siberia," in *Tales of the Foreign Service* (Columbia: Univ. of South Carolina Press, 1978). As I wrote in my article on the intrepid American traveler John Ledyard in the *Dartmouth Alumni Magazine* in October 1980, when Bill Morrison and I visited Yakutsk in Siberia's far north, I was perhaps the first Dartmouth alumnus to visit there since Ledyard, who reached Yakutsk in 1787 after a three-month journey from Moscow.

Peter Bridges and John Steinbeck in
Tbilisi, Georgia, October 1963.

covered with green baize, and the Russians asked Edward Albee where he
would like to spend the next month. Florence, he said. Ha ha, they said.
Really, Mr. Albee, they said, what are your travel desires? Florence, he repeated; he was quite serious. It was some minutes before he agreed to go on
to Leningrad with the Steinbecks, after a stay in Moscow.

Before the Steinbecks and Albee had visited Moscow and Leningrad,
with Luers and me in tow, my wife and I had accompanied the Steinbecks to
Kiev, together with a functionary of the Soviet Writers' Union. Mary Jane
had to return from Kiev to Moscow because of her duties as embassy commissary manager. I was to go on with the Steinbecks to Georgia and Arme-
nia, but our embassy phoned me in Kiev to say that the foreign ministry
would not agree to my travel to Tbilisi and Yerevan. I told John Steinbeck,
who quickly wrote out a paragraph and told me to send it where I thought
it would do most good. I looked at what he had written:

> In refusing a permit for my friend and colleague Peter Bridges to travel to
> Tbilisi with me on grounds of his diplomatic status, the Soviet Foreign
> Office has apparently overlooked the fact that I, too, am sent to represent
> my government and my nation. Since I have no wish to violate Soviet
> regulations, it is with deep regret that I must advise my friends in the
> Republic of Georgia that I will be unable to visit them.

I told John Steinbeck that this was deeply flattering but that of course
they must go on without me. No, he said; I want you to send this. So I sent
it as a telegram to Mikhail Smirnovsky, the head of the USA section in the
Soviet foreign ministry. Next day we heard from Moscow that there had

Peter and Mary Jane at
Serebryany Bor on the
Moscow River, spring 1964.

been some regrettable confusion and that I might proceed as earlier planned. Steinbeck was as pleased as I was. For once we had outsmarted the cops.[8]

By the summer of 1964, I was nearing the end of my tour in Moscow, and Nikita Khrushchev was nearing the end of his reign in Moscow, although we did not know that. We could see some of Khrushchev's failures, among them his Cuban missile ploy (the Cuban missile crisis had come just a month after we arrived in Moscow in 1962) and his disastrous agricultural policies, which left the country almost without bread in early 1964 in the wake of a single bad harvest. For the first time, I heard people in the Moscow bread stores grumbling audibly about the regime. That might not matter much, given police controls, but the extent to which Khrushchev was supported by top military leaders was also questionable; they had notably failed to back his announcement of troop cuts in late 1963.

What was life like in Moscow during the Cuban missile crisis? It was only after we returned to America that we realized how frightened people at home had been. We certainly knew that it was a grave moment (although

8. Jackson J. Benson gives a good account of the Steinbecks' 1963 Soviet journey in *The True Adventures of John Steinbeck, Writer* (New York: Penguin, 1990), but he is wrong in saying that I sent the cable to our embassy. My own account of the trip to Kiev and beyond is in Amembassy Moscow airgram A-650 to Department of State, November 15, 1963, a copy of which I obtained through the Freedom of Information Act.

David, Elizabeth, Peter, and Mary,
westbound on the S.S. *United States*
after leaving Moscow, September 1964.

only the ambassador and his deputy were privy to all the messages being exchanged between Moscow and Washington); but while the press heightened the war scare in America, Soviet media had no interest in scaring its public and took a controlled tone. Moscow was not a city full of jitters—at least not public ones. One Saturday, with the crisis at its height, my wife and I left our children with friends and went for a long walk. Returning, we noticed that traffic had been stopped along the wide boulevard the U.S. embassy faces. A mob had gathered in front—not a Panama-type mob, just citizens rounded up to stage a protest. With their "Hands Off Cuba" placards, they stood quietly as we walked into the embassy. Only later were they told to throw ink bottles at our walls.

Not long before leaving Moscow, I discussed Khrushchev's weaknesses in a cable I drafted for the ambassador's signature. The cable concluded that Khrushchev would, despite his problems, remain at the Soviet helm for the foreseeable future. Malcolm Toon, who then headed the political section (and who returned to Moscow in 1976 as ambassador), agreed with my draft, Ambassador Foy Kohler signed it, and off it went to Washington.

By September 1964 the Bridges had put Moscow behind them and were on home leave in Illinois. One day I went to lunch at a club in Chicago with my brother-in-law Peter Pizzo and one of his business associates. We had, I confess, two martinis before lunch was served. Suddenly the public address system announced that Khrushchev had been dethroned in Moscow. I excused myself, got up from the table, and disappeared in the direction of the telephones. Years later my brother-in-law told me how impressed he and his friend had been. Obviously I had run to the phone, to call Washington and compare notes on what was happening in Moscow. I hated to tell him that I had gone not to the phones but to the men's room. The drafter of the "Khrushchev Will Stay" cable would not have thought that a very good time to call Washington.[9]

In September 1964 I began working as a midlevel Soviet expert in the U.S. Arms Control and Disarmament Agency in Washington. This agency was separate from the State Department, though housed in the same building; Foreign Service officers can be assigned outside State if the other agency agrees to reimburse the State Department for their salaries, and ACDA was agreeable to that in my case. The Bridges bought a small townhouse on Cathedral Avenue in Washington, across the street from the National Zoo. We could hear occasional lions and African hunting dogs at night, and we had good neighbors, including a slightly older couple with a grander townhouse, Jim and Edith Spain. Spain was a CIA veteran now serving on the State Department's Policy Planning Council; he would later serve as ambassador to Tanzania, Turkey, and finally Sri Lanka.[10]

ACDA conducted our disarmament negotiations with the Soviet Union. It was a quiet place when I began working there; the Soviets had refused to continue the Ten-Nation Disarmament Conference in Geneva, composed of five Warsaw Pact and five NATO governments, because there was no representation from developing countries. At this point Moscow's star rode high in Africa and Asia. Soviet aid flowed into those continents in large amounts, and many Africans and Asians admired Soviet-style socialism.

With nothing much doing in my new office, I went quietly to see a friend in the Peace Corps, and after a pleasant talk with its director, Sargent Shriver, I was offered a job as Peace Corps desk officer for several South American countries. But then Moscow and Washington reached a compromise. The United Nations Disarmament Commission, a body that had met only once before in twenty years, would have a session in New York—and then the Ten-Nation Conference in Geneva would resume as a conference of eighteen, with the addition of eight nonaligned countries.

9. If I failed to predict major events, I had at least introduced jogging to the streets of Moscow in 1962, as Yale Richmond, Moscow's second jogger, pointed out recently on the Internet.

10. See James W. Spain, *In Those Days: A Diplomat Remembers* (Kent, Ohio: Kent State Univ. Press, 1998).

Soon I was spending Mondays to Fridays in New York, meeting with scores of diplomats from other countries and helping shape wordy resolutions that, I thought to myself, bore little relationship to the reality of missile silos in the Dakotas and Siberia. After the Disarmament Commission terminated, the new Eighteen-Nation Conference began, and I left my family for lonely summer weeks in a Geneva hotel. That fall I returned to New York for the United Nations General Assembly. Mary Jane came up to New York one day, and John and Elaine Steinbeck took us to dinner at the Plaza Hotel. The Steinbecks were spending most of their time at Sag Harbor and invited me to take over their Manhattan apartment for the rest of my UN stay. Not only was it a very kind gesture but it saved me the money I would have spent on a hotel room. My wife and I had agreed that when I was away she should use all my salary, ten thousand dollars a year, to run the household and pay the mortgage, while I would survive on the State Department's stingy per diem allowance. I was back in Washington for Christmas, but early in 1966 the Geneva conference resumed, and again I abandoned my family for long weeks.

When I first joined ACDA, its staff included a senior Foreign Service officer named Alexander Akalovsky, a Russian-American who had begun his career as a State Department interpreter. Alex was now a top disarmament expert; he also served as interpreter in the private talks between the Soviet and American delegation heads in Geneva. The eighteen-nation forum was too large for any real negotiations; these bilateral private talks were the only place where much substance got discussed. (The talks were not exciting; neither side was taking much initiative. I had witnessed the signing of the limited test-ban treaty in Moscow in 1963, but it would be years before we ventured to discuss limitations in strategic arms and negotiate what became known as the SALT treaty.) One afternoon in Geneva, I saw Alex Akalovsky and his family off on the train for Moscow, where he was to become first secretary of our embassy. And I was now to be the interpreter in the private talks.

My Russian was better than ever before. My former Moscow colleague Terry Catherman was heading the Russian service of the Voice of America, and he wanted to add a native American voice to those of the Russian emigrés on his staff. So sometimes when I was in Washington I would drive down to the Voice of America on a Sunday morning and read news and commentary in Russian to listeners in the Soviet Union. I had lately passed the Russian-English interpreter exam at the State Department. But in negotiations like the Geneva private talks, the interpreter does not interpret from Russian into his own language, which is easier than the other way around. I was called on to interpret into Russian what my boss said in English. I had mastered the standard disarmament vocabulary in both languages, and I soon found that the Soviet side's interpreter, a skilled graduate of a Soviet interpreting school, was willing to help me out when I got stuck. That happened often.

Our delegation in Geneva was often headed not by ACDA's director, a retired corporate executive named William Foster, but by his deputy, Adrian Fisher. Butch Fisher was a distinguished public servant who had been the State Department's legal advisor and would later become dean of the Georgetown University School of Law. He was also the son of a Tennessee congressman, and during the discussions he liked to tell Tennessee jokes and quote by heart from the "Mr. Dooley" stories written in Irish dialect, decades earlier, by Finlay Peter Dunne. Neither the jokes nor Mr. Dooley translated easily into Russian—sometimes they hardly translated at all—and my Soviet counterpart was little help; indeed, he asked me at some point what language Mr. Fisher was using. Never did I have a more difficult job.

Despite my deficiencies, Messrs. Foster and Fisher liked me, and they made clear that they wanted to keep me on beyond my two-year assignment unless I was needed elsewhere. I could not stand the thought of continued long absences from my wife and children, and I wangled an assignment to a year of Bulgarian language training in Washington to be followed by two years at the embassy in Sofia—and then I heard of a job in the Rome embassy that was going begging.

"What would you say," I asked my wife, "if we were to go to Rome instead of Sofia?" My wife is at once sweet, tough, and practical. In the course of following me to a succession of cities at home and abroad, she has at different times taught soldiers who lacked high school diplomas, interpreted for La Scala and Paris Opera stagehands at the Kennedy Center, managed the large commissary in our Moscow embassy, and run a development company in Houston. Just now she was teaching in an inner-city school in the District of Columbia while working toward a master's degree in education at Howard University. "Go to Rome?" she replied. "I could take that."

I went to see Malcolm Toon, my Moscow boss, who was now deputy assistant secretary of state for European affairs. "Mac," I said, "as you know I am bound for Sofia, but if the needs of the service should dictate that I go to Rome instead, I want you to know I'd be ready to do so."

"I see," he said.

five

Rome and Prague

We were assigned to Rome for a four-year tour of duty. Mary Jane and I had first visited Rome in early 1957 as an American army private with a young wife, on a vacation we could not afford, to escape the drabness of our garrison town in France. Italy had already embarked on its economic miracle, the Romans in the Piazza di Spagna were well dressed, but along the Appian Way the only traffic was a priest walking with a group of children, and many shanties still sheltered poor newcomers to the capital under the ancient aqueducts leading in from the *campagna*. Returning to Rome in 1966, we found Fiats everywhere and a booming economy, major social and political problems, and the opportunity to discuss these problems with a sophisticated class of intellectuals, journalists, diplomats, and politicians. After two months in a hotel, my wife found a remodeled apartment that would almost fit the five of us, in Via dei Banchi Nuovi, the street where Benvenuto Cellini once had his studio. I would rise at six in the morning and take our dog, Seumas, to run four laps around Piazza Navona, the Emperor Domitian's stadium. We discovered that the Italian National Olympic Committee had great sports facilities and courses for children. My wife enrolled our three, and soon David was diving in the same pool where two Olympic medalists practiced, and Lizzie and Mary were swimming two kilometers an afternoon. Life was good for us, those years in Rome.

There were some problems. I had been assigned to Rome on short notice, with no chance to study Italian before arrival, and few Italians spoke English. I told myself I would convert my Spanish to Italian, but that took time. Meanwhile I went to call on Luigi Barzini. He was a Liberal Party member of the Chamber of Deputies, a writer whose book *The Italians* was a

Peter and Mary Jane in front of the
Rome embassy, December 1966.

recent best-seller in America, and (not least) a graduate—who spoke perfect
English—of Columbia University's journalism school. Barzini gave me tea
and an hour's disquisition on Italy's many weaknesses and complexities—and
its strengths. What stayed with me was mainly the conviction that this was a
country with a potential much greater than I had realized and a future that
was problematical; but then, so was America's.

Initially, my main responsibility as a political officer in Rome was to report on the Italian Communist Party, the PCI. The job was made more difficult
by the fact that I was not permitted contacts with that party, lest this disturb
our friends in Italy's other parties and give cachet to the Communists. I began
to acquire a number of friends among Italian journalists, non-Communist
politicians, and foreign ministry officials—I was also reporting on the course
of Italy's relationships with the Communist world. But the Communists
could not be ignored. After I had been some time in Rome, it was clear to
me that if Italian politics continued on its present course, the Italian Communists would be in the government within a decade. Our political section

was headed by an astute officer named Samuel Gammon, who agreed that the time had come to open a dialog with the PCI. If, he said, we were to send a cable to Washington recommending we make contact with the PCI, it would be distributed all over the place, Congress would get wind of it, and the answer would come back No. So instead I wrote a "memorandum for discussion," which Sam sent quietly to the Italian desk in the State Department. Soon I was authorized to make contact—one contact.

Louis Fleming was the head of the Rome bureau of the *Los Angeles Times*, and he numbered among his friends and acquaintances both me and Giuseppe Boffa, a native of Milan and the PCI's top journalist. Boffa had served twice as the Moscow correspondent of *L'Unita*, the party's official newspaper; we had both been there in 1963–64 but had not met. Fleming, at the suggestion of Sam Gammon, invited Boffa and me to lunch. It was the beginning of three years of interesting meetings between the two of us. Giuseppe Boffa, who two decades later became an Italian senator, has given a good account of our relationship in his 1998 volume *Memorie dal Comunismo.*[1] He was an astute observer of the Soviet system and was repelled by the repressive ways of that regime, as is clear from his memoir and several major historical works he has published over the years. But while he denounced the Soviet invasion of Czechoslovakia in 1968, he believed—and still believes today—that the 1956 Soviet invasion of Hungary was a necessary act. We talked and argued over many lunches and dinners, but neither had much effect on the other's opinions, although Boffa did somewhat change his opinions about the United States after I arranged for him to obtain a visa despite the prohibition on visits by Communists. In the course of my years in Rome, I met a number of Communists and Communist supporters besides Giuseppe Boffa. They left me sad. Italy badly needed a major opposition force, but it seemed to me tragic that Italians could not devise a Left opposition that was not tied, ideologically and financially as well, to the horrific system that ruled Russia.

After three years in Rome, my wife decided to take our three children to Greece during their spring vacation. Seumas the dog would stay with me in Rome, but our Volkswagen "bug" would be even more crowded than usual, because a friend and two of her children were going along. When they returned, my wife and children were full of stories. They had almost slid off a cliff on a muddy mountain road; they had collided ("slightly" said

---

1. Published by Ponte alle Grazie srl, Milano.

David, Elizabeth, Peter, Andrew
and Mary and their dog, Seumas,
in Val Gardena, Italian Dolomites,
summer 1970.

Mary Jane) with a bus on the quay in Patras. But the big news was that my wife thought she was pregnant.

The birth of Andrew the following December necessitated a change of cars and of housing. We moved from the crowded apartment near Piazza Navona to an old farmhouse on two acres north of Rome. I bought a VW squareback station wagon, which was roomy but had an electronic fuel-injection system, a technology yet to be perfected. One spring evening my wife and I drove into town to a *dopo cena*, an after-dinner get-together, at the house of Luigi Vittorio Ferraris, who headed the foreign ministry office dealing with Communist countries. Ferraris was a brilliant man with interesting friends, and as always at his house we enjoyed ourselves and did not leave for home until almost midnight. We lived near the village of Morlupo, thirty kilometers from Rome out the Via Flaminia. Twenty-two kilometers out, the car stopped dead, and I could not revive it. We began to walk, my wife in high heels. There was almost no traffic on the two-lane Flaminia, and no one would stop for us. But it was a fine moonlit night, and my wife remembers hearing the first nightingales of the year.

After three years in Rome, I was made number-two in the embassy's political section, under a canny and hardworking political counselor whom I much admired, Robert Barbour. While I still followed Italy's far Left, I now became as well the primary embassy contact with the dozen or so geographic offices in the foreign ministry's Directorate General of Political Affairs. It was a great job, and when our new ambassador, Graham Martin, asked me to stay on for a fifth year, I quickly agreed.

After five years in Rome, I was transferred to Prague. It was the end of 1971, three years after the Soviet Army crushed Alexander Dubcek's experiment in "socialism with a human face." It was a time when, Vaclav Havel wrote later, history stopped for the Czechs. Still, I was happy to go. For the first time I would have my own office to supervise, the embassy's political/economic section, and Prague would be interesting, if sad. I went ahead by train in November, then at Christmas went down by train to the Italian Dolomites to meet my family for skiing. My wife had packed up our furnishings at Morlupo and driven the four children to the mountains in the VW wagon. We were sending David to school in America, so after Christmas I would leave my wife and the three other children in the Val Gardena, drive David to the Munich airport, drive on to Prague, then two weekends later drive back to Italy to take the others to Prague. David and I were packing the car when it occurred to me to ask the whereabouts of our new green card, the international car insurance certificate; the old one had expired. "Oh," said my wife, "it's probably still in the Morlupo post office. You don't know how much I had to do the last few days; I just didn't have time to pick it up."

"How do you expect me to cross three borders with no green card?"

"Do your best," she said.

At the Brenner Pass neither the Italian nor the Austrian guards asked to see more than passports. At the Austrian-German border, the Germans asked for the insurance card. I tried to explain. No use; I had to buy a temporary red insurance card, and it was expensive. The Grenzpolizei guard was unpleasant to the point of being insulting. He walked around the car and informed me that since it had no Italian "I" sticker on the rear, I would have to buy one of those, too, for ten marks. Nonsense, I said. I was bound for Prague and within a week I would have Czechoslovak diplomatic plates to replace the Italian ones. He was relentless, and I paid up. Next morning David boarded the plane in Munich and wished me good luck at the Czech border. Thanks, I said.

The Germans caused me no trouble at the border station at Bayerische Eisenstein. Beyond was the Iron Curtain: a line of antitank obstacles, a plowed strip no doubt full of mines, and a high wire fence with guard towers. I drove slowly up to the Czech border guard. *"Dobry den,"* I said, "Good day." *"Dobry den,"* he replied. *"Dokumenty, prosim."* I produced my documents, including the German red card; I spoke no Czech, I said, but perhaps we could use Russian. He smiled, agreed, and said, "I know the Germans made you pay a lot. We'll make you pay, too—but not nearly so much!" I decided that there must be something left of the human face among the Czechs, despite the hold that Moscow had on them.

That turned out to be the case. The Czechoslovak police state was an efficient one, but we managed to make a number of friends. The Czechs were keeping their heads down—the Charter 77 dissident movement would not be founded for several years—but whatever sympathies had existed in Prague for Soviet-style socialism had vanished with the 1968 invasion. I had never served in a country where there was such a natural liking for Americans.

My embassy section was responsible not only for political and economic reporting but for trade promotion, and a lot of American companies were taking a new interest in Central and Eastern Europe. I made the rounds of the economic ministries and state foreign-trade organizations and got to know a lot of Czechs. These had survived the thorough purges after the 1968 invasion, and if they were not Communists (but a number were), they stayed close to the official line when they saw Americans.

There were worse types. The Czech nation had produced at least a few Quislings, spiritual descendants of the amoral bureaucrats whom Jaroslav Hasek caricatured in *The Good Soldier Schweik*. Once, I met at a reception the director of Prague's Ruzyne Airport. My Czech was improving, but my Russian was still better; he spoke no English but was fluent in Russian. We talked in Russian, and he told some joke that he said he had heard from a Soviet Air Force friend. Suddenly I realized that I was talking with the traitor who, while Alexander Dubcek and his reformers lay sleeping, had guided down to Ruzyne in the dark the scores of Soviet transports full of the tanks and troops that by dawn had reduced Prague again to servitude.

We spent not quite three years in Czechoslovakia. The winters were gray and smoky, and one could imagine Franz Kafka tramping those cold Prague streets. The summer woods were green and inviting, and we hiked Bohemia's incomparable network of trails. I immersed myself in Czech history and came to admire greatly the old professor-politician Tomas Masaryk, who had created independent Czechoslovakia in 1918 when Austria-Hungary crumbled. Masaryk's successor as president of Czechoslovakia in the sad Communist 1970s was Ludvik Svoboda, a general who had been installed after the 1968 Soviet invasion but who for a brief time looked capable of standing up to Moscow. Such hopes soon faded.

In 1973, a group of American senators came to Prague. This was the first congressional visit since the invasion, and the foreign ministry told us that the president of the republic would be pleased to receive the Americans. Our delegation was headed by Richard Schweiker of Pennsylvania. When we briefed the group before their call on Svoboda, Senator Schweiker asked me if the president of Czechoslovakia had ever been in the United States. Not to my knowledge, I said. During the First World War, we knew, Svoboda had been an officer in the Czechoslovak Legion, formed in Russia from Czechs and Slovaks who had deserted from the Austro-Hungarian armies. The Legion had eventually had to fight its way past the Bolsheviks in Siberia on its long way home to Europe. In the Second World War, Svoboda and other Czech officers had fled to the Soviet Union after the Nazi occupation of Prague.

The meeting with President Svoboda began pleasantly, but I was sorry to find that Svoboda had with him Vasil Bilak, one of the most pro-Soviet of the current Czechoslovak leaders. Senator Schweiker said he understood the president had never seen our country. "To the contrary," said the president. "When our Legion finally sailed from Vladivostok in 1920, I was on a ship that went through the Panama Canal to Norfolk, in Virginia. When we reached Norfolk my comrades and I learned that the ship had been sold and would not continue to Europe. We were stranded, but I had a Czech friend who had a farm in your state—Pennsylvania—so I went up there and worked on the farm for some months, until my friend decided to go back to the old country and sold the farm. If he hadn't sold the farm, I'd probably still be in Pennsylvania."

Meanwhile Vasil Bilak had been stirring in his seat. I expected he would say something foul. He said, "I must add, Senator Schweiker, that I too have Pennsylvania connections. My parents were married in the chapel at Moravian College in Pennsylvania!"

Afterward I apologized to Richard Schweiker for having misinformed him. No matter, he said, no matter at all—but what a complex place this is.

We were surprised to learn, in the summer of 1973, that Secretary of State William Rogers would visit Prague on his way home from a conference in Helsinki. No foreign minister of a NATO member country had come to

Above: Peter Bridges, Communist Party general secretary Gustav Husak, U.S. secretary of state William Rogers, U.S. assistant secretary of state Walter Stoessel, interpreter, Foreign Minister Bohuslav Chnoupek, Prime Minister Lubomir Strougal, Prague, 1973.

Left: Mary, Andrew, Mary Jane, Elizabeth, and David at the embassy Fourth of July reception, Prague, 1973.

Prague since the 1968 Soviet invasion had brought an end to Dubcek's more liberal regime. The authorities had been pleased to see our senators; they pulled out all the stops for Mr. Rogers. The foreign minister hosted a pleasant, informal dinner for the secretary in a restaurant in the Old Town. Afterward our ambassador, Albert Sherer, and his wife, Carroll, asked my wife and me to join them and Mr. Rogers for a drink in their garden. We all knew that Henry Kissinger, the national security adviser, had already won the dominant position in our foreign-affairs machine. Kissinger was handling relations with Moscow, but it was said that he had left Eastern Europe, which he thought unimportant, to Rogers. I was fascinated to hear Mr. Rogers say that President Nixon had really not wanted him to come to Prague but that he had nevertheless thought he should come. Not many weeks later Rogers resigned his post. I have always wondered whether Kissinger might have mentioned Rogers's Prague visit to Nixon as one further reason why Kissinger should now become secretary of state, as he did in September 1973.

Before we left Prague in June 1974, we spent an evening with a Czech couple we liked. They were doing well under the current regime: she edited a fashion magazine, he worked for a foreign-trade company. But they had made it clear to us earlier that they hoped for something better for their nation's future. This last evening it was time to be franker than we had been before. "What parting thoughts," I said, "will you leave me about the future? The Hungarians are deciding to make their way out of the Leninist mess. What of the Czechs?" The husband replied that he would like to leave me with a parting thought. The younger generation of Czechs were not deceived about the world; most of them were both physically fit and healthy minded; they loved their country. He could not say how long it might take for change to come—but the ultimate future of the nation was assured. I said I could then go home with some hope. And I did.

Before we left I had new evidence, if I needed it, of the contortions of this police state. My wife and I had become friends with Miroslav Holub and his attractive young wife. Holub was a poet and microbiologist whose poetry later became well known, in translation, in the West. He had been one of the signers in June 1968 of the brave "Two Thousand Words" manifesto, drafted by the writer Ludvik Vaculik. One evening we invited the two Holubs to dinner, as we had done before. He came, she did not. Soon after this, a Prague newspaper published a letter from Holub apologizing for his signature on the "Two Thousand Words." When I next saw him I said that I could imagine what pressure he had been under to recant. "No," he said, "I didn't write or sign that letter. It is an StB production. [The StB was the Czechoslovak version of the KGB.] It was forged by someone who knew intimate details about me. In the end I realized that the source was my wife. She is a police spy. And I have left her."

six

Long Years at Home

We returned to Washington in 1974 for what the Department said was to be a four-year tour of duty. I was confident that after no more than two or three years I would have a crack at a DCM job in some embassy abroad. In the event, we spent seven straight years in our country. They were in some ways difficult years. Our three oldest children had been abroad for eight years, and when they entered public school in Arlington, Virginia, they felt like strangers. They adjusted to America, and by 1978 all three were in college, two in Ivy League institutions and one at McGill University in Montreal. That was well and good, but the late 1970s were years of double-digit inflation in college tuition as in other areas, and my government salary increased much more slowly. Fortunately, my wife had settled on a new career in real estate. A main recollection of those years is that each time I became seriously overdue on a college bill, she managed to sell a house.

My first job back in the State Department was in Personnel, running a small, new unit on Foreign Service personnel policy under Nathaniel Davis, the director general of the Foreign Service, a dedicated and indeed inspirational officer who years earlier had been my supervisor on the Soviet desk. Soon I was sent out of the Department to spend two months at the Murphy Commission. This was a joint executive-legislative body created to study and recommend reforms in the federal foreign-affairs bureaucracy. Its head was Robert Murphy, our most distinguished senior diplomat. The commission was looking thoroughly into the State Department's personnel system, and the day after I joined it I was sent back to the department to ask some piercing questions. Unfortunately, the commission failed to take a piercing look at the increasing number of other federal agencies that claimed a share in our foreign relations. No real reforms resulted.

My commission boss was Jim Clark, a canny bank vice president who had spent years in the Bureau of the Budget. He came to me one afternoon and said that he had been putting together appendices for the commission's final report. He had just realized that he was lacking one appendix: he wanted a one-page chart that would show the progress of a Foreign Service officer's career. He would be grateful if I could produce such a chart in the next couple of hours. I said I could do that. I had one question: was I illustrating the career of an exceptionally successful officer or of a middle-ranker? Fairly successful, he said. I sat down at my typewriter and by day's end gave Clark a chart, which was reproduced without change in the published report. Only a relatively small number of senior Foreign Service officers ever became ambassadors, but I showed my fairly successful officer ending his career after being named ambassador to a small country at the age of fifty-two. A decade later, at fifty-two, I became ambassador to Somalia.

Some months after returning from the commission to State, I took on a new personnel job as head of the Office of Performance Evaluation, known as PE. The Foreign Service, like the military but unlike the civil service or most other American organizations, promotes individuals not to a job but to a rank. The promotions are decided on by annual selection boards, which rank all officers in a particular class on the basis of their performance files. The files' main content is annual efficiency reports. In earlier years, a supervisor would rate a subordinate, the supervisor's chief would add a reviewing statement, and the report would go to PE without the subordinate having seen it. In Moscow, as I learned only later, Jim Moran had written a fairly stiff report on my performance in General Services. Worse, his superior, a dour New Hampshireman who liked neither me nor Moscow and left there after a year, had added to the report a damning (and in my opinion totally unfair) review that won me an admonition from the 1964 selection board to shape up or leave the Service.

I had, then, a particular interest in improving the evaluation and promotion process. Together with my colleagues Alfred Haynes, a black civil service officer who had served in PE for a decade, and Dufour Woolfley, a white Foreign Service officer who had graduated from Tulane University's law school, we studied possibilities. By now the system permitted the officer being rated to see the report and to add his or her own reflections and comments. We needed something more to provide the boards with an adequate view of an officer; we recommended using assessment centers to test an officer once or twice in a career. These had been pioneered by the Office of Strategic Services in World War II, had been used for over a decade by AT&T and other major corporations, and were now being used by the Internal Revenue Service to help choose both first-line supervisors and senior officers. In the end, Personnel agreed to introduce such techniques, not for promotion but for recruitment. Today, a Foreign Service candidate takes part in several group exercises as part of a full-day assessment.

My own bad report from Moscow had no lasting effect. In 1975 I was promoted to Class Two, then the lowest of the senior ranks in the Foreign Service, roughly equivalent to brigadier general. Next year I left Personnel to become the third of three deputy executive secretaries in the department's executive secretariat. This was an organization of not quite a hundred people located on the seventh floor near the offices of our top leaders —the secretary of state, the deputy secretary, and the counselor of the department. Our job was to make sure that these three, plus the several under secretaries, got the paperwork they needed: timely reporting on the world's problems and clear recommendations on what, if anything, we should do about them. Our operations center ran twenty-four hours a day to keep on top of crises, and our secretariat staff traveled with the secretary and deputy secretary to maintain their constant links with Washington.

The third deputy's job was not taxing, but I had a promise of promotion later to become second deputy—until Cyrus Vance became secretary of state in 1977. Vance's executive assistant, a Foreign Service officer named Peter Tarnoff, got the secretary's agreement to changes that left me in third place. I told Tarnoff I wanted out. I had no place to go, but the new secretary of the treasury, W. Michael Blumenthal, remembered our executive secretariat from his days at State and decided he needed one at Treasury. Treasury had no one with obvious credentials to head such a group; I had some credentials but knew almost nothing about Treasury operations; I volunteered and got the job.

Mike Blumenthal made clear to his Treasury colleagues that I was a senior officer of his department and that what I demanded of Treasury bureaus I was demanding on his behalf. Our small secretariat, much smaller than that at State, had to pound on some bureaus to get what it needed. In the end we ensured that the secretary was well prepared for his congressional appearances and public statements and well briefed about the financial and business world. For some years both CIA and State had been doing overnight briefing reports for their principals, and we started a daily report at Treasury—a five- or six-page brief, prepared overnight, for Blumenthal to read at breakfast. He readily agreed that it satisfied his basic needs for information, intelligence, and analysis. In the fall of 1977, the secretary embarked on his first foreign trip as a cabinet member, a whirlwind trip to nine European and Middle Eastern cities in thirteen days, on one of the two Boeing 707s used for presidential Air Force One flights. I could have sent one of our two midgrade staff officers with him, but I decided to go myself, since I had had no similar experience while in the State Department secretariat. When we took off from Andrews Air Force Base, there were still many details to pin down for the secretary's schedule. I worked hard; in the first week of the trip I slept a total of twelve hours. At least from the administrative point of view, the trip was successful; the Europeans, however, were scornful about our lack of a clear energy policy—a German treasury official told me we still acted like all the world's oil came from Texas—and our Saudi and Gulf friends were disinclined to do any favors for America.

One day, as I was accompanying Mr. Blumenthal to Capitol Hill, he told me that he been, if briefly, a career Foreign Service officer—to my knowledge, the only former FSO who ever became a cabinet member other than Lawrence Eagleburger, who was briefly secretary of state at the end of the Bush administration. Blumenthal had entered the State Department in the Kennedy administration with a political appointment as a senior trade negotiator and later had become a deputy assistant secretary of state; he had then been given career status in our service. "After some time," he said, "I asked where I could expect to go next. They told me I could probably become ambassador to some small country. I thought about that for a while and decided that I did not want to sit somewhere in West Africa with little to do but urge the local government to vote with us in the United Nations— which they were not going to do. So I quit."

"Well," I said, "I'm sorry you didn't stay in the service; but you haven't done badly."

After I had been a year at Treasury, our secretariat was working well, and Blumenthal had acquired three executive assistants, reducing my own opportunities for direct contact with him. A colleague in the State Department asked me to come back to head State's Office of United Nations Political Affairs, or UNP. I had hoped that I would next go abroad, in some senior position, but UNP was perhaps the most prestigious office in the State Department, and in past years it had been headed by some admirable officers, including Dean Rusk. Blumenthal agreed to let me go and said he would sign an efficiency report on my work if I would prepare one for him.

I drafted a report that described the work I had done, objectively and without the use of superlatives. When he gave it back to me with his signature, he mentioned that he had shared my draft with the deputy secretary, Robert Carswell. I was horrified to see that Carswell had modified it to read in still less superlative terms. The next year, I was surprised to see myself on the promotion list to Class One. Much later, a friend told me he had served on the board that ranked me high enough to get promoted. "You know," he said, "when we read Blumenthal's very straight and frank report, we just knew he had drafted it all himself. There were no superlatives, but it was clear that he thought you had done a fine job and deserved promotion. So we ranked you near the top." I looked at my colleague and thought, what can I say? Best to say nothing at all.

Over the next two years I labored, under great strain, in UNP. The colleague who had asked me to take the job had himself been director of UNP—until he discovered that he could go around his immediate superior, the deputy assistant secretary, to the assistant secretary for international organization affairs. The assistant secretary finally decided he did not need an intermediate between himself and this remarkable officer. He got rid of his deputy assistant secretary and replaced him with the UNP director, who was now intent on sitting on me so I should not try to play the same trick on him. I had no thought of doing so. I ran six miles each dawn, which helped me keep my temper, and profited greatly from having two gifted deputies, Melvyn Levitsky and Thomas Niles, each of whom would later serve as both assistant secretary of state and ambassador.

The work of UNP was difficult. We were responsible for all political questions raised in any UN body. These had mainly to do with the Middle East, usually meaning attacks on our good friend Israel, which we would not tolerate, and Africa, usually meaning attacks on South Africa's apartheid regime, which we too opposed but which we imagined we could pressure into reform. Our successes were rare. Almost no one sided with us in votes on Israel, except Israel. In the case of South Africa, the United Nations had embargoed oil and arms shipments to that country, but we knew the South Africans had been able to buy oil cargoes in Arab states and arms elsewhere— although they produced a lot of arms themselves. I requested and obtained authorization to call in the minister of a NATO embassy and tell him we had learned that his country's state-owned arms manufacturer was selling tens of thousands of rifles to the South African military. He returned some days later to say his government could do nothing about this unless we provided detailed information on the alleged shipments—which we could not do without compromising the source of our intelligence.

Our work in UNP was further complicated by the fact that our UN ambassador—Andrew Young, when I entered UNP—had cabinet status and so could and often did go around UNP, indeed around the whole State Department, directly to the president. In September 1979 Ambassador Young resigned after it came out that he had had an unauthorized contact with a representative of the Palestine Liberation Organization and had not reported the contact. He was replaced by another African American, Donald McHenry, a former Foreign Service officer and from my point of view an excellent choice. But Don McHenry too sometimes went around the State Department to seek President Jimmy Carter's approval for one action or another.

I finished my stated two years in UNP and moved to the Bureau of European Affairs, to become director of the Office of East European Affairs, known as EE. Life became considerably more pleasant. In UNP, for almost every move we planned we had to seek the concurrence of many others inside our own bureaucracy even before trying to get other governments to support us—which was one reason Andy Young and Don McHenry found it convenient to go straight to the president. In EE, however, my deputy—Bill Farrand[1]—and our seven desk officers and I were dealing directly, often without interference from other bureaus or agencies, with six foreign embassies in Washington and were sending instructions to six American embassies in central Europe and the Balkans.[2] Five of our countries were members of the Warsaw Pact and Moscow's poor imitation of a common market, COMECON, and our relationship with most of them was less than warm. But I had decided when I was in our Prague embassy that this region was the most interesting part of the world. Soon after taking over EE, I spent a month visiting our six embassies and several consulates there. It was late autumn, a miserable time to visit countries in that region, but I came back to Washington more fascinated than ever with their history, present predicaments, and future possibilities. President Tito had died several months before my visit,

1. Farrand served later as ambassador to Papua New Guinea and then as a deputy high representative in Bosnia under the Dayton peace accords.

2. The countries we dealt with were Poland, Czechoslovakia, Hungary, Bulgaria, Romania, and Yugoslavia. We also followed affairs in Albania, with which we had no diplomatic relations, and we maintained good relations with the Washington legations of Estonia, Latvia, and Lithuania, which the Soviet Union had occupied in 1940.

and the world wondered whether Yugoslavia would stay together now that he had gone. After several days of talks in Belgrade and Zagreb, it appeared to me that most leading Serbs and Croats wanted to preserve federated Yugoslavia, although old hatreds remained—which Slobodan Milosevic in Serbia and Franjo Tudjman in Croatia would stir up later, after gaining power.

I spent a year in EE and had only one major disappointment, over Poland. The Solidarity movement was riding high there by the time Ronald Reagan took office in Washington in January 1981. Soon afterward, the question arose of renewing the principal American aid program in Poland, credit guarantees for Polish purchase of American grain, which amounted to a third of a billion dollars annually. I was told that the question had to go to the president. I wrote a memo to go up the line to the White House, urging continued approval for our aid as something very much in our own interest. The memo came back before it reached the president; it was too long, Mr. Reagan would not look at anything longer than a page or two. I rewrote it, emphasizing in one page that the Polish regime under strong Solidarity pressure was evolving in an increasingly democratic and anti-Soviet direction; that a dollar spent on Poland was worth a dollar spent on NATO. Soon I heard that Secretary of State Alexander Haig had gone one day to New York and that in his absence President Reagan had convened the National Security Council and told it he could not countenance American aid to a Communist regime. To me this was absurd, given the Reagan administration's recent decision to continue American grain sales to the Soviet Union, thereby helping to prop up the very people who were enforcing the continuance of communism in Poland.

In June 1981 I accompanied the American delegation to the funeral of Poland's Catholic primate, Stefan Cardinal Wyszynski. Our delegation included two top congressmen, Clement Zablocki and William Broomfield, and the Cardinal Archbishop of Philadelphia, Joseph Krol. Every event we witnessed in Warsaw made clear most Poles' desire to go their own non-Soviet way, as well as their good feelings toward America. When we landed in Warsaw, Cardinal Krol read in good Polish the arrival statement I had drafted; it was carried on prime-time Polish television. The open-air funeral was held in Warsaw's largest square. Ours was the only high-level delegation sent by any Western country. We were seated near the altar amid a crowd of over a hundred thousand, while a huge, rumbling thunderhead built in a brilliant sky. When the funeral ended, it was Cardinal Krol who officiated at the primate's interment in the cathedral crypt. After we took off from Warsaw, bound westward in a little air force jet, the cardinal looked at me and said, "You know, Peter, funerals are not supposed to be fun—but I kind of enjoyed this one!"

I agreed. And despite Mr. Reagan's views on Poland, I was enjoying my job. But I had been seven long years in Washington, a very long time for a Foreign Service officer—and then Max Rabb asked me to become his deputy in Rome.

seven

The Way to Africa

My conversation from Rome with Bob Oakley about going to Somalia was not all that needed to be done on that subject. I went to Ambassador Rabb and told him that I had put myself in for an ambassadorship. He said that he would be sorry to lose me but would not stand in my way. After this, I called the Department's personnel bureau to confirm my interest in being considered for the job. Within a couple of weeks, I heard that I was the Department's candidate for the job. But then I heard that the Thursday Luncheon Club, a group of black Foreign Service officers, had told Secretary of State George Shultz that not enough black officers were being given ambassadorships. Mr. Shultz decided to put forward to the White House the name of Richard Fox, a black officer who had been ambassador to Trinidad. Dick Fox was a friend of mine and a very able officer, which made the news easier to take. More news was forthcoming: in July, Dick Fox decided to retire. My name went forward.

Most of our embassies in Africa had at one point or another been headed by a political appointee, but all eight of our previous ambassadors to Somalia had come from the career Foreign Service. It had never been a choice post, and I doubted that any Reagan campaign contributor wanted to go to Mogadishu now. Sure enough, in September I heard that the White House had agreed to name me. On Saturday, September 29, I spent the morning reading cables in the embassy and the afternoon strolling through Rome with my wife. When we got home, my fourteen-year-old son, Andrew, told me he had taken a call from Camp David; they would like me to call back. I thought I knew what that meant; the president had adopted the pleasant habit of telephoning people who were being offered senior positions. Soon Ronald Reagan was on the phone, saying that he hoped he

Peter Bridges escorts Sandro Pertini, president of
the Italian Republic, through the U.S. exhibition
at a Turin auto show, October 1984.

wasn't disturbing me while I was busy at something. I assured him he wasn't.
He said that he would like me to serve as ambassador to Somalia. I said I'd
be honored to do so.

Processing presidential appointments takes time, and the White House
was busy with an election. In October the State Department cabled that my
appointment would be announced on October 29; later, however, a friend in
the Department called me to say that the White House had decided that it
would not look good for the president, even though he was sure of reelection, to be making new appointments just before the country voted. On November 14, ten days after Mr. Reagan won a second term, he named me
ambassador to Somalia. The Senate was in recess, and I was urgently needed
in Somalia—Oakley had left there in August—so I would proceed without
delay on a recess commission; my Senate confirmation hearings would come
later. The Department gave me ten days to wind up my affairs in Rome,
and the Sunday after Thanksgiving I flew to Washington to get briefed and
be sworn in. It was difficult to leave Rome, in many ways. I had served twice
in the Rome embassy, for a total of eight years, and my first time there had
been almost three decades earlier, when I was an army private in France,
and my wife and I had come down to Italy by *wagon-lits*, three months before our oldest son was born.

It was not quite nine on Monday morning when I lugged my two suit-
cases into the C Street entrance of the State Department. I had begun my
professional life in this building, and most of my close friends were members

of the Foreign Service. I had been fortunate in choosing this career and in the career's having admitted me to its ranks. But, I thought to myself, I really hated the State Department. I despised its cumbersome bureaucratic organization. At the beginning of the Reagan administration I had written an article for the *Foreign Service Journal*, under the pseudonym of "Joel Barlow," that criticized the proliferation of top posts in the Department as well as the proliferation of other agencies claiming an interest in managing our foreign affairs.[1]

I thought of this article now as I passed the plaque in the lobby that listed American diplomats who had died in tragic or heroic circumstances. The second name on the list was Joel Barlow, America's first hostage negotiator, who had died in Poland in 1812; I had used Barlow for a pseudonym as a secret joke. Before writing my article I had worked hard but in the end unsuccessfully against the proposed Foreign Service Act, writing for the American Foreign Service Association in April 1979 a report that made clear that the elements of the proposal affecting senior career officers were nothing but a sham. The proposal was supposedly intended to improve our cadre of senior officers, but the fact was that this was a fine cadre; the proposal simply ignored the central problem, which was that both Democratic and Republican administrations gave their supporters top diplomatic posts as political plums. It was politicization that prevented our best officers from rising to the top positions they deserved. No other major country maintained such a spoils system. I wrote a still stronger paper on this score in June 1979 to my friend Philip Habib, then our top career officer, who gave it back to me, saying it was "too hot to read." In the end, my efforts and those of my friends failed. The supporters of the new act convinced Carter's secretary of state, Cyrus Vance, that this could be Mr. Vance's major contribution to American diplomacy; it was approved in 1980. Perhaps, I thought then, I was too frank and my career, like Barlow's life, would end early. Perhaps it was a good thing that I had gotten out of Washington early in the Reagan administration, which politicized our diplomacy even further than Carter had done.

It was not just politicization and the bureaucracy that I hated. I hated this State Department building itself. Most of it had been built in cheap-modern style in the 1950s, with low ceilings and long, linoleum-floored,

1. "On Managing American Diplomacy," *Foreign Service Journal*, February 1981. After leaving government I returned to this subject in two further articles: "U.S. Foreign Service Suffers from Politics," *Los Angeles Times*, November 30, 1986, and "Disentangling the U.S. Foreign-Affairs Mess," *Christian Science Monitor*, November 3, 1987.

windowless corridors. It looked like a hospital, not the foreign ministry of a world power. I took the elevator to the fifth floor and walked down the blue-striped, shiny corridor to my new base in the Office of East African Affairs. My new desk officer was there: Christopher Murray, a bright and energetic officer who at thirty already had one tour of duty in Africa behind him. He had made a full set of appointments for me: State, AID, CIA, Defense, and the U.S. Information Agency.

In the next two weeks I learned all I could about American involvement in Somalia. Our total aid to the country was running at around $120 million a year, the largest set of American aid programs in sub-Saharan Africa. About twenty-five million dollars of this was military. We were supplying defensive weapons to the Somali military—and only defensive ones, I was pleased to hear—for Somali use against frequent incursions from Ethiopia, and we were also supplying a lot of other materiel and training. On the civilian side, we were providing food for hundreds of thousands of Somali refugees from Ethiopia; we were providing financial aid to the government; and we were involved in various economic development projects. My new embassy had a very large staff, almost as many Americans—218, plus 179 family members—as in the Rome embassy. I knew something would have to be done about that.

As soon as possible I met with Jim Bishop, a thin, dour Africanist who was the deputy assistant secretary responsible for Somalia, among other countries, in AF, the Department's Bureau of African Affairs. (There were roughly fifty independent countries in Africa; AF had central responsibility for the conduct of relations with most of them. The Maghreb countries from Morocco to Egypt fell to NEA, the Near Eastern bureau. The office of which my new desk officer was a member was part of AF.) Bishop, still in his mid-forties, had already served as an ambassador, to Niger. Three years after our meeting, in 1987, he would become ambassador to Liberia, which soon after his arrival would disintegrate in civil war. In 1990 he was named ambassador to Somalia. By that time our new embassy compound in Mogadishu had been almost completed. One day in January 1991, Jim Bishop and his remaining staff would be evacuated from the new compound by marine helicopters after Somalia, like Liberia, had come apart in civil strife.

Soon I called on the assistant secretary for African affairs, Chester Crocker, a brilliant and harried man who spent much of his time traveling to southern Africa, where Pretoria's apartheid regime remained in place and still controlled Namibia. I had known Chet Crocker earlier, and I liked him. I told him that I would not worry him unnecessarily about Somalia; I hoped that someday he might be able to visit there.

Michael Armacost, the under secretary for political affairs and our top career officer, gave me a few minutes of his time, and what he said reassured me that he had a good understanding of the problems I would face in Somalia. I promised him an overall assessment of the scene as soon as I felt confident I could attempt one.

The director of the Department's Foreign Buildings Office, Harvey Buffalo, talked to me about resuming work on the planned new embassy at Mogadishu. In the 1960s, when the Somalis were newly independent and our bilateral relations were good, the Somali government had given us a large piece of land in an area that was then beyond the city limits. We had begun to build a new chancery, or office building, and a new residence for the ambassador, but we had stopped in the 1970s after Somali-American relations had gone bad—and after we discovered that the general contractor was incompetent. Now relations were much improved, the Department had a fourteen-million-dollar appropriation from Congress, and Buffalo thought I could expect to see construction resume within a year.

I had decided that when I met with officers of the Agency for International Development, or AID, I would simply listen carefully to what they had to say and ask questions. I could see already that it would take me considerable time to understand and judge the complex set of AID programs. I admitted to myself, though not to others, some prejudice against AID. I had served in one other embassy with a large AID element, that in Panama. As I have described in an earlier chapter, it had been distressing to see scores of AID Americans who understood little about Panamanian society—and most of whom spoke little Spanish—claiming to teach Panama how to improve its public administration, agriculture, and educational system. But that had been many years ago, and perhaps AID had improved. It had, from what my AID colleagues told me now. I would have to wait until I arrived in Somalia to be able to judge for myself. But I did not think the great size of the AID staff in Somalia was a good augury, even though we clearly needed a considerable number of people to run an operation that spent almost a hundred million dollars a year.

I took time to see Dr. Martin Wolfe, the tropical-disease expert in the Department's Medical Division. He assured me that relatively few members of our Mogadishu staff had been stricken with serious ailments. There had been some cases of dengue, and a few of malaria, but fortunately the malaria parasite in Somalia had still not developed resistance to the standard antimalarial drug, chloroquine. It did later.

After a number of calls in the State Department, AID, CIA, USIA, and Defense, I went to Personnel to find out just what I was going to get paid. Personnel confirmed my understanding that because of the cap on federal salaries, I would get no raise in pay with my promotion to ambassador; my salary would remain just under seventy thousand dollars a year. Well, I wasn't in it for the money, but Washington certainly was niggardly. Some months later in Mogadishu, comparing notes with my neighbor the French ambassador, whose small embassy did far less than ours, I would decide that all in all he probably earned about twice what I did.

Bob Oakley and his wife, Phyllis—she had entered the Foreign Service with me in 1957 and was now desk officer for Afghanistan—had kindly invited me to stay with them in their pleasant Washington home. One dawn, a military sedan picked me up there and drove me to Andrews Air Force Base. There a little T-39 jet was waiting to fly David Newton, who was going out to head our embassy in Baghdad, and me down to MacDill Air Force Base near Tampa. This was the headquarters of the U.S. Central Command, or CENTCOM, created out of what had originally been the Rapid Deployment Force, intended to oppose possible Soviet expansion beyond Afghanistan into Southwest Asia.

At CENTCOM, Newton and I met Gen. Robert Kingston, who had joined the army as a private and had just won his fourth star, and his staff of a half-dozen generals and admirals. They briefed us on how CENTCOM would respond if the Soviets ever moved beyond Afghanistan, which they had occupied since 1979, toward the Indian Ocean littoral. The problem, I muttered to David Newton during the smoothly delivered briefing, was that the army divisions that CENTCOM said it would use were the same divisions that we would need in Europe if a confrontation developed with the Soviet Union. Not many years later, Bob Kingston's successor once removed, Gen. Norman Schwarzkopf, led a brilliant American victory in the Persian Gulf. CENTCOM was fortunate that by that time the Soviet threat had disappeared and it could use American units from Europe against Iraq.

CENTCOM's area of responsibility included the Horn of Africa— Somalia, Ethiopia, little Djibouti—and that was why I had been invited down to Tampa. In 1984 our military was emphasizing the strategic importance of the Horn. It was this, far more than humanitarian concerns, that led us to give Somalia so much civilian as well as military aid. The Reagan administration's basic policy had been laid out two years earlier, in National Security Decision Directive 57 of September 1982: "The Horn of Africa is important to the United States primarily because of its strategic location with respect to the Persian Gulf/Southwest Asia region."[2]

I was not convinced, before I went to Somalia, that the strategic importance of Somalia was quite as great as Washington said it was. Zbigniew Brzezinski, President Carter's national security adviser, admitted in his 1983 book *Power and Principle* that when he was in the White House he had even believed in the possibility of a domino effect in the Red Sea region—that the strong Soviet position in Ethiopia and South Yemen was a serious and direct political threat to Saudi Arabia. I had not read Brzezinski's book in 1984; if I had, I would have said Nonsense. It should be noted that Brzezinski's view that the Soviets had a grand design in Africa and the Red Sea was not shared by others in the Carter administration, notably Secretary of State Vance. A decade later, after the Soviet Union had collapsed, the longtime Soviet ambassador to the United States was to confirm that "the Kremlin had no far-reaching global plans in that region."[3] Nevertheless, the Soviet Union would clearly seize on local opportunities to increase its influence in the region, and clearly that was against our own interests.

We had every reason to maintain a military presence in the Indian Ocean. This presence had a long history, although some of Bob Kingston's CENT-COM general officers did not seem to know it; it dated back to American frigates that had cruised that ocean in the early nineteenth century. But I confess that I also thought, in late 1984, that we were unrealistic in contemplating the possibility of conducting a conventional war in that region, against the Soviets, it was assumed then—no imaginable scenario of 1984 would have envisioned us fighting Saddam Hussein's Iraq.

Many of my colleagues and I had long thought that we had been fools in Vietnam to violate the old dictum that America should never fight a land war in Asia, even though we had done so in Korea. I thought we would be equally foolish to attempt a major campaign in the equally distant Gulf. I do not mean to say that I thought the Gulf was of secondary importance to the United States; it was vitally important, above all because of its oil. But while we needed to be prepared for some sort of military action, we simply

2. The full text of NSDD 57 is in Christopher Simpson, *National Security Directives of the Reagan and Bush Administrations* (Boulder, Colo.: Westview Press, 1995).

3. Anatoly Dobrynin, *In Confidence* (New York: Times Books, 1995), p. 403. See also Cyrus Vance, *Hard Choices* (New York: Simon and Schuster, 1983), pp. 84–92.

did not have enough divisions to fight an Indian Ocean war, given our force commitments in Europe. I supposed that a full-scale Indian Ocean war would lead quickly to a nuclear confrontation. I concluded that our strategy must therefore aim at avoiding war, primarily through seeking stability in the countries of the region and close American relationships with those countries. Besides, I did not think there was much chance that the Soviets would try to extend their occupation of Afghanistan into Iran or Pakistan, despite talk—some of it, to be sure, Soviet talk—about Soviet interest in acquiring frontage on the Indian Ocean.

Not only our military but Moscow's put high value on the Horn of Africa.[4] Soviet military involvement in Somalia had grown quickly after Somalia became independent in 1960. This had largely to do with Somalia's differences with neighboring Ethiopia. In 1897 the British, with a protectorate over northern Somalia, had agreed to Ethiopian control over the Ogaden, a huge area of grasslands that were traditional grazing areas for nomadic Somali clans. In the 1930s Somalia had been Italy's base for the invasion of Ethiopia, and the invaders had included not only divisions from Italy but six thousand Somali troops and many more Italian-trained Somali irregulars. There was no love lost between Somalis and Ethiopians, and Ethiopia was undoubtedly Somalia's greatest external problem—although the sizable numbers of ethnic Somalis in northeast Kenya and in what is now Djibouti caused friction with those countries as well. The five-pointed star on Somalia's flag was a revanchist one; it symbolized the dream of bringing together under a single flag the Somalis who inhabited not only the former Italian colony and former British Somaliland but good parts of three other countries.

After independence the Somalis decided, not surprisingly, to build a strong military. In 1962 the prime minister of the Somali Republic, Abdirashid Ali Shermarke, went to Washington and asked President John Kennedy for military assistance. Kennedy responded that the United States did not want to fuel regional conflicts. "Ah," said Shermarke, "but you are supplying arms to Ethiopia."

As a result of Shermarke's Washington visit, the United States, together with West Germany and Italy, offered Somalia ten million dollars to strengthen its internal security if it would promise not to seek military aid elsewhere. Instead, in 1963, Shermarke went to Moscow. Khrushchev, whose regime

4. It was not only the Pentagon that held this view in America. For example, in its issue of August 22, 1977, *Time* had pronounced the Horn of Africa to be "of enormous strategic importance."

was already the largest provider of civilian aid to Somalia, offered Somalia a fifty-five-million-dollar program of military assistance: [5] weapons, Soviet advisors to teach their use, and training programs in the Soviet Union for hundreds of Somali officers. Throughout the 1960s the Soviet presence grew in Somalia. Then came 1969. Shermarke, now the president of the republic, was assassinated by one of his bodyguards while visiting the north at a time when the prime minister, Mohamed Ibrahim Egal, was out of the country. The armed forces took over. Their commander, Mohamed Siad Barre, made himself president, proclaimed "scientific socialism," and turned still closer to Moscow. By the 1970s there were at least three thousand Soviet military and civilian advisers in Somalia, and the Soviets were building major military bases there.

The Soviets were then also building up their military position in Ethiopia, where Mengistu Haile Mariam had proclaimed socialism and turned, like Somalia, to Moscow after deposing Emperor Haile Selassie in 1974. The United States had tried but failed to maintain its military relationship with Ethiopia after Mengistu took over, delivering a squadron of F-5E fighter-bombers as recently as the summer of 1976.

Then the Somalis went to war with Ethiopia. It began in 1977 with guerrilla action—which Siad Barre's regime in Mogadishu aided and abetted—by the Somalis who inhabited the Ogaden grasslands of eastern Ethiopia. The Soviets and their Cuban clients tried to prevent conflict, but Siad Barre told Fidel Castro and Mengistu that Somalia would continue its course toward Ethiopia "while all Somalis have not received freedom."[6] Within several months a full-scale war was going on between the two countries. The Soviets may well have felt that the Somalis had betrayed them; in late May or early June 1977, Somali defense minister Mohamed Ali Samantar, visiting Moscow, had told Leonid Brezhnev and other top Soviet leaders that the Somali leadership would not on its own initiative unleash an armed conflict with Ethiopia.[7] Initially the Somali army, equipped with hundreds

5. For details see Alexander Erlich and Christian R. Sonne, "The Soviet Union: Economic Activity," in *Africa and the Communist World*, ed. Zbigniew Brzezinski (Stanford, Calif.: Stanford Univ. Press, 1967), pp. 66 and 74–75.

6. The quotation is from a report of March 18, 1977, to Moscow from the Soviet embassy in Addis Ababa. The text, from the National Security Archive at George Washington University, is available on the Internet at http://www.seas.gwu.edu/nsarchive/CWIHP/BULLETINS/68-9a9.htm.

7. Ibid., Report (date uncertain) from Central Committee, Communist Party of Soviet Union, to Central Committee, Socialist Unity Party [of East Germany].

of Soviet-made tanks supplied earlier by Moscow, captured most of the Ogaden. In September 1977 the Somalis captured the key town of Jigjiga. The way lay open to two major cities, Harar and Dire Dawa, whose loss would be disastrous to Ethiopia. This caused a quandary for Moscow, which wanted to maintain its strong position in both countries. Finally the Soviets made a definitive choice. On October 19 the Soviet ambassador in Addis Ababa announced that the Soviet Union had stopped arms shipments to Somalia and was providing new "defensive" weapons to Ethiopia. Numbers of troops from Moscow's satellite Cuba and numerous Soviet military advisers arrived in Ethiopia.[8]

Now Siad Barre was in a quandary. The Soviet Union and Cuba had been furnishing Somalia's own main military support. But on November 13, after an all-day meeting with his chief cronies, Siad Barre announced that Somalia was breaking off diplomatic relations with Cuba (though not with the Soviet Union, which was permitted to keep its Mogadishu embassy open with a reduced staff), was expelling all Soviet and Cuban military personnel and advisers, and was closing down the Soviet air and naval stations in Somalia. Siad gave the Soviets just three days (some accounts say four) to pull all their thousands of troops and advisers out of his country. My Italian friends Gianluigi and Luciana Mutto, who for many years managed a banana plantation south of Mogadishu, told me that they had never realized how many Russians were in Somalia until the convoys of GAZ trucks came down the highway, full of blond passengers bound for Mogadishu airport.

Later, in February 1978, Ethiopian and Cuban forces under Soviet command went on the counteroffensive and forced the Somali army out of the Ogaden. Hundreds of thousands of ethnic Somalis came with it, flooding into Somalia. To add insult to injury, one of the Soviet commanders had earlier been Siad Barre's top military adviser in Mogadishu. A reliable source told me later that no one had ever seen Siad Barre so enraged as when he learned this.

Even before the Ogaden war, in the early summer of 1977, Siad Barre had sensed a Soviet tilt toward Ethiopia and had approached the United States for arms and economic aid. Washington had decided that the farthest we could go was to see if our allies could provide help; the Somali invasion of

8. Former Soviet ambassador Anatoly Dobrynin says two thousand Cuban troops and one thousand Soviet advisers were sent (Dobrynin, p. 403). Other sources say that there were as many as twenty thousand Cubans; see for example William H. Lewis, *Beyond Constructive Engagement* (New York: Paragon House, 1986), p. 80.

the Ogaden removed our willingness even to do that much.[9] Eventually, in 1980, we came to terms with Somalia's president, and U.S. military assistance had begun. But the new American ambassador would have to decide for himself what was the proper size and shape of such assistance in the future (though what the ambassador thought might, I realized, have little effect in Washington). I left CENTCOM to return to Washington knowing that the question of Somalia's strategic importance was going to occupy much of my time in Mogadishu. We could not ignore the Soviet presence in Ethiopia and South Yemen, at the southern approaches to the Red Sea and to the Suez Canal. But I was far from sure how key a role Somalia could or should play in any American strategic response to this worrisome Soviet presence. It was, it seemed to me, a long way from Somalia to the Persian Gulf. On the other hand, it was a far shorter distance than that from bases in the continental United States.

Before I went down to Tampa, Jim Bishop had told me that my swearing in as ambassador would have to be a relatively quiet and small affair to avoid irritating anyone in the Senate, which had not been given the opportunity to confirm my recess appointment. That was fine by me. Swearings in usually took place in the Department's grandiose reception room on the eighth floor, and new ambassadors were asked to pay for several hundred dollars' worth of drinks and food provided by a caterer. I always thought it was cheap of the Department not to foot the bill, particularly for career officers who if not rich (and I was one of the great majority who were not rich) had lots of demands on their salaries at such a time. I was therefore happy to avoid the occasion.

On December 5, 1984, a group of forty friends and colleagues plus my cousin Harry watched as my friend Douglas Harwood, assistant chief of protocol, administered the oath of office to me in the outer office of Ronald Spiers, the under secretary for management. Bob and Phyllis Oakley were there, together with two other former American ambassadors to Somalia, Roger Kirk and Donald Petterson, and the Somali ambassador to the United States, Mohamed Haji Nur. I greatly admired Ron Spiers, a brilliant officer who had served three times as an ambassador and who was outspoken in his defense of the career service against the continuing politicization of top jobs. He made some brief remarks, saying kind things about me and adding that he was glad to see the excellence of Dartmouth graduates recognized; we were fellow alumni of that college.

9. See Vance, pp. 72–75 and 85–88.

Then it was my turn. I said that I was sure my father, who had died two decades earlier, would be particularly pleased if he could know that I was becoming an ambassador. He had been an American businessman who began a long international career by shipping out as a seaman on a tramp steamer. He had spent most of my kindergarten year in Africa, and I could imagine him in Nairobi and Mombasa and Zanzibar on that trip in 1937; but, I said, I did not think he could ever have imagined, sitting in colonial Mombasa, that one day his son would be the American ambassador in a nearby place, a country that was then under colonial rule but was now a country with almost a quarter-century of independence behind it. I also said what I thought needed saying to the Somali ambassador, that I was pleased that the relationship between our countries was so good and I would do all I could to improve the relationship further; I looked forward to arriving very soon in Mogadishu.

Then I told Ron Spiers—and I meant it also for others not present—that I was honored as a career officer to be the first ambassador appointed by the president since his reelection. I hoped it might be an augury for the future. Our service was rich in talent, and I had a number of colleagues who were at least as well qualified as I to serve as ambassador to Somalia or to other countries. I hoped the president would draw on that talent. And so I ended. My friends congratulated me, and Chris Murray broke open the champagne he had bought for me for thirty dollars across the street. I told myself that it was not a bad price for such an occasion.

eight

Big Embassy, Poor Country

I would really have liked to go to Mogadishu by ship, down the Red Sea and around the Horn of Africa, Cape Guardafui, into the Indian Ocean. Big moves are best done slowly. When I had been transferred on short notice from Rome to Prague in 1971, I had gone by train; I would have taken a bus if there had been one. It always seemed to me that one could best understand where one lived and worked if one proceeded there overland or by sea. There was no chance of doing that now. For one thing, the passenger ships that had linked Italian ports with Italy's Somali colony, a leisurely three-week trip in the 1930s, sailed no more. But in any case, Somalia had now been without an American ambassador for several months, and Somalia's president was beginning to say that this meant the Americans were paying less attention to Somalia. Besides, what would they say on Capitol Hill if, with a hurried recess appointment in my pocket, I did not hurry? So I hurried.

I flew from Washington to Rome on December 6, the day after I had been sworn in. After two nights with my wife, Mary Jane, and our four children (and after one last hike in the Apennines with my wife and Italian friends), I flew out of Fiumicino airport at midnight on Sunday, December 9, 1984, on an Alitalia Airbus, bound for Mogadishu via Jiddah and Addis Ababa. My wife worked in Rome for the Internal Revenue Service, and she and our youngest son, Andrew, would come down in June after tax season was over and school was out. It would be years before parents and children would all be together again; in the next several years, the six of us would find ourselves on four separate continents.

I woke at dawn as we were coming down over dramatic gorges and small, poor-looking villages toward Addis Ababa's airport. My first look at East Africa. Until the nineteenth century, as I had read recently in the *Corriere della*

Sera, 40 percent of Ethiopia had been covered by forest; now only 4 percent was. I could see only small patches of woodlands. The city of Addis Ababa appeared below us. I caught sight of what must be the headquarters of the not-very-effective Organization of African Unity. We swung around the city and came down. When they opened the door, the Ethiopian air was cool, at eight thousand feet above sea level. A different climate awaited me down by the sea at Mogadishu, two degrees north of the equator.

A year later Alitalia stopped flying to Somalia, after Somali debts to the airline reached a point that Alitalia's chairman, Umberto Nordio, found intolerable. He was pressured, he told me later, by the Italian government to keep on flying to the former colony. He had told foreign ministry officials that if it was a case of Italian national interest, they could reimburse him for the Somali debts. They would not; he stopped service. For now the Airbus still flew, but it took an odd route. Mogadishu was seven hundred miles southeast of Addis Ababa, but we took off and flew northeast. We could not cross the Ethiopian-Somali border because of the continuing, if intermittent, hostilities. So we flew up to Djibouti, turned right, and started south down a thousand miles of Somalia. There were no clouds. I looked down on a reddish world with no villages or roads, only occasional vehicle tracks. There must be vegetation; I could not see it. There had been two years of drought.

Here now was a little river full of tight bends, the Webi Shebeli, flowing down from the Ethiopian highlands. Soon it would dry up completely and stay dry until it rained again in Ethiopia, in April or May. Even when it flowed, the Shebeli never reached the sea. It flowed toward the coast, toward Mogadishu, but then curved southwest to run parallel to the coast. Eventually it died in marsh and sand before its waters could reach the Indian Ocean. There was reason to believe that long ago, when Ethiopia had been forested, the Shebeli had flowed to the sea. Now its waters failed, and somehow, I suddenly thought, that was like Somalia, beset by drought, lacking a steady flow—but that was enough philosophy, we were descending.

We came down low over a sprawling city, curved out over a blue ocean and in again, and landed at the airport just inland from a beach where waves were breaking. On the edge of the runway were carcasses of many planes: a Vickers Viscount, an ancient DC-3, an old, brown Soviet biplane. I thought to myself, the eighth-poorest country in the world.

I was met by my old friend and new deputy, John Hirsch, who had been acting as our chargé d'affaires these past four months since Oakley left. The Somali chief of protocol, Abdi Haji Liban, was also there, and he greeted me warmly. I had been wondering if Mogadishu would feel like Panama, my only previous post near the equator, which had been always hot and sultry. Well, this equatorial sun was very hot, but the day was not sultry, not with this strong wind, the northeast monsoon, which blew for half the year.

By the terminal building all the chiefs of embassy sections had gathered to greet the new boss. I shook their hands, but this was no place for a meeting. I told them we'd get together a little later, and meanwhile thanks for coming out to greet me. Here now was my official sedan, a light-blue Oldsmobile, and here was my new driver, Scerif Ahmed Maio. He was, I knew from Oakley, a fine man. Scerif and I soon became friends, indeed comrades.

I had come to Somalia with little idea of what the country looked like. I had over the years read a number of books on Somalia, and just recently I had devoured hundreds of pages of briefing papers. Unfortunately, neither the books nor the briefing papers had offered much in the way of photographs. I knew what Somali people looked like, having met occasional Somali diplomats through the years. Sure enough, the people I saw now on the Mogadishu streets, as we drove to my new home, were of that same race—tall, thin, and dark skinned, with fine teeth and features that looked Nilotic, or in some cases European, but decidedly not Bantu. What no one had told me was that Somali men wore, along with European-style shirts and cheap flip-flops, a kind of sarong. I asked Scerif what the garment was called: *macawis*. This became my first Somali word. The women, some of them very attractive, wore long dresses, shawls made of bright cloth, and gold jewelry. A few though were dressed somberly, all in black, and had veiled faces. Scerif explained that these were women from Hamarweyn, one of the older parts of town. It was very old, I knew; I had read of an Arabic inscription in the Hamarweyn mosque that equated with the thirteenth century A.D.

Nor had anyone told me to expect to see so many animals wandering through the streets—handsome goats, ugly fat-tailed sheep, small brown cows. The streets were also full of vehicles, almost all Japanese-made except for occasional Land Rovers and some old red-and-yellow Fiat taxis. The town was not unattractive. The walls were whitewashed; there were shade trees. We passed a mosque, and then the handsome but incongruous Gothic cathedral that the Italians had built in the 1920s, and then the still more incongruous Roman-style arch of triumph, which bore a Fascist inscription to Crown Prince Umberto of Savoy, who had visited here in 1928. Scerif pointed out the unimpressive chancery building of my new embassy, and we continued north up the shore road to the semi-suburb called the Lido.

Left at the Lido circle, up three hundred yards of rutted, sandy lanes, past a dumpster in which two goats and two little boys were foraging, and here we were: my residence!

Not such a bad residence, I saw when I entered. It was a pleasant house, and certainly not immodestly grand: three bedrooms, two baths, and a study on one end; a small dining room and big kitchen on the other; in between, a thirty-foot living room. Glass doors at the rear of the living room opened onto a large, roofed patio. At the front of the living room was an open porch, from which a dozen steps descended to a small garden. Beyond the garden was a high wall, and beyond the wall the sandy lane we had driven up and other Lido houses and trees, and then the blue ocean. I found that from the rear patio an outside stairway went up to a roof terrace. Here was a wide view of the ocean, the great blue sky, and this mainly one-and-two-story capital.

Scerif introduced the house staff: a Pakistani Christian cook named Saleem, who would soon come down with malaria and go home to Lahore; a little Somali steward named Cali; and a Somali woman with laughing eyes named Ambia, who was the *boyessa* (the Italian colonialists had decided that the feminine equivalent of a houseboy must be a *boyessa*). I ended my first day in Somalia at dinner with John and Rita Hirsch. He had not been my choice for a deputy but rather Oakley's; I had asked him to stay. Hirsch had been the political counselor in our Islamabad embassy before coming to Mogadishu. Earlier, when I first served in Rome, he had been a consular officer in Genoa. But we had first worked closely together when he was covering Middle Eastern affairs at our mission to the United Nations in New York and I was the director of United Nations Political Affairs in the State Department.

I decided that I would do my running in Somalia at *waaberi*, the early dawn, when it was coolest. The next morning I woke at first light, before six, and it was cool. I rose and put on shorts, running shoes, and my Potomac Valley Seniors Track Club shirt. I walked out, and the ancient Yemeni gate man—not the most dependable of security guards, I thought—saluted me and opened the gate. I ran down the sandy lanes, past the dumpster, where an early goat was already sampling the leavings. At the Lido circle was a well known, indeed infamous, bar where, no matter that this was a Muslim country, Somalis and foreigners could find liquor, whores, and frequently a fight. All was quiet now, but I smelled the stale beer as I ran by the bar and shuffled over a hundred yards of sand to reach the beach.

The ocean was beautiful, with small, quiet waves lapping the land's edge. Far on the eastern horizon, the sun's first rays shone from behind a range of clouds that must be fifty miles out to sea. I ran along the beach, wide and hard at low tide. A flock of twenty sacred ibises flew over me in a V, just a few feet above my head, and headed out to sea. The beach was not deserted. A boy was wading, although every few months a shark would take a victim here. By the water's edge a tall, thin Somali in a *macawis* sat quietly, gazing out at the sea and the glorious new sun.

At seven, after breakfast, Scerif drove me down to the most decrepit American embassy chancery that I had ever seen. It was a shabby, concrete building that had housed our offices since 1957, before Somali independence, when we first opened a consulate at Mogadishu. John Blane, our ambassador to Rwanda, wrote me some months later that as vice consul at Mogadishu in 1957 he had signed the lease on the building, thinking it might with luck last us ten years. In 1984 we were still there, and the place had never been renovated. A former colleague of mine later described it as looking like "some decaying Ottoman hotel or seaman's hostel in the back streets of Istanbul or Alexandria."[1]

At least we had a thoroughly modern telecommunications system; the equipment was of a generation newer even than what we had in Rome. It permitted us to send and receive encrypted cables at the rate of several hundred words a minute. The system was vital. Messages sent by diplomatic pouch took at least a week to reach Washington, and the Somali telephone system worked poorly and sometimes not at all. At Mogadishu one was not tempted to use the phone to discuss sensitive matters with Washington, as happened at other posts. (Years later, the Department developed a reliable secure-telephone system.) The only problem with our fine telecommunications system was that cables sent to SecState WashDC tended to get over-wide distribution, both inside the Department and to other agencies. We could send "official-informal" cables, which were intended to go only to the Department desk officer, but even these over time began to get wider distribution, making frank discussion difficult between Washington and Mogadishu. I knew, though, that I could trust utterly the discretion of Chris Murray, the desk officer, in regard to any message meant only for him.

After I had been in Mogadishu for some months, our ancient office building tried to kill me. One morning I went to call on the minister of agriculture. When I returned, my secretary, Katherine Astala, explained that the

---

1. In his novel (under the pseudonym "W. T. Tyler") *The Lion and the Jackal* (New York: Linden Press/Simon and Schuster, 1988), p. 83.

seat of my chair was punched in because a fifty-pound hunk of concrete roof had fallen through the ceiling onto it. Ms. Astala was, as always, imperturbable. I hoped she did not regret having joined me from Rome, where she had been the secretary to Ambassador Rabb. We made sure no more hunks were about to come down and asked the Department what they could do to speed up the plans for a new embassy.

I could not function as ambassador beyond our premises until I presented a copy of my credentials to the foreign minister, a prelude to presenting them formally to the president. For the moment, then, I busied myself getting to know my embassy colleagues and asking them to brief me further on Somalia and our activities there. The practice in this embassy was for the ambassador to hold weekly meetings of the "country team," which comprised the heads of embassy elements. I had never liked the term, which implied that an ambassador was team captain but not really much above the other members. That was not what international law said. Members of an ambassador's staff, no matter how grand their diplomatic titles, were just members of his retinue. When Max Rabb had introduced me at the first staff meeting in Rome, calling me his alter ego and stressing my full authority, I had responded that I would do my best but that I was simply a member of his staff, even if the most senior one. Now, though, as ambassador in Mogadishu, I did not want to play up my own stature; I didn't think I needed to. I told this country team, remembering troubles in Rome between embassy officers from different federal agencies, that I wanted them to work closely together, no matter who paid their salaries. I wanted them to bring important decisions to me, through John Hirsch as a rule, but I wanted to allow them as much autonomy as possible. I added that I planned to send frank reports and recommendations to Washington. While I wanted the embassy to work closely with Washington, I had no further ambitions, and I did not need to play up to anyone.

The Department had agreed that after I had presented my credentials, I could return to Rome for a few days to wind up my affairs. Perhaps I could get there in time for Christmas with my family. Max and Ruth Rabb were planning a large farewell reception for me and my wife. The minister of interior, Oscar Luigi Scalfaro, with whom Max Rabb and I had worked closely on terrorism and other matters—and who had kindly told me privately that he hoped one day I would return to Rome as American ambassador to Italy—was offering me a luncheon. Scalfaro's remark was flattering, but I knew I would never be ambassador in Rome. What neither Scalfaro nor I could know then was that the minister himself was later to become president of the Italian Republic, serving until May 1999, when he was eighty.

I spent my first weekend in Somalia, and a number of later weekends, touring the countryside with Scerif by Oldsmobile or jeep. After one left behind the whitewashed villas of the wealthy—there were quite a few of these—one could believe that Somalia was as poor as reported. The countryside was arid, with scattered acacias, occasional villages of small huts, and now and then a string of loping or grazing camels with one thin boy in charge. Many Somalis were still nomads—over half the nation, it was said, though there were no real statistics. The nomads roamed for hundreds of miles through the bush in small family groups with their camels, goats, and sheep. Their staple was camel's milk, which could be kept for days in charred containers.

The loss of vegetation in Somalia was extremely serious. There were too many animal mouths and too many people on the land. I had no instructions from Washington on population questions. The Reagan administration did not want to be criticized at home by those who opposed not just abortion but contraception as well. Fortunately, some African leaders were beginning to wake up to the problem. In 1985 I read in the Kenyan press several speeches by President Daniel arap Moi in which he told his people plainly that too many children would eat up any increase in Kenya's gross domestic product. Look at the Europeans, he said. They are economic successes, and how many children are there in a European family? Just one or two. Unfortunately for Mr. Moi's campaign, Pope John Paul II visited Kenya and preached to a crowd in Nairobi about the joys of procreation and fecundity. And Kenya's population continued to explode, not just because of the papal sermon; Daniel arap Moi's continuing trend toward repressive ways no doubt lessened Kenyans' interest in his advice.

Many Somalis took what one might call a Reaganesque approach to population. Eventually I raised the population question with Siad Barre. I had no instructions from Washington to do so, but I was curious to know Siad's approach to a population explosion that, I thought privately, could eventually produce a national tragedy of one sort or another. Somehow I was not surprised when Mohamed Siad Barre insisted that his country was underpopulated. We need, he said, more young men for soldiers to defend ourselves against Ethiopia.

It was not only Siad who professed to be unconcerned about the problem. Educated Somalis pointed out to me that children were useful in nomad families. A boy of ten or twelve was entrusted with a string of camels and would go off alone with them for days in search of forage. Girls took care of goats and sheep and helped their mothers. I understood this, but people were turning away from nomadism, crowding into the capital, where life was at least a little easier. Mogadishu's population had been seventy-five thousand in 1960, and now in 1984 it was at least a million, many or most of them without steady work. There had been no accurate census, but when I called on the mayor, he told me that the city's population was growing 9 or 10 percent a year. That seemed likely. Everywhere were cafés or bars where young men sat all day drinking tea and talking, for want of anything else to do. Yet the average Somali woman, according to the best statistics I could find, still bore seven children, one of the highest fertility rates in the world.[2]

The growth of the capital had an appalling effect on the environment. By the end of the 1980s, not long after I had left, the city of Mogadishu was consuming an estimated 156,000 tons of charcoal each year for cooking and, on cooler nights, for heating. To provide the wood to make all that charcoal, almost all the scanty woodland within sixty or seventy miles of Mogadishu had been destroyed. Denser riverine woodlands, not just along the Shebeli but as far away as the Juba River, more than two hundred miles south, were being intensively harvested.[3]

Mogadishu's unemployed young men worried me from the beginning. They were a recipe for trouble in any country—crime now in Mogadishu (there was a lot of burglary) and something worse in the future. The civil strife that broke out in Mogadishu several years later, after I had left, would draw on these idle young men for its heedless, deadly gunners.

On December 12 I was asked to call on the new permanent secretary, that is, number-three, of the foreign ministry as a prelude to seeing the minister and later the president. I was not surprised to find the Somali Ministry of Foreign Affairs housed in the shabbiest ministry building I had ever seen. At least there was a decent tile floor, and the walls were painted, which I soon found was more than one could say for several other Mogadishu ministries.

The permanent secretary, Ahmed Mohamed Adan, was a tall, handsome, and polished man who had just returned to Mogadishu from several

2. But not the highest; the fertility rate in Ethiopia was about the same. The rate in Rwanda almost a decade later was reported to be still higher, 8.5 children per woman (*World Health* 47:3 [May–June 1994]).

3. *Encyclopedia of World Geography* (New York: Marshall Cavendish, 1994), vol. 16, p. 2289.

years in New York as Somalia's permanent representative to the United Nations. Earlier he had served twice as ambassador to the Soviet Union and as ambassador to the United States. Part of his first Moscow tour had coincided with my service there in 1962–64. We agreed that we must have met at Moscow diplomatic receptions. His new embassy, as I well remembered, had been just across a little square from the residence of our ambassador. I had not thought of it at the time, but now it came to me that the Soviets had probably paid for the construction of the Somali embassy.

The following day I paid a brief but important call on the foreign minister, Abdirahman Jama Barre, the president's foster brother. I handed him a copy of the remarks I intended to make when I saw the president and a copy of my credentials—a letter from our president to Somalia's president, naming me ambassador, along with another letter announcing that my predecessor, Robert Oakley, had been recalled. Now, under Somali practice, I could function freely, making contact with other ministers and officials; but I would feel fully accredited only when I had been received by Mohamed Siad Barre.

That evening I went to the International Golf and Tennis Club for a dinner that had been arranged for the American community to meet the new ambassador. There were perhaps a hundred people, including spouses, from private aid organizations as well as the embassy. I spoke to them for ten minutes, wondering what opinion they might have of me. A reserved opinion for now, I supposed.

Within the next several days I made the acquaintance of five more government ministers. Then I received word that the following evening, December 19, the president would receive me and my credentials at Villa Somalia, once the residence of Italian colonial governors and now the president's heavily fortified office and residence complex. I reviewed an honor guard, walked into the most elegant building in Somalia, and met the man who had been running Somalia for fifteen years. Mohamed Siad Barre had been born into a nomad family in the Ogaden at a time when birth records were unknown there. He told me once that he was younger than Ronald Reagan, who was then seventy, but if so, I did not think he could be more than a month younger.[4] The Somali president was tall and thin, with a small, square mustache—I wondered to myself, Chaplin or Fuehrer?—and he spoke

4. The *New York Times*, which once reported Siad's year of birth as 1919, eventually decided that he was born sometime between 1912 and 1920. See the *Times* for March 10, 1978, and January 3, 1995.

Peter Bridges presents
his credentials to Mohamed
Siad Barre, president of the
Somali Democratic Republic,
Mogadishu, December 1984.

good English to me, although I had supposed we would speak Italian. Siad
had served in the Italian colonial police, and during the decade just before
independence, when Italy administered its former colony under UN mandate, Siad had spent two years at the Carabinieri academy near Florence
and had eventually risen in the police to the rank of chief inspector. After
Somalia became independent in 1960, Siad became one of several deputy
commanders of the new Somali army, and when in 1965 the commander in
chief died in office, Siad succeeded him and remained in that position until
his 1969 coup. Siad's earlier career had perhaps shown little promise; two
senior Somali officials told a friend of mine that Siad's promotion to lance
corporal in the colonial police had been a long time coming.

The State Department had cabled me main points they wanted me to
make to the president and left the rest to me. Several days earlier, Siad had
signed a long letter to Reagan that expressed gratitude for American aid to
date but appealed for an increase in our overall assistance. He said correctly
that Somalia was continuing to experience extreme economic difficulties.
Beyond this, though, Siad described continual attacks by Ethiopian forces
that, he suggested, were the prelude to a diabolical Soviet plan to use Ethiopia to destabilize Somalia.

The presentation of my own credentials was not the occasion to discuss possible Soviet plans. I told Somalia's president that Somalia was important for us; I was the first ambassador appointed since President Reagan's
reelection. Stability in the Horn of Africa and the peaceful development of
Somalia were high priorities for Washington. The Department had told me
to point up the size of our aid programs. I did so but then went on to say that
what we were doing should complement Somalia's own efforts; we wanted

Somalia to help itself on the economic front. I was personally delighted to be here, and I intended to travel widely and meet as many people as I could. I said this last because I was not going to let Siad Barre and his people restrict my contacts, as I was sure he would like to do.

Siad[5] replied that he deeply admired President Reagan; Somalia was "an allied country," and he hoped for much greater American support. He warned me about what he called Quislings and traitors. There were a lot of them in any country, and they spewed out misinformation. When I wanted the facts I should come see him, at any time. He might ask to see me rather late at night; such were his habits.

I was thinking hard as he spoke. I knew about his habits from my predecessors; Siad worked through most of the night before going to bed—as Iosif Stalin once had—and he had often called in my predecessors after midnight. Somalia from our point of view was a friendly country, not an allied one. I was certainly not going to agree to stay clear of "Quislings." So I said that I had just come from three years in Italy, a country closely allied with the United States, but I could not imagine any president of Italy speaking of our president in warmer terms than he had just used. As to assistance, we would do what we could. I intended to report to Washington frankly and accurately on Somalia, and to do this I intended to see a broad range of people. I hoped this would not occasion reports to the president that I was seeing Quislings. And I looked forward to seeing the president frequently, and I would come willingly at any hour.

So we parted. Tom Hull, who headed our U.S. Information Service, had invited me to a film showing together with a number of Somalis. Soon I was sitting in the Hulls' garden watching *It's a Wonderful Life*. And so it was: Jimmy Stewart on the screen, the Southern Cross above us, the smell of flowers in the air, and I had just been matching wits with the president of Somalia. I thought I had come off all right.

5. Somalis have no family names. Instead, a Somali has a given name followed by the name of his or her father and then the name of the paternal grandfather. Thus the president's father was Siad, his grandfather Barre; he might be referred to politely in conversation by his first name and patronymic, that is, Mohamed Siad. Nor was it impolite to call someone by his first name alone; I was often called Peter. But the Western press, and Westerners generally, long referred to the Somali president as Siad or Siad Barre, and I have done so in this book. Most people in Somalia are also given nicknames, which in some cases the individual adopts and uses but that in other cases is only used behind the person's back. The president's nickname was one of the latter: Af Weyne, or Big Mouth. I never learned what my own nickname was—but I knew I had one.

By the time I left Mogadishu for Christmas in Rome, I had met several more Somali ministers and a number of other foreign ambassadors. The thought came to me that since our aid program was larger than that of any other country, larger than those of the United Nations and the World Bank, I was in Somali eyes the most important foreigner in that Texas-sized country. I was not sure I liked that thought, although I could see that we were doing good things in Somalia, on both the civilian and the military sides. At this point I had learned more, on the civilian side, about our food aid than I had about efforts to promote Somalia's development.

As best we could judge, almost all the estimated half-million Somalis who had fled Ethiopia in the wake of the 1977–78 war were still in Somalia. Almost all of them were living in camps up and down the country that were run by the agency of the UN High Commissioner of Refugees, UNHCR. These refugees were fed by another UN agency, the World Food Program; the United States was the largest donor of food to WFP for Somalia. It was moreover a private American agency, CARE, whose Somalia director was an experienced and likable American named Mike Kamstra, that kept thousands of tons of WFP food in safe storage in its Mogadishu warehouses and maintained a fleet of 150 heavy trucks to deliver the food to the camps.

On the military side, we were helping Somalia defend itself against Ethiopia, whose large units of troops and tanks along the border were a serious threat. Ethiopia, in addition, was giving close combat support to units of Somali dissidents that were periodically coming over the border, probing Somali defenses. For some time, too, the Ethiopian army had been holding on to two towns, Balenbale and Goldogob, which were without question inside Somalia.

Siad Barre would have liked us to replace the eight hundred tanks the Soviets had provided him that he had lost invading Ethiopia. We would not do that. Instead we approved the transfer to Somalia of a hundred older, smaller, American-made M-47 tanks that had been in the hands of the Italian army for many years; after we had them rehabilitated, they were good for defense but not for a new invasion of Ethiopia. We also provided him two dozen TOW antitank missile systems and about sixty 106-mm recoilless rifles that, mounted on jeeps, could also be used against invading Ethiopian tanks. The list also included seventy-five 81-mm mortars, 160 40-mm grenade launchers, two dozen machine guns, three thousand M-16 rifles, 130 trucks, a half-dozen 155-mm howitzers, and a number of other items. The howitzers are the only item that I regret our having furnished. They were never used against invading Ethiopians; instead, some of them were used a couple of years after I had left Somalia to batter the city of Hargeisa in the north of Somalia, which was held by the antiregime Isaq clans. At the beginning of 1991, the howitzers were used against dissidents in Mogadishu itself.

I had never liked military dictators like Mohamed Siad Barre. And there was a rapacious side to the Somalis. Siad Barre's insistence that Somalia needed still more American aid was echoed by every minister that I called on, and I already knew enough to realize that many of their requests were not justified. William Fullerton, the British ambassador, a canny Arabist with a wife from Brooklyn, told me to read Richard Burton's 1856 account of his first visit to Somalia. Burton said Arabs called Somalia *Bilad wa issi*, the Land of Give Me Something. "The longer you are here," said Bill Fullerton, "the more you will think that name is apt." He was right. I decided, as I took off on the midnight flight for Rome, that as soon as I returned I would need to spend a lot of time with Louis Cohen, the AID director in Somalia, to make sure I understood—and could in good conscience support—AID's large and complicated set of developmental aid programs. I had, I knew, a lot to learn.

nine

Aid, with Scandals and Defects

After I left Mogadishu for Rome, a sizable armed force from Ethiopia crossed the Somali border in the north. I cut short my stay and returned to Somalia. I was sorry to miss the Rabbs' reception and lunch with Minister Scalfaro. Just after my return the defense minister, Mohamed Ali Samantar, summoned me and ambassadors of other friendly Western countries. I knew what this was about. There had been new skirmishing on the border, and I had learned that two days earlier Samantar had called in the ambassadors of Arab countries to say that Somalia was being attacked and needed help. Our intelligence on the border situation was far from complete, but I doubted that Ethiopia was launching a full-scale attack. In fact it seemed to me unlikely that they would do so, given other circumstances. Mengistu, the Ethiopian dictator, had just been in Havana and Moscow, and there were indications that these visits had not gone well. It did not seem likely to me that the Soviets would be spurring him on at this point to attack Somalia or that he would try to blackmail Moscow by invading Somalia and then demanding more arms. Mengistu had civil war and famine on his hands in Ethiopia. I could imagine continuing small-scale probing by both the Ethiopians and the Somalis along their long common border, but nothing too serious.

There was, however, the complicating factor of the Somali dissidents. Siad Barre had antagonized the largest group of clans in the north, the Isaqs, and many of their men had gone over the border to join the largely Isaq Somali National Movement, or SNM. The Ethiopians, and the Libyans as well, were giving the SNM their support. It was conceivable that the Ethiopians might be encouraging stepped-up SNM activity against Somalia in order to destabilize Siad Barre's regime.

I was interested to find at the defense ministry that the group of "friendly Western ambassadors" whom Samantar had called in included the representative of the European Community (how many divisions did the EC have?) and the ambassador of the People's Republic of China (which was no longer providing Somalia military aid, although it had done so earlier). I had brought John Ryan, our defense attaché, with me, and he took full notes as Samantar briefed us and a Somali major with a pointer showed us on a wall map the obscure but not unimportant places the minister was mentioning. Samantar's conclusion was the same as what I knew he had told my Arab colleagues: the Ethiopians seemed to be grouping for further, more massive attacks, and Somalia needed new help from its friends. From what he had just told us, so far at least, the attacks had not been massive.

I was about to ask the minister a question when my new British colleague, Bill Fullerton, asked just that question. Why did the minister think that the Ethiopians were going to mount a major attack when they themselves faced major insurrections in Tigre and Eritrea, as well as a terrible famine? Samantar gave a logical if not convincing answer. The Ethiopians, he said, might well be cooling the Eritrean conflict; most of the Western famine aid was "undoubtedly" being diverted to the Ethiopian army, making it easier for the Ethiopians to go on the offensive; and the Ethiopians' Soviet allies, as well as Mengistu himself, much wanted a change of regime in Somalia.

As we left I told the defense minister that I would immediately report to Washington what he had said. John Ryan and I went back to the chancery, and after a talk, we cabled home what Samantar had told us. I did not recommend that we increase or even accelerate our military assistance, which in any case would have been difficult to do. By a week later, the Somalis themselves seemed to have decided that the situation was less than critical: Samantar left Mogadishu for a long trip to six foreign capitals. Soon we ascertained that the invaders had not been Ethiopians but Somalis from the dissident northern clans—armed and aided, to be sure, by the Ethiopians.

I had come back to Mogadishu with a viral infection, and after cabling Washington about the military situation I collapsed on my front porch with a book I had found on an embassy shelf, *The Periplus of the Erythraean Sea*. This was an English translation of a work written apparently in the first century A.D. by a Greek-speaking mariner who was a resident of Egypt. It was a gazetteer of the Red Sea and the Indian Ocean, which the ancients called the Erythraean Sea. The first half of the work described the coast, ports, and seaside trading marts that a mariner would find if he sailed southward down the African coast of the Red Sea, then beyond the Strait of Bab el Mandeb along the coast of northern Somalia to the Cape of Spices (the Horn of Africa), and down into the Erythraean Sea, the Indian Ocean. The writer gave detailed lists of trade items brought to this coast from the Roman world—coins, wine, tunics, glassware—and items exported from here—myrrh, various forms of incense, ivory, tortoiseshell, slaves. It appeared that this coast, where I sat now, was what the author called the Courses of Azania. Mogadishu was perhaps what the author referred to as Sarapion. I had long agreed in my mind with the scholars who thought that Somalia was probably also the Land of Punt, where Egyptians had sailed for ivory, incense, and slaves two thousand years before the *Periplus*, although other scholars located Punt in what is now Eritrea.

Sitting on my porch, I raised my eyes and looked out at the great ocean. The northeast monsoon was blowing strongly this afternoon. I could imagine the traders coming down this steady wind two thousand years ago with cargoes from Alexandria and Rome. I thought of Isak Dinesen's Gothic tale "The Dreamers" and her adventurous Lincoln Forsner on a dhow sailing south of Mogadishu. Somali dhows still sailed the Indian Ocean from small ports in the north. Perhaps someday I too could sail this clear blue sea.

I got well and called on Siad Barre's second vice president, Hussein Kulmie Afrah, an older man with a quiet way. He was, I knew, in government as senior representative of the Hawiye clans, who lived in the region that stretched north from Mogadishu several hundred miles. (The later Mogadishu "warlords," Ali Mahdi and Gen. Mohamed Farah Aydid, were Hawiye leaders.) As the months went on, I gained the impression that Kulmie did not accomplish much. In good part this may have been because Siad Barre, who could tolerate no rival, would not let him do much. But Kulmie had attractive ideas about developmental aid. He thought that his sunny, windy country would do well to develop, with foreign assistance, wind and solar power rather than beg occasional oil cargoes from the Saudis, as they were doing now.[1] Somali villagers should

1. The question was later discussed by Rodolfo Pallabazzer and Abdulkadir A. Gabow in "Wind Resources of Somalia," *Solar Energy* 46:5 (1991). They concluded that "the wind resource is good enough in Somalia, especially along the coast, to supply the people with basic energy needs."

be taught to make adobe bricks, such as he had seen on a visit to Arizona, rather than use precious wood. There was an enormous potential for coastal fisheries; small harbors could be built at modest cost, as well as rough roads to link these places with existing roads inland. Above all, he thought, the green revolution could come to Somalia with higher-yielding grains and better animal breeds. This all made sense to me.

Soon I got to know the Catholic bishop, Monsignor Salvatore Colombo, whose cathedral I had passed when I first came to town. He had served here since soon after his 1946 ordination in Milan. His flock comprised only several hundred Somali Catholics plus a thousand Italians. Siad Barre permitted no Catholic proselytizing but was happy to accept Catholic aid. There were sixty Italian and a dozen Indian nuns in Mogadishu, and they provided the only corps of skilled nurses in the city hospitals. The Caritas agency was rehabilitating a hundred village wells, installing Austrian-made hand pumps that were sturdy, easy to repair and required neither electricity nor diesel fuel, always scarce commodities in a Somali village. If, the bishop said, he had learned anything in his decades here, it was to keep aid projects simple if they were to outlast the foreigners who came, most often for brief periods, to set them up.

I continued to see Bishop Colombo for as long as I was in Mogadishu. In July 1989, three years after I had left, the bishop was murdered in his cathedral just as strife was beginning in the streets of Mogadishu. The nuns all left the country. The cathedral, a cool and lovely place where I once attended midnight mass at Easter, was vandalized and burned. The perpetrators may have been inspired by anti-Christian feelings, but I saw it all as just part of the great horror visited on Somalia, almost all of its victims not Christians but Muslims.

China, I found, had made major civilian aid contributions to Somalia in past years, as well as providing some military aid. The Chinese had built the big Mogadishu soccer stadium and also the city's women's hospital. The hospital, I heard from doctors, was well designed and quite functional. This was said to be in good part because the Chinese had put careful study into how to build a hospital building for this particular climate and this particular society. More recently the Chinese had become more economic minded, and what one saw now in Somalia was not large Chinese aid projects but a Chinese construction company building a highway with World Bank funding.

I began, as I had planned, to spend considerable time with the director of our AID mission, Louis Cohen. Lou was an experienced senior officer and a sensible man who ran the largest element in our embassy, so large that AID people did not like to be called part of the embassy. I had learned after reaching Mogadishu that the AID presence was considerably larger than the figures that I had been given in Washington, which did not include over forty Americans who were AID contractors and resided, most of them with families, in Mogadishu. In contrast to what I had seen of AID in Panama years earlier, most of our AID staff in Mogadishu knew Africa. But an AID officer said to me quietly one day, "We spend most of our time in meetings and far too little in the field."

Lou Cohen could see AID's failings better than I could. He did not much disagree with Kulmie's and the bishop's ideas, but our AID program was what it was, and it was hard to get Washington to change course. It was Cohen who brought to my attention in 1985 one development project that he recommended we terminate immediately. I was quick to agree. The project was to set up health clinics in a dozen Somali towns where there were no clinics and no trained medical personnel. The American company that had won the contract was to provide buildings for the clinics and train Somalis to staff them. It had shipped to Somalia the prefabricated clinic buildings, but the contract did not require the company to send staff to erect the buildings, and the Somalis had proved incapable of doing so. There was more. The buildings were designed to be air-conditioned; with low ceilings and small windows, they had to be air-conditioned to be used in the Somali climate. But, as the bishop had noted, electricity was at best a scarce item in a Somali town. Even if there was a town generator, there was often no fuel to run it. Air-conditioning a building in a Somali town was totally out of the question—and so was this aid project. We terminated it, saving the American taxpayer perhaps as much as had been wasted.

Unfortunately, life with Louis Cohen was not without friction. Much of the friction had been built in by Bob Oakley's predecessor, Don Petterson, who as ambassador in 1981 had (on instructions from Washington, not of course on his own initiative) negotiated a U.S.-Somali aid agreement that provided for an AID "mission" with almost independent status. This agreement was not unlike similar agreements we had concluded with other African countries. Still, I would never have agreed to its terms, because I set a high value on coordination; this agreement was in effect a license for the AID director to operate almost without reference to me. Indeed, he often did so. I told Lou that regardless of what he might have done under my predecessors, I did not want him meeting with Somali government ministers—even if, as he said, it was often the minister who requested the meeting—without first consulting me, so that I could either join the meeting myself or at a minimum give Lou my thoughts beforehand. As he well knew, I had, like every other American ambassador, a letter from our president that made clear my authority over all U.S. government elements in my country of assignment, other than military units directly subordinate to a military command. I added that I was not talking to him as the State Department's man, because I was not that. I was the president's man. I had worked not only in the State Department but in two other federal agencies in the course of my Foreign Service career, and I had believed particularly strongly in the need for coordination since my assignment as the executive secretary of the Treasury Department. Lou said he understood. Nevertheless, he continued to see ministers, and even Vice President Kulmie, without prior reference to me. Eventually I brought the problem to the State Department's attention, which I would have preferred not to do, asking that it be discussed with AID/Washington.

This was, fortunately, the only serious difference that I had with Lou Cohen, who died several years later in Washington after a distinguished career. I found, as Lou and his staff educated me in what AID was doing in Somalia, that many of our developmental aid programs, which concentrated on agriculture and animal husbandry, made good sense. We were pushing the green revolution, as Kulmie urged. We were helping Somali farmers import seeds that increased yields by 50 to 75 percent; we supported an artificial insemination program that had already improved cattle herds; we were (together with other donor governments) teaching Somali herdsmen in the central rangelands, which covered 25 percent of Somalia's land area, how better to protect that fragile environment, threatened by increased herds of camels, sheep, and goats. But the question, as we all knew, was whether the effect of these aid programs would outlast AID. When the Americans left, as someday we must, would the Somalis carry on with the improvements or revert to traditional ways?

This was not, of course, a question for the Americans alone but for all the other foreign aid donors as well, and for the Somalis. Other donors, I soon found, were making mistakes similar to ours. The European Community provided an expensive network of several dozen automatic, diesel-powered weather-reporting stations that for the first time would provide the ministry of agriculture with nationwide temperatures and rainfall figures. The stations were too sophisticated, and there was no more fuel to run them than there had been for our village clinics. Only one or two of the stations ever sent in data.

Two of my best non-Somali friends in Mogadishu were Andrew and Judi Macpherson, an Australian couple. Macpherson was a dry-country agriculturalist who had learned his business by farming with his father in Australia. He and Judi had spent several years in Somalia working for an Australian development company that had World Bank funding; they had only recently moved to Mogadishu from a small southern village. Macpherson and his company were convinced that southern Somalia had considerable untapped potential for rain-fed farming. He was showing Somali farmers how they could raise not just sorghum but corn, at least in years with average rainfall. But he had learned that it took a long time to make Somalia's small farmers change their ways, as it does in any peasant society—I thought of pre-1917 Russia. And there was always the danger that along the way something important, something elementary, might not get learned. Andrew had a management intern, a bright, young graduate of the Somali National University who had studied agronomy and was good at office work—but who, Andrew discovered one day, had never seen a screwdriver and did not know how one worked.

I soon decided that the sensible thing for us to do was to concentrate heavily on Somali education. As happened elsewhere in colonial Africa, the British and the Italian colonial administrations in Somalia had done pitifully little to educate young Somalis—and the British had done less than the Italians. In British Somaliland, a year before the Somalis gained independence in 1960, few more than 2 percent of Somali children attended school. This was not in any way due to parents' disinclination to have their children educated; there were many times more applicants than places in the protectorate's two elementary schools.[2]

After independence, the new government put considerable emphasis on education. In 1963, when the U.S.-Somali relationship had not yet gone downhill, AID had built the teachers' college at Lafoole outside Mogadishu. It still functioned, but, as I found when I went there, the Somali authorities had spent almost nothing on maintenance, and the buildings were in bad shape. Fortunately, AID had recently thought of a way to remedy the situation. Funds to renovate the buildings were being provided by Somali shillings generated by our new program to auction off food aid to local

2. Abdi Ismail Samatar, *The State and Rural Transformation in Northern Somalia, 1884–1986* (Madison: Univ. of Wisconsin Press, 1989), p. 72.

wholesalers. (The auction program seemed to me eminently sensible; it helped prevent the imports of American grain from depressing local food prices and lessening Somali farmers' interest in marketing a crop.) But AID was not focusing on education in Somalia. And yet, I thought, if we were to help the Somalis effectively to master their many problems and become truly independent—whereas economically, at least, they were becoming ever more dependent on donor governments—we should put all possible effort into teaching them what they needed to know. That might be called simplistic; I thought it fundamental. I raised the subject with Washington. I was not saying that public education was all that our assistance should aim at. We could not ignore, for example, public health or sound local economic policies. Students in villages ridden with schistosomiasis (as many were) were not likely to learn much in school, and Somali farmers' disinterest in marketing crops was due less to American grain imports than to Siad Barre's decision some years earlier to freeze food prices. But AID/Washington liked the present mix of programs. There were too many constituencies, and too many contractors, who found the present aid scene comfortable or, in the case of the contractors, profitable. So I got nowhere on increasing aid for education.

We were not the only foreign donors interested in Somali education. A new campus for the Somali National University was being completed, with European Community and some Saudi funding, at the edge of Mogadishu, just beyond the site of our new embassy. Soon after my arrival I went with Tom Hull of USIS to call on the university's rector, Mohamed Gani Mohamoud. The rector's office was in a handsome, round building surrounded by other new buildings that would house twelve of the university's fourteen departments, spread across a campus of almost two hundred acres. Across the road from the main complex were student dormitories and the political science building, which had been provided by the Chinese government. About 80 percent of the construction had been completed when I called on the rector, and almost all of it would be complete by the time I left Somalia. There were three thousand students. In most departments the language of instruction was Italian; the teachers' college used English, and two departments used Somali and Arabic.

I was in no sense anti-Italian, but the longer I stayed in Somalia the more I wondered about this use of Italian in the university. In earlier years it would have made better sense. After Somalia became independent in 1960, Italian had continued to be the main language of instruction in both elementary and secondary schools in the part of the country that had been an Italian colony.

There had been no choice; Somali had first become a written language only in 1972, when Siad Barre decreed the use of the Latin alphabet—after long debate as to whether to use the Latin alphabet, the Arabic, or the 'Osmaniya script (invented earlier in the century by a Somali). In the first years of independence, a young Somali entering the national university or going to Italy for a higher education, as a number of Somalis then did, was likely to be well prepared in the Italian language. (Later I would befriend a Somali minister whose wife, a charming woman, spoke good English and almost perfect Italian. She had learned her Italian in a school taught by Italian nuns in Brava, south of Mogadishu.) But now, in the 1980s, things were different. All Somali schools were taught in Somali. Most students entering the university had to spend most of their first year simply learning Italian. Somalis were in general excellent linguists, but clearly someone new to a foreign language was going to have difficulty pursuing a higher education in it. How much learning would really sink in and stay with the student later?[3] The same question could be asked about the use of English at the Lafoole teachers' college. But English had become the world language, and Somali graduates would find it a useful tool and probably continue to improve their knowledge of it, while Italian was not much spoken anywhere else in Africa or the Middle East, except for Ethiopia—which I did not suppose many Somalis would be visiting in the coming years.

There were Italians in Somalia who agreed privately that an Italian-language Somali university did not make the best of sense. But, as they pointed out, there was no practical alternative. Somalia still lacked enough Somali professors; it made sense to provide higher education in a language that, if not a world language, was more widely spoken than Somali was. More importantly, the Italian government was providing the needed professors. I got to know several of these professors quite well. They were, like most Italian professors I have known, interesting and well-prepared people. Moreover, they liked to come teach in Mogadishu, at least for a time; it was a good deal. Most came on a six-month contract. Unfortunately, relatively few of them returned for a second tour, although they were well paid:

3. Years earlier my wife and I had been befriended in Moscow by several Nigerian students who hoped to transfer to American institutions from Lumumba Friendship University. They were in a somewhat similar linguistic predicament. They had had to spend their first year of higher education learning a new language, Russian, and it was clear that, partly but not entirely because of the linguistic problem, they were not getting the educations they wanted.

five thousand U.S. dollars a month, several times what professors were then paid in Italy, and free of tax.

If America were someday to decide to put more effort into educating the Somalis or helping the Somalis educate themselves, it would clearly have to be a long-term endeavor. The new campus that the Europeans and Saudis were paying for was going to need outside help for many years, not only in teaching staff but in maintenance. As we left the rector, Tom Hull asked Scerif to drive us into town so that I could see the old campus of the university. The old campus consisted of a double row of buildings, and they were in bad shape. Hull commented that though they looked about thirty years old, they had in fact been built just eight years ago. The authorities of the eighth-poorest country in the world did not think they could afford maintenance. So things corroded, cracked, and stopped working. If that happened to the new university, as I thought likely—since the Europeans did not, apparently, intend to maintain the place—I did not suppose that anyone would find funds to build yet another new campus. Well, the university as a whole would not stop working. It was just that, little by little, windows would get broken and microscopes would cease to function and laboratory sinks would stop up and wall switches would fail to turn on lights, and the rector would run out of typewriter ribbons with which to report the piteous state of affairs. But by then, I thought to myself, the country's population would presumably have doubled again, as it had done in the quarter-century since independence, and the problems of higher education would pale (perhaps they did already) in comparison with the problems of finding Somalis enough to eat.

By 1985 our position as top aid donor was being eclipsed by the Italians. It began with Marco Panella, head of the Italian Radicals, one of the smallest parties in the Italian Parliament. The Radicals had successfully championed divorce and abortion in Italy. In the 1980s Panella needed a new cause, and he found it in foreign aid. Italy was one of the seven top industrialized countries but was doing little to help the third world. Panella began hunger strikes: not long ones, but enough for media coverage. He shamed the country, and Parliament appropriated over two billion dollars for additional foreign aid. It was decided to spend most of this on Italy's former colonies. About a billion dollars was allocated for projects in Somalia. Other Italian parties got involved. The Radicals were outside the governing coalition; the Christian Democrats and the Socialists ran it. Christian Democratic interests would handle aid projects in Ethiopia; the Socialists, whose leader Bettino Craxi was prime minister, would work Somalia.

This became a dirty scene. Italian firms linked to the Socialists got the Somalia contracts, working through the Italy-Somalia Chamber of Commerce, headed by Craxi's brother-in-law Paolo Pillitteri. A quarter of a billion dollars was spent on an unnecessary road in northern Somalia. Many more millions went to renovate a useless pharmaceutical plant, several large fishing boats that never went to sea, and a fertilizer plant that never produced a bag of fertilizer. A former Somali minister testified later in Italy that 10 percent of the money had gone into the pockets of Siad Barre's family and cronies.[4] In 1985–86 my good friend the Italian ambassador, Mario Manca, could no doubt sense the corruption in the air. We all could. But clearly the schemers were not going to take into their confidence this ambassador, who had won a reputation for standing up to bad guys when as consul general in London he had acted heroically during a terrorist incident. Later some other Italian officials were investigated for corruption in the aid system; Manca went on to serve with distinction as ambassador to Denmark.

In addition to the various operations in Somalia sponsored by the Italian government, there were a number of resident Italian business people and a few Italian farmers like our friends the Muttos, who, as mentioned in chapter 7, had a banana plantation south of Mogadishu. The total number of Italians permanently resident in Somalia in the mid-1980s was perhaps a thousand. There had been many more before the Second World War, most of them living in Mogadishu, which in 1938 numbered about twenty thousand Italians in a total city population of fifty thousand.[5] A number of the Italians who settled in Somalia had first gone there for Mussolini's invasion of Ethiopia and had stayed on because prospects seemed better for them in the colony than in 1930s Italy. One of the remaining farmers, a man I knew slightly, was an Italian Jew who moved to Somalia when the Duce instituted anti-Semitic laws in Italy in the late 1930s and who was, fortunately, left alone by the colonial administration.

The Germans—both the Federal Republic of Germany and the German Democratic Republic—contributed significant aid to Somalia, as I

4. See Wolfgang Achtner, "The Italian Connection: How Rome Helped Ruin Somalia," *Washington Post*, January 24, 1993. The last Italian ambassador to Somalia, Mario Sica, who arrived there in 1990, gives a defensive account of Italy's aid programs in his *Operazione Somalia* (Venezia: Marsili Editori, 1994).

5. *Guida dell'Africa Orientale Italiana* (Milano: Consociazione Turistica Italiana, 1938), p. 565.

commented to the East German ambassador when I paid a polite call on him one day. Well, he said, the GDR was not at this point providing significant amounts of aid. Yes, I said, but you built the worst prison for political prisoners in East Africa, at Labataan Jir near Baidoa, and it still functions. The GDR ambassador was a pleasant, elderly man and had probably not expected that Labataan Jir would come up during my courtesy call. But I wanted to make sure his government knew that we knew they were the builders, so I stayed on the subject until I finished my tea, then left.

The West German aid role was a more positive one. The Federal Republic furnished, as did the other Western Europeans, considerable amounts of technical assistance to Somalia, but its most significant program was assistance to the Somali National Police. In contrast to the hated National Security Service, or NSS, which was the Somali equivalent of the Soviet KGB, the national police continued to enjoy a generally good reputation throughout the country. Several of its top officers had been trained by the British at Sandhurst, and indeed its dress uniforms were British-like; they even carried swagger sticks. Unfortunately, the commander of the police, Gen. Mohamed Abshir Musse, had been imprisoned by Siad Barre almost immediately after Siad took power in 1969. Siad released General Abshir only in the final months of my tour in Somalia, and I had the pleasure of meeting him several times. Abshir was not broken by his years in prison, and he was delighted to know that we had mutual friends in Liv and Miggs Pomeroy, who had served in our embassy in the 1960s. Later, after Siad had fled Mogadishu and civil war began in Somalia, General Abshir would play a key role as de facto administrator of the northeast of the country, maintaining relative calm and prosperity there.

The continuing West German assistance to the national police stemmed from a major incident in October 1977. Palestinian terrorists hijacked a Lufthansa jet loaded with passengers and in the end made the pilot fly it to Mogadishu. Bonn had cut off official assistance to Somalia five years earlier, after Siad Barre recognized East Germany. Now, though, Bonn instructed its ambassador at Mogadishu to tell Siad Barre on the most urgent basis that if he would give West Germany a free hand in dealing with the hijacking, the Federal Republic would renew assistance to Somalia—and it would be generous. Siad agreed. Within hours, a German antiterrorist team killed three of the four hijackers and recaptured the plane as it sat at the end of the Mogadishu airport runway. Ever since then the West Germans had remained true to their word, providing the national police with training, weapons,

and equipment. The German vice minister of defense, Peter-Kurt Wuerz-
bach, visited Mogadishu twice in 1985. He assured the Somali authorities
and, separately, me that the Germans would consider themselves in debt to
the Somalis for a long time to come.

For the first part of my tour in Somalia, the West German ambassador
was Martin Florin, still in his forties and a veteran of over a dozen years in
Africa. We had each spent an academic year in the other's country, mine on
the study of Soviet affairs and his at Harvard. We found we agreed on most
things, including the likelihood of a worse future for Africa, a continent he
knew far better than I could ever hope to. (In 1990, after he had left Somalia for a long leave of absence in Finland, Florin and two friends published
in Germany an excellent primer on the continent, *Afrika Transparent.*[6]) One
of Martin Florin's complaints was that he had never yet found a way to visit
the long coast north of Mogadishu toward the Horn. Perhaps, I told him, I
could some time arrange a way for the two of us to go there.

---

6. Published in Baden-Baden by Nomos Verlagsgesellschaft, 1990.

ten

Dams, Drugs, and Dictator

The defense minister, Mohamed Ali Samantar, was also the first vice president and so presumably the number-two in Somalia. Well, he was, and he was not. Samantar was a Tumal. The Tumal were one of several low-caste groups, Somali-speaking but looked down on by the regular Somali clans. Traditionally the Tumal worked as smiths and shoemakers. Some scholars thought that they might be a remnant of pre-Somali, Bushmen-like, aboriginal inhabitants of the land. Certainly Samantar was not a typical Somali in appearance; he was lighter skinned and much shorter than most of his compatriots. It seemed clear that one reason Siad had Samantar as his number-two, aside from the fact that Samantar had been one of Siad's partners in the 1969 coup, was that a Tumal could not aspire to rule Somalia.

We knew that Samantar had been close to the Soviets in the years before the Ethiopian war. So of course had his boss and most if not all of the other top Somali leaders. But there were rumors that Samantar in particular was still pro-Soviet. I kept this always in the back of my mind, but we had no reason to believe the rumors, and I found Samantar frank and easy to deal with. Years after my tour in Somalia ended, I learned that Fidel Castro had told East German leader Erich Honecker in early 1977, after Castro visited Mogadishu, that Samantar had "held to leftist positions," in contrast to the interior minister, Ahmed Suleiman (of whom more later), whom Castro described as a representative of the right wing. Castro had at the same time taken a clear dislike to Siad Barre—this was several months before Cuban and Somali forces began fighting each other in the Ogaden—saying, "I have made up my mind about Siad Barre, he is above all a chauvinist. [His] socialism is just an outer shell. . . . Siad Barre really thinks that he is the summit of wisdom."[1] (This from a man who clearly has had no doubts about his own wisdom!)

Each time a top U.S. military official would visit Mogadishu—Deputy Secretary of Defense William Taft; two successive CENTCOM commanders, Generals Robert Kingston and George Crist; once even the commander of the Seventh Fleet, Adm. Paul McCarthy, who was based in Japan—I would take the visitor to Samantar for a meeting between just the three of us. Samantar spoke good English, but he would tell the visitor that his English was weak and his Italian better, and that he would therefore speak Italian and ask Ambassador Bridges to interpret for him. The first time he did this, it irritated me; I was not in Somalia as an interpreter. But then I decided I enjoyed it. As I translated for the visitor what Samantar was saying, Samantar of course understood me and so knew whether I was being accurate—which, it seemed to me, might also tell him something about my general reliability as a channel to top people in Washington. At the same time, the visitor was using me, at least to some extent—since Samantar's comprehension of English was in fact less than perfect—to convey his thinking to the minister. Of course I could and did interject what I liked. For me there was something almost humorous, and indeed enjoyable, about such occasions.

In August 1985 I spent a full and interesting day with Samantar during our annual Bright Star military exercise. This involved our forces and those of several countries in the region, notably Egypt and Somalia. In 1985 we sent for the first time a trio of C-130 transport planes on a non-stop flight from Egypt south to Somalia, carrying American paratroopers. Samantar invited my wife and me to fly out to the air base at Bale Dogle, a hundred miles inland from Mogadishu, to watch the paratroops drop. Mary Jane and I arrived there at dawn. It was cool, with the monsoon wind blowing strongly across the long runway that the Soviets had built for their own as well as Somali use. The C-130s appeared on schedule and dropped their men from several hundred feet, directly above the runway. Was it possible that the pilots did not know about the monsoon? Clearly they did not, and most of the men drifted in the wind and landed, contrary to plans, in the thick bush. Fortunately, only one of them broke his

1. Transcript of meeting between Honecker and Castro in East Berlin, April 3, 1977. Text available at the National Security Archive website.

leg. But the main thing for the Somalis was the direct demonstration of American involvement in Somalia—we assumed that the Soviets and Ethiopians could detect the flight. Samantar was very positive and polite in his appraisal of the exercise.

After the drop, Samantar took us back toward Mogadishu in his Land Rover, and we called at a small tent camp near the Shebeli River where American and Somali officers were together working out a Bright Star paper exercise. But that was not the defense minister's idea of a proper headquarters. In fact, when Samantar had paid a visit to CENTCOM headquarters in Florida, before my arrival in Somalia, he had become enamored of the modern furnishings and high technology in the new headquarters building. This, he decided, was what a proper defense minister needed. The Pentagon agreed with him, and several million dollars of our military assistance funds went subsequently to build a high-tech command, control, and communications center for Samantar in Mogadishu. It was, like many other instances of foreign aid, too high-tech for Somalia, and the center was far from finished when I left Somalia. The delays, and also an unfortunate increase in the cost, were on the American side, not the Somali. The center was originally to cost two million dollars and to be ready in 1985. Samantar and I finally held a groundbreaking ceremony in 1986, with some expectation the project might be completed in 1987 at a cost of six million dollars. I did not care about providing the defense minister a seat of proper elegance, but there was also a question of providing his ministry with the capability to order a timely response to an incursion by Ethiopian MiGs.

Siad Barre once or twice demoted or transferred Mohamed Ali Samantar, as he did other members of his regime to reduce the chances of their becoming real rivals to him and to remind them, not that they needed reminding, that Siad was Number One. When Siad was finally dethroned and fled Mogadishu, Samantar had been for some time without a job, living in his sumptuous Mogadishu villa, where, as I remembered well, he had twice entertained my wife and me. Samantar had no reason to believe that the new group of Mogadishu leaders would see him as anything but Siad's man, and he too fled, taking his family south in a Land Rover. They were attacked on the way, and Samantar was wounded. He nevertheless kept on, and they reached Kenya and eventually Italy, where until recently Siad Barre's interesting former sidekick was living, I understand, in comfortable circumstances. At the end of 1998, I was surprised to learn from a Somali acquaintance that Samantar had moved to northern Virginia.

Soon after my arrival I met, and came to like and respect, the vice minister of defense. He was a big, fine-featured brigadier general named Aden Abdullahi Nur. He had been born in the Northern Frontier District of Kenya, peopled almost entirely by Somalis. As a young man he had enlisted in a British colonial unit that was sent to Malaya in the late 1940s to fight the communist guerrillas. Hard jungle fighting, he told me, but we were good fighters. In 1963, some time after his unit had returned home, Kenya became independent. Aden Abdullahi became a platoon leader in the new Kenyan army, but as a Somali he fell under suspicion and was reduced to private, eventually leaving the army and becoming a game warden in a Kenyan park on the border with Tanzania. Enough was enough. He crossed the border and made his way to Dar es Salaam, where the Somali embassy arranged his passage to Mogadishu. Soon he had a commission in the Somali army and, notwithstanding his experience fighting communists in Asia, went to the Soviet Union for four years' training. It was, he said, good training but a difficult experience. A lot of Russians had a strong dislike for black Africans, and he never forgot being mugged on the street one night; he was sure the mugging was race inspired. I told him that his was a real soldier's story and that I heard only good things about him from our own military officers. I said, and meant it, that though I had not met many African military leaders, I doubted any were better than he.

Military leaders were one thing, military dictators another. As I have said earlier, I did not like dictators like Mohamed Siad Barre, although as ambassador I did my best to maintain a close official relationship with the head of a government to which the United States was giving very substantial aid. After Siad Barre fled from Mogadishu, and eventually from Somalia, he died in exile in Nigeria in January 1995. He was a tough, indeed ruthless, man, and he deserves considerable blame for the Somali tragedy. The civil war that erupted and dethroned him was to a considerable degree a reaction against the later days of his rule, when Siad had surrounded himself with cronies and bodyguards from his own clan, the Marehan. His was a regime that excluded effective participation by other groups of clans, a regime that was not based on the strong democratic traditions of Somali pastoral society. It also became, as the years passed, an increasingly corrupt regime.

And yet, one must give Mohamed Siad Barre his due. Both before and after his 1969 coup, the forces he commanded profited hugely from Soviet military aid, and after he became president he let the Soviets build up a strong military position in Somalia. But that changed; and how many leaders in Africa, or on any other continent, would have had the courage then to expel thousands of Soviet advisers—many of them enmeshed in Somalia's police and military—as Siad Barre did in 1978?[2]

Nor, from what I know, had Siad always been the corrupt and cruel dictator of later years—the years when I knew him. For perhaps five years after the 1969 coup, Siad's Somalia was run by a kind of coalition between his military junta and a group of civilian professionals, including engineers, economists, doctors, and lawyers. There was a considerable amount of what might be called revolutionary enthusiasm and also substantial popular support for the regime. But this civilian-military coalition ended in 1974–75; a number of the civilian professionals were imprisoned, some for many years. Siad's regime had been strict from the beginning. Now it turned more repressive, more corrupt, and more centered on the interests of his own Marehan clan and the allied clans of the Darod group.

Siad's strengths never included a good understanding of economics. His Soviet-encouraged "scientific socialism," which in its early years enjoyed the support of many educated Somalis, had seriously discouraged farm production (and central Somalia produced considerable amounts of sorghum as well as other crops) by putting a lid on market prices. The lid came off, after considerable American pressure, just before I arrived. There was also a panoply of state-owned enterprises that made no economic sense. Some of them, however, did make business sense—family business sense. Quite aside from the rakeoffs I have mentioned on Italian aid projects, by the 1980s Siad Barre had put much of Somalia's export trade in the hands of family members and cronies. When I was in Somalia, world prices were high for leather and hides, but the Siad-controlled company that exported hides remained more interested in keeping control than in maximizing sales. The same was true for incense, harvested from trees in northeastern Somalia and available from very few other places in the world except Yemen, across the Gulf of Aden.

Siad also seems to bear responsibility for the serious damage done to Somalia's once-considerable export trade in live animals. This trade had a long history. The original reason for Britain's seizing control of what became its Somaliland Protectorate had been to provide a meat supply for its coaling

2. In 1977 President Muhammad Gaafur al-Nimeiry of Sudan expelled all his Soviet advisers and asked the Soviets to reduce by half their embassy staff; in Sudan, however, there were ninety Soviet advisers, not thousands as in Somalia. See *New York Times*, May 20, 1977.

station and base at Aden. More recently, animal exports to Saudi Arabia had increased, and tens of thousands of live camels, sheep, and goats were exported yearly. In 1979, however, Siad's finance minister, Abdillahi Ahmed Addou (of whom more later), apparently decided, or perhaps Siad decided for him, that the major animal exporters, centered at Berbera in the north, were enemies of the regime. Perhaps it was so; many or most of them were Isaqs. In any case, they had been enjoying a tax-free regime at Berbera, and they profited from it; so indeed did the country as a whole, which otherwise had little enough to export. Addou closed down the Berbera trade, on what he claimed were fiscal grounds. One former Siad supporter, Mohamed Aden Sheikh, wrote later that this was "the drop that made the glass run over"[3] and led the Isaqs into active opposition and then full-scale revolt.

Siad's regime may also, in regard to live-animal exports, have accomplished something unusual in economic life: dampening demand as well as supply. By the time I reached Mogadishu in 1984, the Saudi market for Somali cattle had dried up, although some sheep and goats were still being exported. The reason that Saudi officials gave for this was that Somali cattle herds were infected with rinderpest, an animal disease endemic in East Africa. I finally determined a year after my arrival, through a German veterinarian, Dr. Herbert Schels, who was the chief representative in Somalia of the United Nations Food and Agriculture Organization, that the Somalis, with FAO help, had brought rinderpest fully under control. I put the FAO representative together with the Saudi chargé d'affaires, Mohamed Said Abduljawar, who said that he would report the news to Riyadh; I have no doubt that he did. I also informed our embassy at Riyadh and suggested that they too inform the Saudi authorities, and no doubt they did. There was no result. Well, there were credible reports that influential Saudi businessmen had signed contracts for large-scale imports of meat from other countries. Perhaps that was the whole of the story. But I always suspected that Siad's bad treatment of the Isaq exporters in northern Somalia, coupled with the overall negative impression of Siad Barre among conservative religious circles in Saudi Arabia (of which more presently), was the main reason for the Saudi cutoff of Somalia's main export item.

Mohamed Siad Barre's great dream was to leave behind him, as his chief monument to the nation, a high dam on the upper Juba River in southern

3. In *Arrivederci a Mogadiscio* (Roma: Edizioni Associate, 1991), p. 99.

Somalia. The Juba flows down from the Ethiopian highlands, and unlike So-malia's other river, the Shebeli, it flows all year. I flew down one day to see the proposed dam site near the village of Bardera.[4] From an engineering point of view, it was a very good site, where the river flowed through a relatively nar-row gap in a long, two-hundred-foot-high limestone ridge. But there were two serious problems. The first problem, which Lou Cohen of AID soon brought to my attention, was that the surrounding countryside, which was supposed to benefit from irrigation water coming from a big reservoir behind the dam, was stony country and not much good for farming. Farther down-stream the land was better. There was already irrigated agriculture there, and the Chinese had begun a project at Jilib, on the Juba, to develop a large rice-growing area—but this would not depend on waters from the future reser-voir. The Chinese, I heard, were displeased with delays on the Somali side of the rice project. It looked like it would be years, with or without a dam, be-fore the Juba valley began to produce a large food surplus.

The other problem regarding the planned dam, which I may have been the first to point out, had to do with the other intended use of the dam, as the site for a large hydroelectric station whose power would be transmitted several hundred miles overland to Mogadishu. This would largely remove Somali dependence on imported oil, and that was a laudable aim. But the countryside to be crossed by the transmission lines was mainly nomad country. I envisioned the local sporting types using the insulators for target practice—and there were plenty of arms and ammunition in the country-side—and then, after the line was down and the power cut, stealing the cables to sell for scrap.

Siad Barre did not see it that way. The Egyptians, after all, had the Aswan Dam, and the Italians even now were building the largest dam in Africa, in Mozambique. So Siad had created a Ministry of Juba Valley De-velopment, headed by one Ahmed Habib Ahmed. The likable minister and his deputies made the rounds of Western capitals looking for a half-billion dollars to build the big dam. We ourselves estimated that a dam might cost as much as a billion.

Our own position on the dam was not wholly negative. Siad Barre had asked Ronald Reagan for American support when the two met in Washing-ton in March 1982, during the only visit Siad ever made to the United States.

4. It was the Italian colonialists, and not Siad Barre, who first conceived of a Bardera high dam in 1930. Glauco Licata, "E finalmente tutti si sentirono somali," *Corriere della Sera*, June 11, 1985, p. 7.

In 1983, after long debate on the dam inside the State Department and AID, the United States had decided on a position of "limited involvement." This meant that we could foresee a possible need for a dam but would not commit ourselves until a number of studies, some of which we would fund, had been completed. In the next three years, we would spend over eight million dollars on these studies, ranging from local soils to possible socio-economic impacts of a dam. In 1985 AID/Washington decided for reasons I could not comprehend to look more favorably on the dam project. I went to a World Bank meeting in Paris with this news in my pocket. There the Germans, as well as other Europeans, raised a long series of hard-nosed questions about the dam project, questions that—since European as well as U.S. funding would undoubtedly be needed—put the matter in serious doubt, where it stayed until the country collapsed.

Mohamed Siad Barre, like all but a small handful of Somalis, was a Sunni Muslim. He was not in good repute among strict Muslim leaders. For one thing, he was reputed to have been once a heavy drinker. For another, he countenanced relative freedom for Somali women, and there were even two women vice ministers in the Somali government. There were reports that puritanical and influential Wahhabi figures in Saudi Arabia put considerable sums of money into the hands of Somali religious sheikhs to preach against Siad Barre. But Siad had the police power. In January 1975 he executed ten sheikhs who opposed his granting equal inheritance rights to women. Siad did not, of course, want a reputation for being a bad Muslim; he wanted a maximum amount of aid from Arab as well as other quarters. An Arab ambassador whom I came to know well told me one day that the president had asked him to obtain a copy of a film on the life of the Prophet that had recently come out in Cairo. Siad had told the ambassador that he was now spending much more time on Islamic subjects. My Arab friend commented to me that he thought Siad had not really changed his ways, although he had apparently stopped drinking, and that the film request was most likely meant for show. Since my Arab friend was no doubt saying the same thing to other Arab ambassadors in Mogadishu, I concluded that Siad Barre was probably doing himself more harm than good with his new pose of piety.

One of the two women vice ministers, and one whom I came to know and respect, was Raqiya Haji Dualeh Abdalla. I respected her even before I met her, for her brave book *Sisters in Affliction*, which had been published in London.[5] This was a frank treatise and a strong attack on the almost

5. By Zed Press in 1982.

universal practice in Somalia of female circumcision and infibulation. This means, in simple English, that when a Somali girl is somewhere between six and twelve years old, she is held down by female relatives while a woman operator cuts off her clitoris with a razor blade and then sews up her vulva, traditionally with thorns, leaving only a small outlet for urine and, later, menstrual flow. This causes a little girl terrible pain and often results in serious infection, but it offers a bridegroom proof that his bride is a virgin. Raqiya's book had little initial effect on this practice, but it was a brave beginning.[6] When I first met Raqiya, I remembered what Rita Hirsch, my deputy's wife, had said to me earlier: A great evil is done to Somali women, and yet they tend to be lighthearted, sprightly, and smiling—and in some cases, I could add, also very lovely.

Female circumcision in Africa is, of course, not limited to Somalia or to Islamic societies. It is said to be viewed with abhorrence in Saudi Arabia and the Gulf states, but unfortunately it has sometimes received support from Islamic sources. The Grand Sheikh of Al Azhar University in Cairo was quoted in 1995 as saying, "Girls who are not circumcised when young have a sharp temperament and bad habits."[7] In 1997 an Egyptian court issued a ruling, sought by Islamic doctors and scholars, that overturned a ban on female circumcisions.[8]

Female circumcision and infibulation have become better known, and more sharply criticized, in the United States in the wake of greater African immigration into this country and the continuance of these practices among Africans here. I know of only one case involving Americans while I was in Somalia. An American woman had married a Somali and moved to Mogadishu with her husband. They had one daughter, and when the child reached eight or ten, the mother learned that her in-laws intended to have her circumcised and infibulated. Worse, the girl told her mother that she wanted it done, to be like the other girls. The horrified mother decided to take her daughter back to the United States. She succeeded in getting herself and her daughter out of the country only with great difficulty.

Again as regards Siad Barre, he deserves credit for banning the cultivation, sale, and use of *qat,* a narcotic leaf that is chewed in East Africa and Yemen. *Qat* chewers gain, after several hours, a feeling of well-being and mental alertness, but the aftereffects include insomnia, inability to

6. See also the account in *Aman: The Story of a Somali Girl* (New York: Pantheon Books, 1994).

7. *Washington Post,* April 11, 1995.

8. *Los Angeles Times* dispatch from Cairo, in *Denver Post,* June 25, 1997.

concentrate, and anorexia.[9] The *qat* trade revived in Somalia even before Siad's overthrow, but for as long as I was there it was strictly banned. A European who had lived for a number of years in Mogadishu commented to me that the ban had at least one visible effect: employees of ministries began to come to work almost on time. How much they accomplished at work was another question.

Alas, said the Somali deputy minister in charge of sports programs when I called on him one day, we would like to develop more sports programs so that our young people's attention is diverted from even thinking about things like *qat*, but we lack funds for infrastructure.

Nonsense, I replied, you don't need money. Somalis are good runners; why not start a series of runs in Mogadishu? Suddenly I had an idea. In Washington my wife and I had been devoted members of the Potomac Valley Seniors Track Club. The average club member had dozens of commemorative T-shirts from the races he or she had run, and often extra running shoes. I got in touch through the State Department with Sal Corrallo, the club president. Sal quickly got the club to sponsor a collection among Washington runners of T-shirts and shoes (which we insisted had to be new or nearly new) and shipped them to me through the Department. Within a couple of months, the American embassy and the Somali Ministry of Labor and Sports began to cosponsor a series of races, both in Mogadishu and in other towns, including Merka and Balaad, in which top finishers were awarded shirts and shoes. They became big events. I reported to Sal Corrallo that a race in Mogadishu in March 1986 included eight hundred adult runners, who did eight kilometers, and three hundred children, who ran a shorter course. It was a good program—and it didn't cost millions, or even many hundreds, of dollars—and it was fun to meet on my morning runs a Somali runner wearing a T-shirt from a marathon in Saginaw or Seattle.

From the first days of my mission in Somalia I began a kind of dialog with myself about Siad Barre's harsh regime. Perhaps we could not make him turn less dictatorial; but should I not at least say something to him about political prisoners? We knew, though it was never publicized, that the Labataan Jir prison, which the East Germans had built, housed a number of former top officials as well as less prominent people. From what we heard, conditions for them were very bad.

9. Abdullahi Sheikh Elmi, "Khat Consumption in Somalia," in *Proceedings of the First International Congress of Somali Studies*, ed. Hussein M. Adam and Charles L. Geshekter (Atlanta: Scholars Press, 1992), p. 846.

I had no instructions to raise the subject, but I did so anyway in early February 1985, during the course of a long meeting with the president. The occasion for the meeting was a letter that I had been instructed to deliver, from Ronald Reagan to Mohamed Siad Barre, in response to a letter Siad had addressed to our president the previous December. Reagan's letter was a strong statement of U.S. support for Somalia. Siad was glad to have it. He talked to me for a long time, and eventually he began to complain of slanderers in the West who spread lies about Somalia. Siad especially had it in for the BBC's Somali service, which he said had stooped so low as to interview Somali dissidents who had hijacked a Somali Airlines plane to Addis Ababa shortly before I came to Somalia. He wished people would tell the truth about Somalia.[10]

I said I thought most people did. The Somali government was widely credited for the way it had faced up to the tremendous refugee problem and also to its economic and financial crisis, which, as Mr. Reagan's letter noted, was not entirely of Somalia's own making. But, I went on to say, there was also the question of how Somalia's internal regime was viewed. I knew that dissidents had invaded northwest Somalia from Ethiopia and that the Somali armed forces had repelled them, as was their duty. However, as other Somali officials had confirmed to me, a number of civilians had been executed. There were also a number of Somalis in prison for political reasons, facing unknown futures. It was not, I knew, for a foreign ambassador to tell a president how to run his country, but I thought the president of Somalia would want me to be frank—and to be frank, I said, the picture was not very pleasant. I would add just one point, which was that at a time when the world was receiving daily reports of the cruel and repressive nature of the Ethiopian regime, Somalia could only benefit if it demonstrated to the world that things were different here.

I am not sure how many ambassadors have talked frankly to presidents. I knew of two cases where frank American ambassadors had been expelled by another African dictator, Mobutu Sese Seko in Zaire. As I waited for Siad Barre to reply, it came to me that perhaps I might be back in America in time to go to New Hampshire and climb Mount Moosilauke in June, in

---

10. Although I did not say so to Siad (who probably knew it anyway), the BBC Somali service was said to be staffed largely by Isaqs, employed presumably because they came from what had been British Somaliland. The result was, as best I could judge, not only justifiable BBC criticism of Siad's harsh regime but also a certain amount of bias against non-Isaqs. Almost all Somalis who had shortwave radios listened to the BBC Somali broadcasts.

the fresh green of the leaves—and that I'd rather be there than sitting here in Villa Somalia chatting with a dictator.

Siad Barre replied simply and not sharply that I did not understand. Of course there were dissidents, and they were treated according to the laws. (I thought to myself that perhaps they were; Siad had introduced draconian laws that, for example, provided the death penalty for organizing a strike.) "But," continued Siad, "one of the leaders of these supposedly principled people is a man who served as a minister of the Somali government for over a dozen years, until I decided that he should be moved to another post that lacked the ministerial title but paid the same salary. At that point," said Siad, "this man declared that everything that we were doing was wrong, and he went to Addis Ababa to join our enemies." Siad added that he himself had put much effort into national reconciliation and that the situation was much better, as I could see for myself when I visited the north, as he understood I hoped to do. I said I did indeed hope to do so, and soon.

Since Siad himself had raised the question earlier of accurate information on Somalia, I went on to ask him what I could report to Washington about possible changes in the Somali government; there were rumors. Well, he replied, Siad's not sick, and Siad's not leaving the country, even if you've heard rumors about this. I said that what I had heard the previous day, from two other foreign ambassadors, was that they knew for a fact that Siad was in poor health and planning an extended trip to the United States. I had told them that I knew nothing of this; that Siad Barre had not approached us for a visa, but that I would probably give him one if he wanted one. Siad laughed and said that he might make some changes among the party, government, and parliamentary leadership. As the months went on, so did rumors about Siad's possible departure.

I discussed political prisoners with a top Somali official one other time, in December 1985, again without any instructions from Washington. I did so because there were rumors that several of the former top officials imprisoned in Labataan Jir, including a former foreign minister named Omar Arteh (who was well known though not always liked in the West, and who had been in prison since 1982), might be tried and sentenced to death. This time I saw Adan, the permanent secretary of the foreign ministry. I told him that I had no instructions from Washington but that rumors abounded that Omar Arteh and others, who had spent three years in jail without trial, were to be tried now and given death sentences. I said, exaggerating somewhat, that the situation was of deep concern to the Reagan administration and that I would like to know what I could report to my government beyond rumors. A day later, Adan telephoned me to say that he had talked with "the responsible judge"—I wondered if that meant Siad Barre—who had told him that the investigation was continuing and that it kept turning up new evidence of misdeeds. For a second I wondered if I had hurt rather than helped these poor men; but I knew that at least one Arab ambassador had also weighed in on their behalf, and I decided it was a good thing I had too. I told Adan that I wanted to be kept informed. I reported all this to the State Department, as I had done after my earlier discussion with Siad Barre. Each time I was told in reply that the Department agreed I had done right. I was never asked, or told, to do anything more.

Subsequently, after my departure from Somalia, these once-prominent prisoners were tried and sentenced to death, and then had their sentences commuted. My guess is that Siad never intended to execute them.[11] In 1991, after Siad fled from Mogadishu, Omar Arteh became briefly the prime minister of Ali Mahdi's interim government. Soon, though, Omar Arteh decided there was no place for Isaqs like himself in this new Hawiye-run regime; he took a leading role in the Somaliland Republic that the Isaqs proclaimed in the north, in what had been British Somaliland. Later he moved to Saudi Arabia.

I did succeed in getting two Somali prisoners freed during my tour in Somalia. Whether they were political prisoners is a matter of definition. In March 1985 I was shocked to learn that two of our embassy's senior Somali employees had been arrested and were being threatened with ten to fifteen years in jail for having allegedly defamed the president of their country. There was reason to believe that they were the victims of accusations made by a couple of other Somali employees, whom we had fired for cause. I sent our admirable consul, Christopher Costanzo, to call on Gen. Mohamed Jabril Musse, the dreaded head of the murderous National Security Service. Costanzo told Jabril that I was seriously disturbed by these arrests, that I believed the men were the victims of false charges—and that I wanted them released. Jabril said that he had no reason to disbelieve the witnesses against them, but finally he agreed to release the two men, on the condition

---

11. The commutation came a few days after the Voice of America service to Africa broadcast an interview with me in which I strongly urged that the death sentences be changed. But I have no reason to believe that the interview had any effect on Siad Barre. See *USIA/USIS Newswire*, no. 99 (February 24, 1988).

that no matter what they had done or not done in the past, they must utter no disloyal statements in the future.

These employees of ours were Somali citizens, living under the rule of this regime—diplomatic immunity did not extend to national employees—so I agreed. After their release, the two agreed that whatever they had said in the past, they would be careful in the future. I had no doubt that they would. I had educated myself on Siad's draconian legislation, mentioned earlier, dealing with supposed crimes against the state. Law No. 54 of September 10, 1970, provided not imprisonment but the death penalty for a string of loosely described offenses, for example, "an act detrimental to the independence, unity or security of the Somali state." From what I knew, not even Soviet law was so severe.

One day Consul Costanzo told me that the daughter of Omar Arteh, the imprisoned ex-minister, was applying for a job in our embassy's consular section. She was the best candidate for the job; should he hire her? Definitely, I said. Some time later Costanzo heard complaints about this from his Somali official contacts. Tell them, I said, that we hired the daughter, not the father. So he did, and she kept on working.

There was one type of prisoner in Somalia I had to leave mainly to others—the prisoners of war. Almost a decade after Somalia's war with Ethiopia, each side was still holding prisoner a number of the other country's soldiers. There were about two hundred Ethiopian prisoners in Somalia, and in addition the Somalis were holding one captured Cuban officer. The International Committee of the Red Cross began to interest itself in this problem. It sent representatives to both Addis Ababa and Mogadishu to try to arrange an exchange or, short of that, ensure that the prisoners were being treated in accordance with the Geneva agreement of 1949 on war prisoners. The representative sent to Mogadishu was an able young man, a Swiss citizen like all such ICRC representatives. We met frequently. The United States had no great interest in a possible prisoner exchange, but it would be a civilized act that might in a minor way help lessen tensions between Ethiopia and Somalia. Unfortunately, the Somali regime was even less interested in the subject than was Mengistu's Soviet-backed regime in Addis Ababa. I finally discussed the matter quietly with Defense Minister Samantar, suggesting that an exchange could help Somalia's good name. I got nowhere. Worse, my ICRC friend told me that the Ethiopian prisoners and the sole Cuban were being treated badly by their Somali jailers, and that as a result the Cuban had gone out of his mind. But aside from the ICRC and the families of the prisoners, no one really cared very much.

eleven

New Gazas, New Greed

Early in 1985 two critical questions faced us—"us" meaning the United States, other major aid donors, and Somalia itself. The first of these was financial. The finance minister, Mohamed Sheikh Osman, had told me and other Western ambassadors that the Somali government faced a financial gap of perhaps one hundred million dollars for 1985. If this was true, and we thought it might be, it was a horrendously large gap for a country with an economy the size of Somalia's. The World Bank called a meeting of donor governments to discuss the matter in Paris on January 23. Lou Cohen wanted to attend as the top U.S. representative. I wondered if I would do well to attend myself, but the usual pattern was for the AID director to represent us, and in the end I decided that it was better that I stay at my new post.

The meeting resulted in pledges totaling about eighty million dollars from Western governments, which, coupled with a probable twenty million dollars from the International Monetary Fund, looked as if it would keep Somalia financially afloat for another year. The Arab governments, which were taking a generally negative view of their fellow Arab League member Somalia—not that Somalia was remarkable among them for corruption or repression—had not even attended the Paris meeting. Before long I learned that the Arabs had been particularly miffed because the Somalis had, incredibly, failed to send representatives to an earlier meeting that the Arabs had called on the question of aid to Somalia. (I did not initially believe this report, but Siad Barre subsequently admitted to me that it was true—the fault of incompetent subordinates, he said.) In any case, the Paris meeting had been something of an initial accounting exercise. As Paul Daley, our embassy's economic officer, warned me, the more immediate problem was that Somalia's national bank was close to running out of cash.

The other critical question for Somalia was the drought that continued to afflict this part of East Africa. Normally there were two rainy seasons in Somalia: the lesser rains of autumn, called *dayr*, and the greater rains in spring, or *gu*. The rains in the autumn of 1984 had been scanty, and prospects for the sorghum and corn crops were poor. Minister of Agriculture Bile Rafle Gulaid, and subsequently Siad Barre himself, asked me to get a shipload of grain to Mogadishu on an urgent basis. I reported, and supported, this request, but experience showed that at best it could take us several months to deliver such an unscheduled shipment. Much, therefore, depended on whether the *gu* rains began as they should in April or early May and whether they were enough to break the drought. There were areas in the northeast where, from what we had been told (and the data were at best scanty), no rain at all had fallen for a year or more. It was true that rains in the northeast were never abundant, and almost no crops were grown there; still, the situation now was exceptionally bad, and many people were moving out of the region with their herds. The situation in Ethiopia was still worse, and the drought and ensuing famine had led to a huge outpouring of aid to Ethiopia from around the world, including the series of Concert Aid, and then Band Aid, concerts to raise funds.

I was fortunate to have an early opportunity to discuss food relief with James Ingram, the Rome-based director of the United Nations World Food Program, when he visited Mogadishu in February 1985. Ingram was a former Australian ambassador who had made a good name for himself running the international agency that was concerned with obtaining food supplies for the world's starving people. The United States was planning to contribute about thirty thousand tons of food, mostly flour, to WFP in 1985 for distribution, through CARE's logistical operations, to the hundreds of thousands of refugees in camps in Somalia. This would amount to a quarter of all the WFP shipments for these refugees. As to the urgent shipload for which the Somalis had appealed, Washington had informed me that the best we could do was get a ship to Mogadishu in April. Ingram told me that WFP had fortunately just been able to divert to Somalia a ship bound with ten thousand tons of wheat for India, where it was not critically needed. He went on to criticize American procedures; it took the Americans months to arrange a shipment, and diverting shipments from other countries was complicated and costly. I was willing to admit we were slow, but it was also true that the Somalis sometimes came at us with requests we had not anticipated and that sometimes proved unjustified. This particular request clearly had been justified, and I would see if anything could be done to speed up procedures in the future. But I knew that WFP itself often worked slowly.

Ingram asked me if there was a long-term solution to the refugee problem in Somalia. I replied I was still relatively new to my job and was not sure. We were considering the possibility of putting some money into refugee resettlement projects, but I did not think the United States government would ever make funds available to resettle more than a small number of Somali refugees. Recently the Somali authorities had been talking about the need to convince refugees to settle on the coast and become fishermen. I had, however, looked into what had happened after the previous drought, in 1974–75, when many Somali nomads had been resettled in fishing and farming communities. Of the fifteen thousand whom the authorities had tried to make into fishermen, only three thousand remained on the coast. Perhaps a few had returned to live in the grasslands; most had probably ended up in the capital. The fact was that most Somali nomads despised fish and fishermen and had no liking for farming. I supposed, I said to Ingram, that we must give some help to resettlement projects, but once we had been able to get an accurate count of the refugees—and so far we had not—the international community might perhaps start cutting slowly back on its aid to these poor people, forcing them to find a new life where they could. If they continued to be fed in the camps, the camps would become permanent fixtures with ever-growing populations, like those of the Palestinians in Gaza, still in camps after thirty-five years. We did not want new Gazas in Somalia. Yet one had to ask whether the poor people would simply begin to starve if the world cut back on its subsidies. They would not find much welcome in their traditional pasturelands, which were under Mengistu's rule and still suffering from drought. Nor would anything good come from further increases in Mogadishu's population. As Ingram could see, I had no good answers.

It was important for me to get to know Somalia at first hand. Soon I crossed the equator for the first time, flying to Kismayu, Somalia's southernmost port. The equator was two hundred miles down the coast southwest from Mogadishu, Kismayu was thirty miles beyond the equator, and the Kenyan border was a hundred miles beyond Kismayu. Somalia was a large country, twice as large as Italy, although its population was a tenth of Italy's. It was the size of the five states of Ohio, Indiana, Illinois, Michigan, and Wisconsin together, but it contained one-eighth as many people.

This was my first ride in the new twin-engine C-12 Beechcraft of our defense attaché office, which the Pentagon had decided we needed in order

to keep in touch with the Somali military and with our own defense cooperation programs in Somalia. Washington had told me that the ambassador
could use it too, and now I did so, together with three navy men, two of
them visitors from Norfolk and the other an embassy officer, Jim Dell, our
resident officer in charge of construction. At Kismayu port we were finally
going to rebuild the quay that AID had built in the 1960s and that had soon
begun to crumble because of salt in the water used to make the concrete.
This was the most embarrassing page, from my point of view, in the vexed
history of U.S.-Somali relations. Matters had been worsened by long delays on the repair project, delays mainly on our side—delays within our
Agency for International Development—even after Congress had provided
funding. Finally AID had agreed to use the U.S. Navy, which knew how
port facilities should be built, and the navy was on the point of seeking bids
from U.S. construction companies.

Kismayu had an airport with a paved runway more than two miles long,
built by an Italian construction firm in the 1960s. Next to the great long
runway stood a little terminal building with a sign that said "Kismayo International Airport."[1] The international airport was served by exactly two scheduled flights a week, both domestic—the Fokker F-27 of Somali Airlines
came down from Mogadishu on Wednesday mornings and returned after an
hour—and there were very few unscheduled flights. I would see worse waste
in Africa in coming years, notably an almost unused international airport in
Cameroon on which the French had spent well over a hundred million dollars, at least several times what this field had cost. But our little plane on the
long and lonely Kismayu field would always remain in my memory.

Kismayu port had better natural protection than most anchorages along
the Somali coast, thanks to an island lying just offshore from the town. A
causeway had been built linking the island with the town, and then in the
1960s came our big project. We had built a stone breakwater extending from
the end of the island several hundred yards parallel to the shore, then making
a right-angle turn and continuing two hundred yards in toward shore. On the
inner side of this gamma-shaped breakwater ran the concrete quay, and it was
this that was crumbling and would be rebuilt. It would not be a complicated
job, except for the need to import literally everything and everyone needed
for the job other than a couple of hundred laborers to be hired locally.

The existing quay was, though crumbling, still usable. It was the ships
that were largely missing. There were just five vessels tied up there: two

1. The usual Italian spelling; the Somalis wrote Kismayu.

Somali navy missile boats, acquired from the Soviets a decade earlier and, although still listed in *Jane's Fighting Ships*, no longer functioning; a rusty little Somali freighter, said to be under repair but with no sign of any work being done on it; and two small motor vessels, with refrigerated containers on their decks, that called at villages on the string of islands down the coast, loading fish for a freezing plant newly rebuilt with German aid funds where the Kismayu quay joined the island. The new plant was beginning to export frozen fish to Europe, and Kismayu port did a little more export business than that. Several freighters a year loaded bananas here for Italy and the Arabian Peninsula; two ships were due soon to load cattle for Suez. But the place was pretty sleepy, and one had to wonder about the real prospects for development.

Several days after my flight south to Kismayu, I flew north to Berbera for my first visit to northwest Somalia. From the point of view of weather, it was a good time to visit Berbera, since daytime temperatures were still no more than 90 degrees Fahrenheit; by June, temperatures would reach 115 or 120 degrees, dropping only into the 90s at night. Berbera was a poor and rather decrepit town, but it was a very old one. It is without question the town that the author of *The Periplus of the Erythraean Sea* knew as "Malao" in the first century after Christ, being the only place on that coast that squares with his description: "The harbor is exposed to the sea, [but] sheltered by a projection running out from the east."[2] Late in the nineteenth century, the British made it the administrative capital of British Somaliland. Earlier, in 1855, Richard Burton had described it as just a wretched clump of dirty huts. It was outside Berbera in April 1855 that Burton and three other British officers, who had sailed over from Aden to begin a long exploration through the Somali country, were attacked by Somali warriors. As Burton wrote later, and as the film *Mountains of the Moon* depicts in a fairly realistic way, one attacker "left his javelin in my mouth"; Burton carried the great scar across his cheek for the remaining thirty-five years of his life.

There were still some huts around now in Berbera and not much in the way of hotels. Fortunately, I had been invited to stay in a prefabricated, air-conditioned cabin at the M. W. Kellogg construction camp just outside town. As at Kismayu, our navy was carrying out a large port-improvement project at Berbera, and MWK had the main contract. A decade earlier the Soviets had built a major military base at Berbera, including the longest

2. G. W. B. Huntingford, ed., *The Periplus of the Erythraean Sea* (London: Hakluyt Society, 1980), p. 23.

airport runway in Africa and a concrete quay at the harbor. We were not emulating them; we were not building a base at Berbera. MWK was constructing a sizable addition to the Soviet-built quay and also repairing the shoddy concrete—Soviet work, not our doing—on the existing quay. The quay with its extension would be used by civilian shipping, and it would be a useful addition to the existing port facilities, particularly if cattle exports to Saudi Arabia should someday resume. Meanwhile Berbera port, like Kismayu, seemed a pretty sleepy place, although occasional vessels loaded sheep and goats for Saudi Arabia and Yemen. But of course Berbera would also be available for possible use by our military, as our agreement with the Somali government provided, if an international crisis ever came.

In the evening, a few hours after I had arrived, the acting governor of northwest Somalia came to call on me at the construction camp. He was by profession a police officer and by clan an Isaq, and I knew that he was by reputation a drunkard. His breath reeked. I offered him a cold Seven-Up. He said that he would come by for me at dawn the next day and that we would drive to Sheikh and Hargeisa. I did not have to be concerned about security; he had taken appropriate measures. I said that I was not concerned. He continued to ramble on about security—perhaps the Seven-Up had gone to his head—and repeated several times that I did not need to be concerned. By the time he had left, he had made me think that perhaps I did need to be concerned.

At this point in time, the only organized resistance to Siad Barre's regime was taking place in this region, which, as noted earlier, was and is inhabited mainly by the Isaq family of Somali clans. Several Isaq leaders had fled to Ethiopia, and the Mengistu regime had been pleased to complement its own army's forays into Somalia by arming and outfitting a force of Isaqs to conduct sporadic raids across the border. It was such a raid that had led the defense minister to call in my diplomatic colleagues and me soon after my arrival. More recently, a large Isaq raiding group had been caught in the highlands beyond Hargeisa; its members had been killed by Somali forces. Apparently, from what I had heard in Mogadishu, many or most of the recent raiders were city-dwellers by origin. They had thought, wrongly as it turned out, that they could operate in the northern countryside, far from towns, in winter, when food was very scarce and the nights, at several thousand feet above sea level, got cold.

I could not be sympathetic toward men trying to bring down by violence the government to which I was accredited. Still, I felt sorry for them.

They reminded me of an incident, mentioned earlier, that occurred when I was in the embassy in Panama: the slaughter by Panama's Guardia Nacional of a little group of secondary-school students who, inspired by Fidel Castro, had taken to the hills proclaiming revolution. I could not back those Panamanian students any more than I could back the Isaqs against Siad Barre; but any slaughter of people was a tragedy, and in both instances there had been reason to contest an unjust system and corrupt government.

The governor came back to the Kellogg camp at dawn with a little convoy: an open Toyota truck painted in camouflage colors with a machine gun mounted on top and a half-dozen soldiers armed with AK-47s; a Land Rover for the governor and me; two cars with other soldiers and officers; and finally another truck with a squad of armed soldiers. Nothing to worry about, said the governor, nothing at all. In fact the only thing that worried me was that one of the young soldiers might accidentally shoot off something in my direction. But none did, nor did we encounter any rebels.

From Berbera we drove first up to the town of Sheikh, over a mile above sea level and once, since it was much cooler than Berbera, the little summer capital of the British protectorate. It was from Sheikh, in 1913, that a reckless British officer named Richard Corfield rode out with a mounted force in search of the "Mad Mullah," the greatest figure in Somali history. The so-called Mad Mullah's true name was Mohamed Abdallah Hassan, and he is usually known, and much revered, in Somalia as the Sayid. Despite what the British called him, he was in no way mad. Angry, rather. He had declared a *jihad*, or holy war, against the British and the Christian Ethiopians in 1899, when he found that a Catholic mission at Berbera was weaning Somali boys away from Islam. And he was never defeated until in 1920 the British used a new weapon—the airplane—to bomb him out of his strongly built stone fortress at Taleh, in a distant inland region. He fled into the Ogaden, where he died, probably from influenza, certainly not from British bullets.

Richard Corfield, who was commanding the Somali Mounted Constabulary in 1913, had orders not to engage the Sayid if he found him. Corfield found him, disobeyed his orders and attacked, and, together with a number of other members of his force, lost his life. The Sayid, who was a great poet as well as a great warrior, composed on the subject of Corfield's death a long, fierce poem that I had read at Mogadishu:

Now, Corfield,
That you have embarked on your perilous journey [to the Underworld]

Tell them, if they [the already departed] care to question you about the
Upper world,
How the valiant Dervishes have slain you;
How they have abandoned your rotting corpse,
With its gaping dagger-wounds, to the carrion-eaters.
Tell them how the hyena . . . has dragged your carcass to its grisly den . . .
How crows plucked your sinews and tendons from the bare bone.[3]

I sat at Sheikh at tea in a bungalow that had been the British governor's
summer house and talked with an Isaq elder who said that he remembered
the Sayid from when he was a little boy. But what he remembered better was
shipping out to Hamburg as a young seaman. I would have liked to spend the
day sitting in this cool village asking the elder about the old days. There was
little sense in discussing the present; the elder had no doubt been produced
for my benefit, because his Isaq group still supported the government. But I
had a long way to go, and we parted. *Auf wiedersehen*, said the elder.

Our next destination was Hargeisa, then Somalia's second-largest city.
We drove inland to Hargeisa through an arid country of long vistas that
reminded me of southeastern Montana, where I had once worked on a drill-
ing rig. I had read British accounts of Hargeisa earlier in this century, when
it had been a town of thirty or forty thousand people, which, at four thousand feet above sea level, enjoyed a pleasant climate. The rainfall was not
heavy but enough to permit the growth of trees. Angus Hamilton, reporting on British Somaliland in 1911, had written that near Hargeisa there
were cedar forests, and even "jungles" in the stream valleys. The permanent secretary of the foreign ministry, Adan, had told me that when he was
working for the British in Hargeisa in 1954, he and his friends would go
walking after work in the woods above town. But, he said, he had not seen
the place for years.

I found when I reached Hargeisa that the woods had long since vanished,
cut for firewood and charcoal for a city population that had been seventy-five
thousand at the 1975 census but had multiplied in the ensuing decade and
was now estimated to be four hundred thousand. I also found, driving out of
Hargeisa toward the Ethiopian border, that this was, or rather had been until
recently, a country of small farms. The main cash crop that these farmers had

3. This translation (not the one I originally read) is by Abdi Sheik-Abdi in *Divine Madness* (London: Zed Books, 1993), p. 77.

developed was *qat*, which supplied a thriving market in Hargeisa; one survey indicates that 64 percent of adult males in Hargeisa used *qat* before Siad Barre banned it.[4] The ban had been effective, and the farmers had not found an alternative crop. Most of the fields were now sprouting weeds.

By the time I visited Hargeisa in 1985, not only had the trees vanished but even water was now scarce in the city, and the electricity supply was very uncertain. Moreover, in addition to the regular city population of perhaps four hundred thousand housed in more or less permanent dwellings, the city was ringed with refugee camps. The first of the camps I visited was at Bixin Duul on the way from Sheikh to Hargeisa. It was five miles off the main road, along a rough vehicle track. Until the previous autumn, Bixin Duul had been a small village, located along a watercourse coming down from the mountains, at a point where springs produced a little stream of water even in dry months. But then thousands of new refugees had come streaming over the border from Ethiopia, fleeing Mengistu's forced resettlement program. UNHCR, the agency of the UN High Commissioner for Refugees, had set up a camp at Bixin Duul, and now there were thirty-eight thousand people living there in rough, round shelters, living on flour, oil, and beans supplied by the World Food Program and trucked in by CARE from a warehouse at Berbera. Most of these people were not ethnic Somalis but Oromos, members of the largest ethnic group in Ethiopia, who spoke a language related to Somali and who, to my untrained eye, closely resembled Somalis.

The best thing about Bixin Duul was the camp doctor, a Somali physician named Hassan, a man with a sturdy look whom I sized up as intelligent and devoted. Our people had told me before I left Mogadishu that a number of children were dying at Bixin Duul; Dr. Hassan told me why. When the refugees had been trucked in to Bixin Duul the previous autumn from collection points in the countryside, they had had to scour the surrounding countryside for poles to make the frameworks of their shelters as well as for firewood. In their search for wood, the people had ranged eight to ten miles away from the camp, many of them going up the bed of the watercourse, where there was more woody growth, and there they had defecated in the bed of the watercourse. It had rained in December, and the fecal matter of many thousands floated down and contaminated the camp's water supply. There had been twelve to fourteen hundred cases of diarrhea daily in the last two months. Now the international agencies were setting

4. Abdullahi Sheikh Elmi, p. 849.

up water-chlorination equipment, and Hassan was treating only forty or fifty diarrhea cases a day—but there was a new increase in infectious hepatitis.

Diet was another story. CARE was trucking in enough food to Bixin Duul to provide each inhabitant 1,400 calories a day. In camps nearer to Hargeisa or Berbera, the ration was the same, but people found small jobs to do, and with what they earned they could buy food in town to supplement the ration. Bixin Duul was too far from any town for that, so its people were existing on just 1,400 calories. It was a survival ration, not more.

Dr. Hassan brought me to two shelters where the severe cases of infantile emaciation were being given supplementary feedings of milk several times a day. There were twenty-eight such infants, he said, and a number of them might survive. I looked at them, and it was a heartrending sight. It was in a sense not a new sight, I thought to myself. These were the same hopelessly thin little human beings that one saw in American newspapers or on television, but here they were in the flesh—all too little flesh. The sight stayed with me, and while these babies had been starving before reaching the camp, and while we were sure that the Somali authorities were exaggerating the number of refugees in the country, after seeing Bixin Duul I would think twice before recommending that the international community cut back on food deliveries.

But Bixin Duul was not the worst. The worst of the camps was a place called Gannet, on the edge of the city of Hargeisa, where a mass of probably forty thousand squatters were living in miserable shelters. It was not one of the regular refugee camps; these were all supervised by UNHCR, and like the one at Bixin Duul, they provided a food ration and at least minimal medical and sanitary facilities for the people in them. The situation was different for the people in the shelters at Gannet; they were at Gannet because there, behind high fences, was the food warehouse that supplied the regular refugee camps around Hargeisa. The news had spread in the Ogaden that there was food at a place called Gannet, and it was to Gannet that the people came. The warehouse officials tried to tell them that they should go to a regular camp if they wanted to get fed. But they were often near death after walking a couple of hundred miles out of Ethiopia, so they stayed, and sometimes the warehouse people would break rules and distribute some food. The continued presence of all these poor people at Gannet reflected shocking mismanagement by both the United Nations and the Somali authorities, who between them should have set up, long since, a reception center and transport to take new arrivals to regular camps.

I went to see the people of Gannet on a cold and foggy dawn. It looked, I thought, like a scene from hell. Each family had made itself a kind of shelter with a framework of sticks and whatever covering it could find, most often cardboard from old boxes. At the edge of this community of many thousand small hovels, one could see figures in the cold, thick fog wandering out over the stony ground. I thought at first that they must be scavenging. There were bits of paper on the ground; perhaps this was an old garbage dump. No, the people were walking out to defecate on the ground. Among things lacking in this hell was even a single latrine. Yet here were forty thousand people.

When I got back to Mogadishu, I went to see the head of the Somali National Refugee Commission, Abdi Mohamed Tarrah, and the local UN-HCR representative, and I sent a scathing telegram to Washington and to our mission at Geneva, site of UNHCR headquarters. I told all concerned that the rains were due in a month, and even if drought should continue in much of Somalia there was sure to be some rain at Hargeisa. I was not a sanitary engineer, but I did not need to be one in order to know that rain in such a place as Gannet meant epidemics: mass dysentery, if not worse.

Washington agreed, and we put what pressure we could on UNHCR headquarters. But the representative in Somalia of the United Nations High Commissioner for Refugees was a lazy incompetent, and the Somali authorities shrugged their shoulders and said they did not have shovels to dig latrines. Four months later the UNHCR representative retired and went happily home to his own country—to raise chickens, he said. But in those four months over a thousand people died at Gannet, some from dysentery but most from something worse: cholera.

Throughout my time in Somalia the refugee problem worried me deeply. Eventually, after one of my many discussions on the subject with Lou Cohen and the embassy coordinator for refugee affairs, Frank Pavich (a sensible and patient man in a difficult job), I wrote a long note for myself. It read in part:

Refugees, mainly but not entirely ethnic Somalis, had flooded over the line from Ethiopia on several occasions in the past decade. These floods of people were different from the normal movements of Somali nomads, who over a given year might move hundreds of miles with their camels, goats, and sheep, looking for decent pasture land as the seasons shifted in what was at best a dry country.

1974 had seen disastrous drought in the Horn of Africa, and hundreds of thousands of Somalis had come seeking food and water from the authorities, no longer able to fend for themselves. Many more had come in 1978, fleeing the advancing Ethiopian army, which did not always distinguish between a Somali soldier and a Somali herdsman.

And now, in 1985, many of these people were still living a poor life in refugee camps in Somalia. How many? The Somali national refugee commissioner, Tarrah, insisted that the number was seven hundred thousand. We doubted this strongly. There was evidence that a lot of people had left the Somali camps and gone back to rebuild their herds in the thin grasslands of the Haud and Ogaden, on either side of the border which was long and unfenced and relatively open to nomadic movement, although units of one or both opposing armies could always cause people trouble.

Tarrah and his Commission of course had a bureaucratic reason in seeing the refugee figure kept high. If there were no refugees there would be no Commission—and no Commissioner. Nor would the international community be pouring so many tens of thousands of tons of food aid into Ethiopia each year. Yet even the office of the UN High Commissioner for Refugees was divided on numbers. The UNHCR people in Somalia more or less supported Tarrah's number, while the UNHCR office in Ethiopia said they had counted many returnees. We had asked Washington if aerial or satellite photography could be used, to help get a more accurate count of people in the camps. We had also asked the U.S. Mission in Geneva to tell UNHCR headquarters that it was imperative that UNHCR itself decide what the most accurate figure was. So far, UNHCR had not responded.

My meeting today with Lou Cohen and Frank Pavich was to talk about refugee resettlement. Even if a lot of nomads had left the camps to get back to the pastoral life, a lot had not and it looked like they never would. AID's idea, which was also that of the Somali Government, was that these people would have to be moved out of the camps into some kind of settlements where they could get off the dole and fend for themselves. This meant converting ex-nomads into villagers, into farmers and sedentary animal-raisers and perhaps fishermen. The money and projects AID had in mind could not take care of the necessary well-boring, hut-building, etc., for more than a smallish part of the camp populations. But I agreed with Lou and Frank that we should go ahead.

After they left I sat thinking. The post-1945 world had seen many major changes; one of the biggest had to do with territories and peoples. It had not been too many decades since a nation could take lands by force of arms without a moral objection being raised. Now wars continued but formal borders could no longer be changed. Africa was the best, or worst, example. The new African states still kept to the borders drawn by the colonizers even though they often made no sense ethnically or economically. So it was, I thought, with refugees. It had not been many decades ago that a crowd fleeing war or famine would soon fade from view, either because they would disperse in all directions or because a related group would take them in—or because they would die. The cruel balance of nature had affected people as well as animals. If there were too many Somalis the excess would die off, like lemmings and foxes. And neither Reuters nor UPI had had agents in the Ogaden to report this to the world. Indeed they still did not; awful things still happened in Africa that never reached the world press. My informed guess was that some hundreds of Somalis were still dying each year in tribal fights, quite aside from skirmishes between the Ethiopian and Somali armies or between the Somali army and Somali dissident groups.

But civilized society had decided that human beings could no longer be left to die like lemmings. And so several hundred thousand Somalis remained in camps, and the civilized world fed them, and we would have to deal with them. At least the Somali refugee problem was not as big or quite so complicated as the Palestinian and Afghan problems. But the longer it was with us the worse it would get.

Never, during my tour of duty in Somalia, did we get UNHCR to agree on its own best figure for Somali camp populations. Nor did we make much progress on resettlement. Some months after I wrote the above, Al Edgell, the resident director of the nongovernmental U.S. agency Save the Children, invited me to visit their refugee resettlement project in the Shebeli valley. At first glance it looked laudable. An irrigation canal had been dug and a pumping system installed to draw water from the Shebeli during months when the river flowed. Several hundred acres were being developed for small-scale farms, each of which could support an ex-refugee family on several fertile acres. It was, of course, the same old problem. The pumping system employed a diesel engine, and I did not think ex-nomads would be able to keep it running for long. Even if they could run it, I doubted they would find a continuing supply of fuel, or of spare parts—yet Save the Children planned to leave the project to the Somalis once it was in operation. It could take far more than a couple of years to turn Somali nomads into farmers.

Whatever the rights and wrongs of aid problems, it was a notorious fact that Mohamed Siad Barre and his regime would accept whatever aid was offered them, and wherever they could get it. He took aid from the Catholics (not just Caritas—Somalia had entered into formal diplomatic relations years earlier with the Sovereign Military Order of Malta, which offered to set up a leprosarium in the Juba Valley), and yet Somalia was at the same time a member of the Arab League, from which Siad also accepted whatever he could glean. And although Africans should presumably have been taking the lead in opposing South Africa's apartheid regime, in late 1984 the South African press revealed (after what looked like a deliberate leak from Pretoria) that South Africa's foreign minister, Pik Botha, had visited Somalia and met with Siad Barre. We were not perfectly sure what Siad had wanted from South Africa in exchange for violating the ban established by the Organization of African Unity on African governmental contacts with the Pretoria government—but we were confident that what Siad mainly wanted was arms.

Somalia had two air forces. One was composed of Somali pilots, who flew aging, Soviet-built MiGs. The more reliable, if smaller, one was composed of white pilots from southern Africa—either South Africa or what was then white-run Rhodesia—who flew well maintained, British-built Hawker Hunter jets that the Somalis were said to have obtained from Abu Dhabi. There were also reports that the South Africans furnished artillery and small arms to Somalia, but if so our people never caught sight of them.[5] The white pilots and their jets tended to stay out of sight, but once or twice a pair of them flew over the city, and once, in a Mogadishu hotel, someone pointed out to me two white men who apparently were members of this small mercenary corps. I would have liked to know more about them, but this was one area in which our intelligence fell short. Presumably Siad Barre viewed them as useful primarily as a deterrent to the occasional sorties by Ethiopia's MiGs, which were no doubt better maintained, given the continuing Soviet presence in Ethiopia, than the MiGs of Siad's regular air force.

5. See, for example, an article by Godwin Matatu in *The Observer,* April 28, 1985. This article was incorrect in at least one detail: it claimed that the South Africans had agreed to lengthen "the existing short runway" at the Kismayu airport—a runway that, as noted earlier, was in fact a long one. For what it is worth, the article said that the chief white pilot in Somalia was a South African wing commander named Wilde.

Some years after ending my mission in Somalia, I learned to my surprise that Mohamed Siad Barre's willingness to deal with the Catholic world
had reached beyond the question of aid from Caritas or the Order of Malta.
I found in the papers of William Wilson, our former ambassador to the
Vatican, a letter he had written on May 20, 1985, to Somalia's first vice
president and defense minister, Samantar, who apparently had met Wilson
in Rome through an intermediary—Charles Tyson, a former Reagan White
House official—and had asked for advice on the possibility of Somalia's
establishing diplomatic relations with the Holy See. Wilson wrote Samantar
that "it is entirely possible—and this is only speculation on my part—that
the government of another country may have indicated that they would
sever relations with the Vatican if the Vatican were to establish relations
with your country. . . . [I]f I am able to learn more on this issue, I will pass
it along to you." What country Wilson was referring to is unclear, but presumably it was an Arab state; indeed, one imagines Somalia would have
hurt its relationships with more than one Arab aid donor if it had opened
relations with the Vatican. Wilson should properly have informed me of
his meeting and exchange with Samantar, but he did not do so. This was not
untypical of Mr. Wilson, who later resigned his post after it was revealed that
he had flown secretly from Rome to Tripoli to meet with Qadhafi.[6]

I immediately suspected Somali greed when, in April 1985, the Somali
news agency announced that Somalia and Libya had agreed to resume relations "in consideration of the emphatic necessity to prepare for and face
the problems posed by imperialism and its like." The announcement came
just several hours after I had told Defense Minister Samantar that I had
heard rumors that relations might be restored with Libya, and he had told
me he did not think any definite decision had been taken. (In fairness to
Mohamed Ali Samantar, I must add that he left our meeting to go see his
president, and it is conceivable that it was at this meeting that Siad Barre
first told him he had made a definite decision on Libya.)

I did not need instructions from Washington after learning of the announcement. I went to the foreign minister and expressed my indignation.
The minister should be aware, I said, that there were people in Washington
—the view had been expressed openly in the Senate—who considered that
our country was in effect at war with Libya. And what was this reference
to imperialism? I hoped that the minister could explain this to me; was this

6. The Wilson letter is in box 1, folder 74, William A. Wilson Papers, Georgetown
University Library, Washington, D.C.

a reference to my country? Jama Barre said quickly that of course the reference was to Ethiopian imperialism; no reference to America was intended. The reason, he continued, that Somalia was resuming relations was that Qadhafi had promised to stop providing aid to the Somali dissidents who were raiding into Somalia out of Ethiopia. Later, on instructions, I saw the president, who said that the reference to imperialism meant the Soviets. Oh. He added that the Somalis had made it clear to the Libyans that they must take no action in Somalia against Somalia's friends, which of course meant the Americans. I told him that I had been instructed to say that if there were any terrorist acts against us in Somalia that appeared to have been inspired by the Libyans, the consequences would be "incalculable."

Well, the deal was done. It might be that the question of Libyan aid to the dissidents had played some part. I compared notes with my colleagues in the diplomatic corps. One African ambassador said that he had been told by a high-ranking Somali that the Libyans were paying out one billion dollars for their new link to Somalia, of which one half was going to the Somali treasury and the other half into the pockets of the president and his foster brother, the foreign minister. That sounded like an incredibly large sum, although the just-deposed leader of Sudan, Nimeiry, had recently told the *Washington Post* that he had turned down an offer of five billion dollars from Colonel Qadhafi. A more credible rumor, which I had heard earlier, was that the foreign minister was to receive one million dollars from the Libyans once relations resumed. In any case, if the Somalis had taken Libyan money, the Libyans would want something in exchange, and this might well involve us, no matter what Siad Barre told me.

I heard from several sources that many Somalis were puzzled by the resumption of relations. Qadhafi had supposedly said a long time ago that he would get rid of three Mohameds: Sadat in Egypt, Nimeiry in Sudan, and Siad Barre in Somalia. The first two were gone; would Qadhafi not concentrate on the third? A Somali friend told me that when the foreign minister went to lecture at the university on Somali nationalism and Islam, he was sharply questioned about Libya. One questioner had also asked whether people should now expect a resumption of close ties with Moscow; the minister had reportedly said no.

Somali officials told us that they had informed the Libyans that their reopened embassy in Mogadishu would be limited to a staff of five. Several months after this, in October 1985, I went to see Permanent Secretary Adan at the foreign ministry and told him that we knew that at least fourteen

Libyans were working in their embassy. He protested that this could not be so. I returned several days later to give him the names of the fourteen, who included one "diplomat" involved in anti-American terrorist activities before he came to Mogadishu.

Thus far what I told the permanent secretary had Washington's prior agreement. What I said next did not. I noted that I had on instructions recently warned the president about the possible consequences of any terrorist act against us possibly instigated by Libya. Now I thought I should be more explicit. If any member of my embassy should be killed or injured by what appeared to be terrorist action, I would immediately stop all our aid activities and I would return to Washington to discuss the matter. I had instructed John Hirsch to do the same, in case I myself was killed or incapacitated.

Although I said this to Adan without instructions, I did not think Washington would disagree. When I cabled what I had done, it did agree, fully. No action would have had as much effect on this rapacious Somali regime as one touching its pocketbooks. But if I had waited to get instructions from Washington to say what I had just said, it might have taken weeks if not months, and meanwhile who knew what might have happened to our people in Somalia.

What effect my demarche had was never clear. I think the Somalis must have repeated to the Libyans that they could not tolerate any anti-U.S. action in Somalia. At least the foreign minister, when I raised the Libyan question with him again in late November 1985, claimed that he had called in the Libyan chargé d'affaires. He also muttered something about having sent a message to Tureiki, the Libyan foreign minister—which did not convince me that he had really sent a message.

There was one visible result of my demarches. For a few days an athletic young Somali police lieutenant would appear at my gate at dawn and keep me company on my morning run. That was better than what the Italians had done the first time I became chargé d'affaires in Rome, when Ambassador Rabb had left the country for a week. The Italian police had detailed two agents in a white Alfa Romeo to follow me, in their car, when I went running in the Villa Borghese. Since the Villa Borghese was closed to normal vehicles, it must have been clear to anyone watching that the runner must be some sort of VIP. In a week Rabb would be back, there would be no more Alfa Romeo, and I might have been identified as a good potential target. I told the Ministry of Interior that I did not want any more of that kind of protection.

But I was not well protected in Mogadishu. Nor of course were other Americans, and I was not necessarily the most attractive target. Our marine guards protected only the chancery, and at Americans' residences, including my house, there was only a Somali watchman or two armed with clubs. My watchmen included my ancient Yemeni friend mentioned earlier, who was more likely to get his head cracked than to crack others'. Nor was I exactly unknown in town. That fact had been impressed on me a couple of months after my arrival, when I went running one dawn down the back streets of Mogadishu, feeling pretty anonymous in shorts and T-shirt. On a corner stood a teenager. He looked at me, waved, and said, "*Warhaye*, Peter!"

We also learned in 1985 that the Somalis were dickering with the Soviets. When Siad Barre had sent all the Soviet advisers home in 1978, he had not broken off diplomatic relations with Moscow, but the now small Soviet embassy in Mogadishu was pretty well shut out by the Somali authorities. The Soviet ambassador during my first year in Somalia, a florid gentleman named Boris Ilichev, had previously been the Soviet ambassador to Thailand. When I first went to call on him, he made clear that he had had more to do in Bangkok than he did here and that he had enjoyed Thailand more. I said that I could understand that. He said that he had told the Somalis that Moscow was ready to see relations normalized but that the Somalis harassed his embassy, and he had to spend 60 percent of his time just getting shipments for the embassy out of Somali customs. He was sure the American ambassador did not encounter such problems. Well, I said, he was dead wrong there. (I did not actually spend 60 percent of my time on customs clearances, but despite the best efforts of our administrative officer, I spent much more time on them than I wanted to. Much of this was due to Somali harassment—not harassment for political reasons but harassment from Somali officials looking for bribes, which we would not give them.)

Late in 1985 it appeared that the Somalis must have started listening to Ilichev. We heard that the Somalis had made an approach to Moscow and that as a result several midranking Soviet officials had come visiting, the first such visit to Somalia in seven years. I asked the president about that at our next meeting. He knew, he said, that some Soviets had come, but he did not know what they wanted; they had seen no one. Well, perhaps he did not know what they wanted, but I knew that Siad Barre was lying to me. The visitors had certainly come with Siad's approval, and I knew that they had seen some ranking Somali officials. Still, I was not very concerned about this, despite Siad's attempt to deceive me. Somehow I did not think that

Siad Barre was going to turn back to the Soviets; and I did not think that the Soviets, who were having difficulty in their relationship with Mengistu in Ethiopia, would give much to Siad to get him to resume a client relationship. But it was, of course, something that we needed to watch carefully. Fortunately, the CIA station chief in Somalia was one of the best, and bravest, in the business, and he had excellent sources of information.

twelve

From Siad
to Canal Street

Most ambassadors, in my experience, work hard. For an American ambassador in charge of an embassy of any but the smallest size, the job has several quite different components.

On one hand, the ambassador is called on to be a single actor, the senior diplomatist who, as his president's personal representative, talks one on one with the president, cabinet ministers, and other top people in the country to which he or she is accredited. One must win the trust of these top people so that they come to view the ambassador as the authoritative voice of his or her government, as an authoritative link to Washington. It is not necessarily a question of being liked. The important thing for me in Somalia was not that Siad Barre should like me—and I doubt that he did—but that he should believe that when I spoke about my country's views and policy, I spoke for Ronald Reagan and George Shultz. The occasions when this president and his secretary of state were personally involved with our Somalia policy were very few at best. We would, however, often receive circular instructions, addressed to a number of our embassies and sometimes to all of them, telling us to deliver American views on various matters at an appropriately high level in the host government. Like all cables from the State Department, these cables were signed "Shultz." In Cairo or Brasilia or Rome, our embassy might carry out the instructions by sending a midlevel officer to call on a midlevel foreign ministry official. In Mogadishu, more than once I used these opportunities to go see Siad Barre and tell him that Shultz had instructed me to convey to him new elements of our Soviet or Chinese or South African policy. In a dictatorship like this one, it was important both to convince the dictator that I spoke for the top people and to stay in close touch with him to try to know his mind, to convey our thinking directly to him—since his subordinates might tend to tell him only what he liked to hear—and contest and try to correct wrong things he said about us.

I saw a lot of Somalia's president, mainly at late-night sessions at Villa Somalia. As mentioned earlier, Siad had indicated when I presented my credentials that he would be pleased to see me one on one. As it turned out, there was sometimes, although not always, in the background a Somali official who listened but did not take notes. I decided that I would in general go alone to such meetings, taking John Hirsch, Lou Cohen, or another embassy officer only if the discussion seemed likely to get into detailed questions I might not have fully mastered. I would come home after an hour or two with the president, write down a page or two on what had transpired, sleep the three or four hours that remained until day dawned, go running, and then go down to the chancery and dictate to Kathy Astala, my expert Foreign Service secretary, a reporting telegram to the State Department. After discussing it with John Hirsch, I would cable it to Washington in good time for it to be summarized, if it included any developments of interest, in the report that the Department's executive secretariat prepared overnight for the secretary of state and other top officers.

I made it a point not to take detailed notes in Siad's presence of what he was telling me, since I knew from experience that this could sometimes cause people to speak less freely, but I would jot down occasional names or facts. After a year of these meetings, Siad Barre's curiosity got the better of him. Why don't you take more notes? he asked; Ambassador Petterson always wrote down several pages. Are you really reporting to Washington all the things I tell you? I replied that I had developed an excellent memory, which I knew Somalis could appreciate because they too had developed such memories, since Somali had not been a written language until Siad's administration. If he liked, I would show him my next reporting cable; he would find it comprehensive but also, I warned him, very frank. Better not, in that case, said Siad, almost with a smile.

A second part of the ambassador's role as senior diplomatist is to represent the United States not in private talks with high officials but at public and private functions. Some such functions are useful, many are not; but if the American ambassador is expected to attend and does not, questions can arise as to official American attitudes, even if it is just a question of ambassadorial fatigue. Mogadishu was no major capital, but there were a lot of evening functions, and sometimes I got a little short of sleep. My dawn runs helped keep me going.

I had not been long in Mogadishu when I was invited to a concert at the National Theater, a large and relatively new building in the city center. The protocol office in the foreign ministry told us that the president would attend. It was therefore expected that foreign ambassadors would be there. I had never been inside this theater. John Hirsch had; he said it had bats. I went, and indeed there were big bats. Fortunately, they did not drop anything on the section reserved for their excellencies the ambassadors. The theater was not air conditioned, and it was very hot. After a long half-hour, the president of the republic arrived. I had not seen him before in a public place. He came accompanied by a half-dozen young Marehans from his personal guard, all of them armed with AK-47 rifles. As this entourage walked down the aisle, I thought to myself that I had no confidence at all as to how young Marehan gunners would react should there be some disturbance in the theater. That was not the way I wanted to die. I stayed until the end of the performance—a Somali folk ensemble, quite good—and then I went home vowing that between bats, heat, and the young Marehans I was never going to attend a performance again at the National Theater. Nor did I. If the Somalis thought this reflected an official American attitude, they were right.

The American ambassador is also a senior executive, responsible for what was, in the case of Embassy Mogadishu, a large staff and a large budget. I could and did leave many of the details in the hands of John Hirsch, whom I found to be a capable deputy. Lou Cohen ran AID and ran it well, and the two colonels who in succession headed our office of military cooperation, Charles Collins and George Marecek, were extremely good—better than Lou—about consulting the ambassador about approaches to them from top Somali leaders.[1]

The ultimate responsibility for the embassy was mine. I had no problem with the size of our civilian and military aid programs, but as noted earlier, I had been concerned from the beginning about the size of our American staff. (We also had a large and generally very competent Somali staff; I did not think we had more Somali employees than we needed.) When I discussed this question with John Hirsch, I found that he shared my concerns. Neither of my two immediate predecessors, Don Petterson and Bob Oakley, had thought it necessary to limit growth in our American staff, in years when our programs in Somalia were growing. Now, in general, the

1. Marecek, a tough former Special Forces officer who had won the Silver Star in Vietnam, was much disliked by his subordinates and was removed early from his post in Somalia. In 1997 a North Carolina jury found him guilty of murdering his wife and sentenced him to thirty years' imprisonment. His conviction was subsequently overturned on appeal.

programs had stopped growing, and now, I decided, the time had come to put a lid on the number of Americans.

I had no illusions about my ability to *reduce* American staff, at least on my own. An ambassador has the ultimate authority to send an employee back to the United States for cause but cannot eliminate that employee's position. Washington agencies are fierce about defending jobs. During my tour in the Prague embassy some years earlier, our ambassador had tried to cut a superfluous subordinate position in the defense attaché office; the Pentagon had told the State Department that if the ambassador did not back down, the secretary of defense would take the matter straight to the president. Perhaps it was only a threat, but State had told Ambassador Sherer that it would not support him on that matter, and that ended it.

I asked John Hirsch to draft a cable for me to send to Washington, saying that henceforth I would not permit any additional Americans to be assigned to the Mogadishu embassy. Soon he had a good draft ready, and after sharing it with the heads of other embassy elements, I made a few changes and sent it on its way. The cable emphasized that there was no reason to believe that our Somalia aid programs, or any other programs, would grow in the future. I said that the security situation in Somalia was uncertain and that this was an additional reason for us to restrict our resident staff to those people definitely needed.

For the remainder of my tour in Somalia I stuck to my guns, and no additional positions were created for Americans—despite one unfortunate attempt by the Defense Department to go around me. For some months after my cable was sent, no one contested it, at least so far as I was aware. Then a Pentagon agency announced that it intended to establish a new officer-level position in Mogadishu. The officer was to have duties that, I satisfied myself, others on our staff were already doing well. So I said No, and after a further exchange of messages it appeared that that was the end of it. I was therefore surprised when one day early in 1986 the defense attaché told me, with some embarrassment, that he had received word from his counterpart in Nairobi that a container had arrived at the port of Mombasa, for onward shipment to Mogadishu, containing the household effects of the officer whose addition to our staff I had not agreed to. I quickly cabled the State Department, which inquired and soon cabled me that it was clear that people in the Pentagon had simply ignored what I had told them. The officer had been instructed to continue with his preparations for transfer to Mogadishu, his effects had been packed and shipped, and he himself would be arriving in Mogadishu in several weeks. I felt sorry for this officer, who had been doing what he was told to do, but I sent a cable that made clear beyond any possibility of doubt that the container was to be sent home and that the officer's orders were to be torn up.

Such things had happened before in the Washington bureaucracy. I should, I suppose, then have been a little skeptical about the possible outcome when one morning in 1986 I received a cable that Secretary Shultz had sent to all ambassadors. He was, he said, concerned about overstaffing at our overseas posts, and President Reagan had given him full authority to undertake a program to slim overseas staffs. The secretary wanted from each of us our frank recommendations on a desirable level of American staffing for each federal agency represented in his or her respective embassy.

It is important to say what one believes; it is particularly important for someone who has come near the pinnacle of one's career, whether as ambassador, member of Congress, or president—or corporate executive, or university dean—to be frank and honest about what needs to be done. At a certain point, after all, one has little to lose but one's reputation and self-esteem. So, delighted to have the chance to give Mr. Shultz my honest thoughts, I consulted all the agency representatives in our embassy at Mogadishu and sent in my personal recommendations. I proposed some paring all around, but in the case of our overstaffed AID mission I recommended a cut in American staffing of 50 percent.

Mr. Shultz made no mention of his cable, or the responses to it, in his 1993 memoir *Turmoil and Triumph*. Perhaps it was just as well that he did not. No doubt the secretary thought that he gotten a clear go-ahead from Ronald Reagan to undertake a thinning of embassy staffs, something that was badly needed in every American embassy I had ever seen. But Mr. Shultz might have done well to recall, before sending us these instructions, how his predecessor Alexander Haig had informed the world early in the first Reagan administration that this same president wanted Haig to have primacy as his "vicar" in our foreign affairs. The result was about the same for the two secretaries: no vicariate for Haig then, and a successful defense against Shultz now, by all the agencies outside State of almost every position in every embassy. It was only long after my departure from Somalia and from government service, when Siad Barre's hands had turned much bloodier and the United States had sharply cut back its aid programs, that our Mogadishu staff was finally cut back—after it had again grown, in the wake of my departure, because of construction work on our new embassy.

I tried in Somalia to offer our government my best, most objective thinking on what we should be doing both in Somalia and in the region. By April 1985 I had been four months at Mogadishu. This seemed a good time to offer Washington my main thoughts on our overall relationship with Somalia. I sent Mike Armacost, the under secretary for political affairs, a cable whose thrust I was to see no need to amend during the succeeding thirteen months of my mission in Somalia. I began by noting Somalia's recent approaches to South Africa, Libya, and now the Soviet Union. Some of these approaches might reflect the venality of Siad Barre and his foster brother, the foreign minister; rakeoffs were nothing new in Somalia. The approaches might also reflect a belief on Siad's part that he could not expect any increase in Western, including American, aid. It was also the case that Siad found much of our aid neither as timely nor as useful as it might be; and I sometimes agreed with him on that, though I did not tell him.

As noted earlier, one of the antitank systems we were providing the Somali army for defense against the Ethiopians was a number of recoilless rifles to be mounted on jeeps. Alas, I told Armacost, when the jeeps arrived in Mogadishu we found that almost all of them had defective engines that could not be made to work. These were not Chrysler jeeps but the products of some smaller manufacturer that had come in with the lowest bid. Over forty years after America had started making jeeps, it was seriously embarrassing not to be able to provide an African army with jeeps that worked. There were a number of other failures and delays in both our civilian and our military aid programs. But it was also a case of Siad Barre's not understanding, or not wanting to understand, what we were about. For example, one aim of our military assistance program was to provide the Somali army with a better maintenance and repair capability. We were not going to provide new trucks simply because old trucks were not being repaired; we sent in training teams to teach Somali soldiers to become mechanics and maintenance men. That was very hard for Siad to understand; he just wanted weapons and more weapons.

But, I told Armacost, I did not think that in any case we could ever satisfy the greedy old man. My Western and Arab colleagues were in full agreement (privately, not publicly) that the Somali regime would take all it could get—and show very little economic development as a result. The main thing that a quarter-century of independence had brought Somalia was urbanization and a lot of educated people; few of these educated people had the training or spirit that might incline them to change the country's direction.

Nor could they hope to succeed in changing Siad's policies; it was a very strict police regime.

The main question that I wanted to raise with Mike Armacost was that of our overall interests in Somalia. I told him that some statements about the strategic importance of Somalia and the Horn of Africa were in my opinion exaggerated—which was not to deny that there was some strategic value to Somalia and our position there. I knew that CENTCOM had ideas about a possible United States buildup in the Horn of Africa, in the context of our possible need to contest Soviet forces on the ground in Southwest Asia. I did not say so in my cable, but I continued to exclude in my own thinking any possibility that the Soviets might decide to make a military push for the Indian Ocean. What I did say to Armacost, after doing a little work with a piece of string and a map, was that we needed to keep in mind that any American supply facilities in the Horn of Africa would be a good fifteen hundred miles by sea from Baluchistan, in southern Pakistan, the likely site of confrontation with the Soviet Army if it moved toward the sea. Yet Baluchistan was only four hundred miles from the nearest railhead and supply bases inside the Soviet Union. We would therefore be at a serious logistical disadvantage in a conflict, and the value of possible American supply dumps or other facilities in Somalia was to say the least very questionable.

At the same time, we certainly did not want the Soviets to come flooding back into Somalia. Even if we were not building ourselves a major base at Berbera, the Soviets had built themselves one. If they ever did come back, they would aim to stay, and they would have an easier time controlling Somalia, perhaps having got rid of Siad Barre, than they were having in Afghanistan. Moreover, having Somalia would make it easier for them to stay on in Ethiopia, which still seemed to occupy a key place in Moscow's African strategy.[2]

My ideas about what to do were not profound ones. I told Armacost that I thought we should move cautiously in Somalia and try to stay in concert with other friendly countries that had an interest in Somalia's well-being, particularly the Europeans, the Egyptians, and the Saudis. I could not

2. Soviet strategy in Africa was not necessarily wise strategy, and I suspected it was partly based on tradition. The Russians, a history-minded people, still recalled that the tsarist army had sent to the emperor of Ethiopia military advisers, who helped him defeat the Italians at the battle of Adowa in 1896; nor did they forget the old connection between the Russian and Ethiopian churches. After leaving government, I suggested in an article in the *Los Angeles Times* (April 3, 1988) that the Soviet presence in Ethiopia was in part a kind of romantic exaggeration.

recommend raising aid levels in the present circumstances, and in any case I did not imagine this would be feasible; neither, however, did I think we should reduce our aid or encourage the Congress to think of making cuts. We should, I believed, take a cautious approach to any proposals for new U.S. military facilities in Somalia—and we should keep in mind the fact that Siad Barre would always want some quid pro quo.

I also told Armacost that I did not think that Siad Barre himself would remain in power for many more years. Many, perhaps most, Somalis hoped for a more democratic, and certainly a Western-oriented, regime after Siad departed the scene. It might be, on the other hand, that the younger colonels and generals would take power. They too certainly preferred the West to Moscow, and they might at least initially care more than the present crew about setting their country on a path toward sound economic development. But I feared it was too much to hope that corruption would end in Somalia after Siad.

Neither in this cable to Armacost nor in later ones, nor for that matter in my own thinking, did I predict the bloodshed that would come. Nor to my knowledge did any foreign observer, whether diplomat, journalist, or professor, foresee such a future at that time. I doubt that any Somalis did either. It was difficult for me to discuss with Somalis the prospects for their country's future. I made few Somali friends I felt I could trust completely. This was a police state, and I had to assume that what I said would reach Siad Barre. There were exceptions, one of them a well-placed man who came, like Siad Barre himself, from the largest family of clans, the Darod. My friend was part of a small circle of well-placed Darod people who, as the president was informed, met to discuss ways to advance particular Darod interests. The secret fact was that they were discussing how to create a better, democratic Somalia once Siad was gone. My friend believed, and it seemed reasonable to me, that the old Somali democratic tradition would reassert itself. Initially there would probably be some sort of junta headed by both civilians and military officers; one could hardly exclude the men who had the guns. But the post-Siad future should be brighter, and it did not seem Siad's rule would last very much longer. In 1985 he rebuilt a house at the air force headquarters, which was adjacent to the airport, and he began to spend some nights there instead of at Villa Somalia. The reasonable assumption was that one night—but who knew when?—he would flee the country on one of the two Somali Airlines 707 jets. My friend and I were wrong, terribly wrong. We did not foresee what happened, not soon but five years later—Siad's flight not abroad but to the upper Juba Valley, where he held out for months with his clan allies while the country fell apart and many, many thousands of Somalis died in civil war and famine.

My only other recommendation to Armacost in the spring of 1985 was for radical reform of our management of civilian and military aid. Somalia, I said, was a useful example of how inefficient U.S. aid could help cause disaffection on the part of the recipient. But, I noted, other foreign-aid donors were no more efficient than we—I decided not to mention the sturdy hand pumps that the Catholic bishop had mentioned to me—and even if we could bring off real aid reform, Somalia would still remain the "give me something" country that Burton had described in 1855.

Undersecretary Armacost sent back a brief but positive reply. In the months to come the State Department generally agreed with me on aid matters and in questioning the need for any additional military facilities in Somalia. Many people in the Pentagon were similarly doubtful about this last, and so nothing ever happened on that score despite an interesting 1986 visit, described in a later chapter, by the new CENTCOM commander in chief, George Crist.

After some months in Somalia, I decided that my work was having some limited effect, at least on Washington's perceptions of the Somali scene. I was working hard; although most ambassadors work hard, few work seven days a week, and I myself tried not to do so. Friday was the Muslim equivalent of our Sabbath, and the embassy was officially closed. If, after looking at incoming cables and talking with our CIA chief, I did not see some pressing problem, I went to the beach, with my wife when she was in town. (A good part of the time she was not. She had continued to work for the Internal Revenue Service in Rome, on a part-year basis, after I went to Mogadishu.) I had bought a small, four-wheel-drive Suzuki for personal use, and by midmorning on a Friday we were usually headed out of town with a picnic cooler on the back seat to join friends at what the foreigners called Crab Bay, south of Mogadishu. We would drive twenty-five miles down the rough coastal road, past the airport and then past Somalia's sole refinery, which had been provided by the Iraqis. After some miles of empty country, we would finally turn left off the road and drive a quarter-mile over a track across the sand and dunes, and so come to the sea.

Here was a white sand beach with a protecting coral reef that circled out from the shore and back again. A little island stuck up at the reef's midpoint, several hundred yards from shore. At high tide most or all of the reef was under water; at low tide it was sometimes entirely exposed. There were many

Senate confirmation hearings for five ambassadors, Washington, June 1985; Paul Hare (to Zambia), Edward Perkins (Liberia), Peter Bridges (Somalia), Robert Pugh (Mauritania), Lannon Walker (Senegal). Mary Bridges is visible in the third row, beyond her father's right shoulder.

sharks in this ocean, but a European fisheries expert had said that a shark would not come inside such a reef, for fear of being caught there at low tide. So we swam happily in the delicious light-green water, which was as clear as crystal and almost cool. My wife and I would run a mile south down the beach toward the equator and then run back again, swim again, and pull our lunch out of the cooler and sit under umbrellas, under the great brilliant sky, drinking cold beer and eating potato salad. It was a great release, that beach; a release from all my cares, to dive into that clear ocean. (Sorry to say, two years after we left Somalia the fishery expert's theory was disproved. A shark came inside the reef and took off the leg of a bather.)

As the months went on in Somalia, I cabled the Department more than once to ask when I might be called back for my Senate confirmation hearings. Siad Barre's ambassador in Washington had made him aware that I had not been confirmed, and the president had once suggested to me that he wondered if I was fully an ambassador. So, although my present commission was valid until the end of the present session of Congress, Senate confirmation would be useful. The Department cabled me back that it had asked about hearings; the Foreign Relations Committee staff had replied that the committee had confidence in me and would call me back at the appropriate time.[3] This turned out to be June 1985, after I had been six months in Somalia. There were five of us in the hearing, the other four also career officers named to African posts. There was just one senator present to

3. The chairman of the Foreign Relations Committee, Sen. Richard Lugar, had written me a warm note after I was named to Somalia, recalling a long dawn run we had done together in Rome.

Peter Bridges's second swearing-in as ambassador to Somalia, Mogadishu, July 1985; Consul Christopher Costanzo, Deputy Chief of Mission John Hirsch, and Mary Jane and Peter Bridges.

conduct the hearing, Nancy Kassebaum of Kansas; Africa was not high on the Senate's priority list. The senator asked me a couple of questions about the American presence and indicated that she was satisfied with my replies. There seemed to be no reason why the full Senate should not vote to confirm me. But then Sen. Jesse Helms of North Carolina announced that he would hold up twenty-eight appointments in the foreign-affairs field, including mine, until the Reagan administration gave him satisfaction on the apparently uncertain fate of six conservatives who held political appointments.

I had hoped that my wife and I could pay a call on President Reagan, and she had come to Washington in the expectation that we could do so. It would be at best a brief call, literally a photo opportunity; but it would have the practical result of producing a signed photograph of me with the president, which would be a visible sign for my visitors in Somalia (and I would send a copy to Siad Barre) of my link with the president. The White House said, however, that they would not schedule an appointment until the Senate had confirmed me. That might take months. Meanwhile, I still had my recess appointment. So I saw several people concerned with Somalia in the State Department and other agencies, flew home to Mogadishu, and never did meet Ronald Reagan. Senator Helms eventually got his pound of flesh and released his hold on most of the nominations, and the Senate voted on July 11 to confirm me and twenty-three others. On the evening of July 23, 1985,

Luncheon for Maureen Reagan at ambassador's residence, Mogadishu, July 1985. *From left:* Foreign Minister Abdirahman Jama Barre standing, Maureen Reagan, Peter Bridges.

I was sworn in as ambassador to Somalia for the second time, this time on the roof terrace of our house in Mogadishu, under the great evening sky, with my wife holding the Bible and our youngest son, Andrew, watching while John Hirsch administered the oath of office.

Several days later President Reagan's daughter Maureen arrived in Somalia. She had been heading the American delegation to the United Nations conference on women taking place in Nairobi. I had met her in Washington before the conference, and she had told me that she thought the visit to Somalia would be fun. From my point of view it was, and it was not. We sent the defense attaché Beechcraft to Nairobi to pick up Ms. Reagan and several other members of her large delegation, and my wife and I met her when the plane landed in Somalia. The ending days of the conference had been hectic, and I gathered that neither Maureen Reagan nor her companions had gotten any sleep the night before she came to visit. On the ride into town I decided that she was not just a large lady but one with a short temper. Fortunately, the latter improved. We toured refugee camps south of Mogadishu, Siad Barre's daughter gave a dinner for her, and the following day my wife and I gave a luncheon for her on our back terrace. It was attended by two dozen Somali women, including the two women who were vice ministers, and just two men, the foreign minister and me. That completed the visit. Visits to embassies by presidents' children, like visits by presidents themselves, can be hard to arrange properly, and an ambassador is more likely to suffer than to prosper as a result. But so far as I could learn later, Maureen said nothing bad to her father about her visit to Somalia.

Meanwhile, the long drought in East Africa had ended. In March my good friend the West German ambassador, Martin Florin, had accompanied

me on a five-day trip on a navy hydrographic ship, the USNS *Harkness*, northward up the otherwise inaccessible Somali coast almost to Cape Guardafui,
the Horn of Africa. There by the Horn we had watched the northeast monsoon finally die and the sea turn calm, beginning the month-long period that
the Somalis called *tanganbili*, a Swahili word meaning "two sails," because
with almost no breeze blowing a dhow's sail would flap from side to side.
During this month of calm, the great wind system of the Indian Ocean shifts
180 degrees to begin blowing out of the southwest. It is the southwest monsoon that brings the rains of *gu*, the main Somali rainy season—if the rains
come. On Saturday, April 12, when I was entertaining Capt. Garrett Wanzor
and his officers from the *Harkness* at lunch on our roofed patio, a thunderstorm struck with fury, pouring two or three inches of rain on the city.

The rains continued over much, though not all, of Somalia. By July
central Somalia had turned green. Our eldest son, David, and his wife, Lisa,
had flown to Mogadishu to visit my wife and me and our son Andrew. When
we drove inland to Afgoi one weekend, we found that the Shebeli River,
which had been a dry bed for months, was full to the brim with brown
water. The brown, alas, was topsoil washing down from Ethiopia's denuded
highlands upstream; still, for Somalia this water meant life. Beyond the
banana plantations at Afgoi, irrigated with waters from the Shebeli, stretched
miles of green corn and sorghum. It was a greener, lusher world than I had
dreamed of, even though it would come to dust and brown again in autumn. Moreover, the temperature had dropped with the coming of the southwest monsoon. The sun stayed fiery, but the shade temperature at Mogadishu
was never above 85 degrees Fahrenheit all that July and August. I had read
in old Italian guidebooks, and later I had been told by Mogadishu residents,
that such moderate temperatures were normal in the summer months, yet I
had wondered until now if this really could be so.

As the rains began, the Somali government, with exquisitely poor tim-
ing, announced that it was convening what it called an international conference in Somalia on the drought emergency. There was some envy involved
in this. New billions in Western aid had been pouring into Ethiopia and
Sudan, where millions of people had been facing starvation because of the
long drought. Not so much was pouring into Somalia, and for a good reason: the situation in Somalia was not so desperate. But the Somalis wanted
more aid dollars, so they were preparing a long list of additional aid needed,
they said, because of drought. We had received a preliminary version of
this list. It included many items that had nothing to do with drought or with

the possible consequences of drought, and the total cost of these items was estimated at eighteen million dollars.

The top United Nations representative was supposed to act as local co-ordinator of foreign donor representatives, but he seldom did. Whenever I saw him he was at pains to impress me with the amount of paper on his desk, but I doubted that the paper moved much. It seemed to me that the proposed conference might backfire on the Somalis. At my suggestion, Martin Florin called a quiet meeting of Western ambassadors, at which we all agreed to warn the Somali authorities that they would only damage their government's credibility by proceeding with such a poorly motivated meeting. No matter; they proceeded. No matter, that is, that the drought was broken; no matter that it was continuing to rain. Ah, said a minister to me, perhaps there has been some rain, but it takes time for the grass to grow, and meanwhile the cattle are dying by thousands. I did not tell him that I had just driven two hundred miles through the countryside and had seen a total of two dead donkeys and one dead cow. Nor had any other Western traveler reported the deaths of large numbers of animals.

The Somalis invited donor governments and international agencies to send ranking officials from their capitals and headquarters to attend the conference in Mogadishu. With one exception mentioned below, none did so; all, including ours, were represented by their Mogadishu ambassadors and agency representatives. When we arrived at the conference, we found at each seat the final edition of the Somali wish lists, put together by the Ministry of Foreign Affairs. The lists were much longer than they had been in the first version, and the original total of eighteen million dollars had now become sixty million—and much of this sum had nothing whatever to do with drought. The Ministry of Health, for example, wanted millions of dollars for cholera vaccine and rehydration equipment for cholera victims. But cholera was on the increase not only at the Gannet squatters' camp outside Hargeisa but elsewhere in the country, not because of drought but because of the recent rains; in any case, the international community was already doing a good job of sending in the supplies needed.

One of the commissioners of the European Community, Lorenzo Natali, decided to attend the conference. Natali was Italian, and presumably the special Italian interest in Somalia had something to do with his coming. The Somalis gave him VIP treatment; they flew him inland to Belet Weyn to look at the effects of the drought. They were a little late in doing so. The plane was unable to land at Belet Weyn—because the runway had been flooded by persistent rains. And the ill-conceived International Conference on the Drought Emergency failed to attract even a dollar of additional aid from any government or international agency. The Somali foreign minister complained of "donor fatigue." Well, it was not true that foreign donors were tired of helping to save lives in the Horn of Africa. We would continue to fund food and supplies for the refugees, and we were not cutting back on other aid; but it was fatiguing to hear Somali ministers plead for things they did not need, at a time when aid budgets were harder to defend both in Washington and in other capitals.

Water was always on one's mind in such a usually arid country. A point that Somali authorities failed to make to the world in the 1980s was that a flood, with its largely useless water, could be as tragic as a drought. Years later, at the end of 1997, exceptional *dayr* rains, said to be the heaviest in over a century, killed over 1,600 people in Somalia and at least hundreds more elsewhere in East Africa, not to speak of the dead from the resulting spread of diarrhea, cholera, malaria, and other diseases.[4]

After the First World War, the Italian colonizers realized that some Somali waters—mainly those of the Shebeli River, even though they flowed only part of the year—could be tamed and used for irrigated agriculture. Our Italian friends the Muttos, with their banana plantation near Merka, south of Mogadishu, were one of the vestiges of this era. As Gianluigi Mutto freely admitted, his father had been a Fascist blackshirt who was granted land in Somalia as part of Mussolini's colonization drive. But now in the 1980s, the Mutto plantation was supplying many tons of what was Somalia's only export crop, and the Muttos certainly lived in less than grand style, in a wooden bungalow surrounded by two hectares of lush gardens that reflected not opulence but hard work by the proprietors.

One day I took my family to see a far greater vestige, the irrigated plantations up the Shebeli River at Jowhar, which had been created by Luigi Amedeo, the Duke of the Abruzzi. Luigi Amedeo had been born in Madrid in 1873, when his father Amedeo, younger brother of King Umberto I of Italy, was briefly king of Spain. The father soon abdicated and went home to Turin, where it was clear that neither father nor son had any real hope of succeeding to the Italian throne, given the number of more senior relatives. Young Luigi Amedeo became a naval officer, a climber, and an explorer, perhaps the greatest outdoorsman that the world saw in the last century. In 1897

4. "Flooding Spreads across East Africa," BBC News bulletin, 16:40 GMT, December 10, 1997.

he was the first man to climb Mount St. Elias in Alaska; his polar expedition of 1899–1900 reached farther north than any previous try; in 1909, in India's Karakoram range, he reached higher than any man had ever gone before him, and his record lasted thirteen years. In the First World War, Luigi Amedeo commanded the allied naval forces in the Adriatic, resigning his commission when several ships were lost and supreme command was given to the French. The duke offered to organize and lead a kind of green-beret unit of *arditi*; permission was refused. When the war ended in 1918, the offended duke decided to leave Italy for a new life as a colonial developer—in Somalia. He had first seen the coast of Somalia in 1893, as a young officer on a gunboat sent to put down the Somali clans that were resisting Italian domination. By 1919 he had secured good financial support in Italy—the family name helped—and he began to build a dam on the Shebeli near Jowhar, as well as a series of plantations that soon totaled over twenty square miles of irrigated fields. The project flowered and became a major producer of rice, cotton, and sugar, almost all of which found a protected market in Italy.

Luigi Amedeo was not quite finished exploring. In 1929, when Italian-Ethiopian relations were still good, he secured the approval of Emperor Haile Selassie for an expedition that discovered the headwaters of the Shebeli in unmapped Ethiopian highlands, near a village whose people had never seen a European, and then followed the river's course for eight hundred miles downstream back to Jowhar. Soon he fell ill with prostate cancer. After a final trip to Italy, he took ship for Mogadishu in 1933 and died, less than a month after his return, in his pleasant two-story villa at Jowhar.

When we visited Jowhar in 1985, the enterprise, now state owned, was growing sugar cane on several thousand acres. Salt had built up in the ground, a common problem on irrigated land, and the general manager, Omar Hersi Omar, confessed that the Somalis did not know how to deal with it. The sugar mill, built under the duke's administration, was still working, and the Europeans had supplied some new equipment, but I was asked if the Americans could supply technical advice on the land and also completely rebuild the mill. All in all, it seemed to me that the Jowhar complex probably made good economic sense, but such projects were just not in our budget, and I made clear that we would have to leave them to the Somalis and to the Europeans. I would perhaps have taken a more negative attitude had I known that Siad Barre's regime was employing prisoners—though I think not only prisoners—as farm labor at Jowhar. Whether these prisoners had been justly imprisoned, God knows. Under the Italian colonial administration, the forced labor of men certainly not guilty of crimes had been used both at the duke's Jowhar plantations and elsewhere in Somalia.

We were fascinated to find the duke's villa untouched since his death in 1933 and still well preserved: furnishings, linens, pictures, even an ancient, American-made air conditioner that was no longer functioning. There was also a bust of a very attractive Somali woman. The duke had never married, despite a long romance with Katherine Elkins, the daughter of Sen. Stephen Elkins of West Virginia. Italian biographies of the duke say nothing of his private life. In Somalia, however, he had found this lovely companion, Faduma Ali, who our Jowhar friends said had been with the duke at his end.[5]

In Somalia, I often thought, there were far too many things that tended to go wrong instead of right. In late 1985 a large container ship, the *Ariadne*, Greek owned and flying the Panamanian flag, went aground as it was being towed stern-first out of Mogadishu port to put to sea. The towline broke after the ship had gone beyond the protection that the quay provided against ocean swells. For some reason the ship's engines did not function. Mogadishu had been the first port of discharge for the *Ariadne*, which had come down from the Mediterranean fully loaded. Even after offloading a number of containers at Mogadishu, the remaining containers were stacked four and five high on the ship's decks as the ship put to sea. *Ariadne* took on its port side the full force of the monsoon wind and waves, and they blew it sideways onto the coral reef just off Hamarweyn, one of the old quarters of Mogadishu. This happened near sundown, perhaps an hour before my family and I returned from a pleasant week touring national parks in Kenya. As we drove in from the airport with Scerif, we saw a crowd of people standing by the road in Hamarweyn, looking out over the water. We stopped, got out of the car, and saw the great ship on the reef, all its lights on and canted at a fifteen-degree angle, with horrid creaks and groans coming from the containers straining at their lashings.

In succeeding weeks, as the Somali authorities and the London-based shipowners' association fought bitterly over what to do, the containers began to fall overboard, and the ship began to go to pieces. The London association sent a representative, an Englishman who was a longtime ship's master,

5. A more recent biography of the duke claims that nothing was known of the duke's Somali love before 1987 (Mirella Tenderini and Michael Shandrick, *The Duke of the Abruzzi* [Seattle: Mountaineers, 1997], pp. 160–61). Not so—and our friends Mario Manca (the Italian ambassador) and Gianluigi Mutto (the plantation owner who was also chargé d'affaires of the Order of Malta, which looked after the duke's villa) were fully aware of the story before I was.

to Mogadishu to work out salvage arrangements. Somali officials attacked him so savagely, insisting that the owners were solely at fault and threatening him with imprisonment, that he shut himself in his hotel room and eventually had to be sent back to London. By the time, weeks later, that it was agreed to give a contract to the large Netherlands salvage firm Smit Tak, a number of containers, some of them full of chemicals, had broken open on the harbor bottom. The wreck caught fire, and chemical fumes could be smelled a mile away. We briefly evacuated our embassy chancery and cabled Washington, which quickly sent two Coast Guard officers and two specialists from the Environmental Protection Agency to advise both us and the Somalis. The Soviet embassy sent its staff members' children back to Moscow. My colleague the Romanian ambassador stopped taking his daily five-mile walk along the beach, and I ran inland instead of along the sand. But dozens of younger and older Somalis, despite our appeals to the authorities to stop them, kept diving down to see what they could find of value.

In September 1985 I left John Hirsch to deal with the *Ariadne* and other problems, and I went back to Washington for a meeting of our ambassadors to African countries. Annual meetings of American ambassadors to particular continents have long been the custom—annual, that is, if the budget of a State Department geographic bureau like AF can pay for all the travel. Sometimes it cannot. A multinational corporation might well bring together its top people from around the globe more frequently than once a year, but multinationals are not constrained by a Congress that can be liberal with domestic pork-barrel projects but is forever miserly with money for the State Department.

Our September meeting, in which we were warned that aid money for Africa was becoming more scarce, was my first chance to spend much time with Chester A. Crocker, assistant secretary for African affairs, whom, as mentioned above, I had known, though not well, before I went to Somalia. Chet Crocker was an expert on Africa, and while he was a Reagan political appointee rather than a career Foreign Service officer, he was also a devoted public servant who clearly never mixed any private interest with his official duties. I say this because the Reagan administration was shot through with venal ambassadors and domestic officials, who were a shame to our nation and sometimes an embarrassment to us abroad.

Unfortunately, from my point of view, Chet Crocker, who was the top administration official on Africa, never spent much time on the problems of the Horn of Africa. Always preoccupied with what was then South Africa's ugly apartheid regime, Crocker left the Horn to his deputy, Jim Bishop. Bishop was able enough, but in retrospect it seems possible that if Chet Crocker, or for that matter Secretary of State Shultz, had looked more carefully at Somalia, where we were spending a hundred million dollars a year and no one thought the regime was healthy, one of them might have instructed me to raise with Mohamed Siad Barre the need for political reform in Somalia. I did, as noted, press Siad and colleagues on behalf of political prisoners, although I had no instructions to do so. But I could not have told him on my own initiative that the United States insisted that he democratize Somalia. Someone has commented cynically that African democratization had not yet come into vogue as a Washington subject. The fact is that I did not request any instructions to press democratization.

It was not, let me make clear, that I believed our strategic position in Somalia was more important than the question of democratic reform. We were already pressing Siad Barre to agree to economic reforms, and he did reluctantly agree to certain measures, such as the freeing-up of food prices, which encouraged farmers to produce for the market. Political reform was another matter. I saw no chance of Siad Barre's agreeing to a freer and more democratic political system, on a continent where almost all presidents were dictators. If I had recommended to Washington that we press the old man on democratizing, it would have been a recommendation for show and not for real. I never believed in making recommendations for show.

It was in a sense the lack of democracy in Somalia that finally led Siad Barre's enemies, the clans and groups of clans not well represented in the regime, to bring him down. One can object that sharing power among clans is not the same thing as democracy. One can also object, and many have, that American, British, or Italian models of democracy are not necessarily relevant for Africa, that Africa has yet to develop the right kind of representative government. It is important here to look at the Somali Republic's nine years of independent existence before Siad Barre took over in 1969. From 1960 to 1969, the country had a functioning democratic system. It is true that there was an increasing amount of corruption; the new party system was to a considerable extent based on the traditional clans; ideology and programs for the future ran second to political maneuvering. But political maneuvering was not restricted to Somalia, and even as the 1960s ended, one American scholar could still speak, if perhaps with some exaggeration, of "the vibrancy of national political life in Somalia and the responsiveness of the central government, as well as the basically egalitarian and democratic nature of present-day Somali society."[6]

Even before Siad's coup, the military had posed a problem in Somalia, as shown by abortive mutinies in Hargeisa in December 1961 and in Mogadishu in February 1967. The scholar quoted above admitted that a successful coup could occur in Somalia, "but the evidence suggests that it would be neither welcome nor enduring."[7] He was wrong, at least about the "enduring." He might have added, and I would agree with this today, that a coup was not inevitable. Individuals have often changed the basic direction of a country, and Mohamed Siad Barre was such an individual.

As I have indicated earlier, in 1984–86 it seemed to me and to other ambassadors, and to those Somali friends with whom I could speak freely —and I had some—that Siad would not remain in power much longer. He was old, he had unquestionably cached large assets abroad, and, as noted, he had begun to live part-time in the reconditioned villa adjacent to the airport. It was less defensible than his heavily fortified hilltop residence, Villa Somalia, but it was next to the logical point of departure if he was to make a getaway. I will admit that I thought, as did my friends, that in a year or two Siad would be gone from the scene. Why then try to pressure him to adopt democracy, to which he would in any case never agree? It seemed most likely that the old traditions of Somali pastoral democracy would, after Siad, bring some better sort of rule to the poor country. How wrong I was; how wrong we all were.

The main subject discussed at our September 1985 meeting of ambassadors was apartheid in South Africa. President Reagan had just signed an executive order tightening up American sanctions against South Africa. This had been done principally to fight off bills introduced in Congress that would have carried sanctions much farther and that in the administration's view would be counterproductive. Privately I did not always agree fully with the administration's approach to South Africa, but this time I did. I voted Democratic, but I did not like to see Democratic-sponsored bills that might gain support at home but would not further our purposes abroad. When Chet Crocker told our meeting that he wanted a half-dozen of us to make public appearances on South Africa, I volunteered and was sent off to address audiences in Vermont, New Hampshire, North Carolina, and also Louisiana, where

6. Christian P. Potholm, "The Somali Political System," in *Four African Political Systems* (Englewood Cliffs, N.J.: Prentice-Hall, 1970), p. 189.

7. Ibid., p. 209.

I had been born and had deep roots. We were not, Crocker told us, to engage in any sort of debate; ours should be the calm voice of reason. I understood. I told the several audiences that I addressed in New England and North Carolina, and the *Charlotte Observer* when its editors interviewed me, that what the president had wanted to do in issuing the executive order was to reduce the possibilities for divisiveness in the United States over South Africa; he did not want to have to veto legislation that in the main he agreed with. As Chet Crocker had said recently, Americans were builders and not destroyers, and that was true for our policy on South Africa. But our judgment was that political reform had to come in South Africa if it was to avoid a cataclysm.

When I reached New Orleans, I found that the *Times-Picayune* had reported that Ambassador Bridges had come to town to "debate," at the Plimsoll Club, Marc Morial, a young lawyer who was the son of the city's black mayor, Ernest "Dutch" Morial. The younger Mr. Morial, who a decade later himself became the mayor of New Orleans, got pretty heated. I kept in mind Chet Crocker's instructions and resisted a strong temptation to return the heat. Several members of the audience came up to me afterward to say that I had won the nondebate on points. Two days later I was back on the Indian Ocean, another world—and, I thought, in some ways not a worse one.

thirteen

Anxieties, Artifacts, and Bases

My predecessor, Robert Oakley, told me before I first went to Mogadishu that I would do well to spend some extra effort on raising morale among embassy staff. It did not surprise me that morale was not at its highest in Mogadishu, which had the reputation for being one of the most difficult posts in the Foreign Service. The reputation was not entirely deserved. Most staff were adequately housed. There was an embassy commissary, and food supplies were more than adequate. Health conditions were not too bad in the foreign community, and we had a skilled Foreign Service nurse in our embassy plus the half-time services of a young American doctor, a black Harvard graduate whose wife worked for AID. There were swimming facilities and a club, and for people with children there was an eight-grade American school that was both well managed and well taught. In addition, our government paid Americans (except for the ambassador) 25 percent extra for serving in Somalia, and their way to and from Europe for vacation was paid once a year. The way was Somali Airlines, not the best of carriers, but its old 707s at least got good maintenance from Lufthansa at the end of the line, in Frankfurt.

Airline security was a slightly different question. A Somali 707 had been hijacked by dissidents just before I first arrived. Now when the twice-weekly northbound flight was ready for departure from Mogadishu in late evening, the passengers' checked bags were put on the tarmac by the plane, and the passengers had to identify their own bags before they could be loaded into the baggage compartment. One evening my wife and I took our son Andrew, returning to school in Rome, to the airport and found that the foreign minister and the prettier of his two wives were taking the same flight. The boarding call came, and the passengers identified their bags and boarded the plane. Soon all the people and all the bags but one were on board. One large, unclaimed suitcase remained on the ground. The baggage handler shrugged his shoulders, put it on board, and the flight took off, carrying this most uncertain piece of cargo, the country's foreign minister, and our son.

All in all, our people in Somalia were far from content. In part this had to do with security, not so much on the airline as in town. The Somali National Police might enjoy relative respect among the Somali people, but Mogadishu was not the safest of cities. To celebrate the fifteenth anniversary of his coup, in October 1984, Siad Barre had ordered a large-scale amnesty for prisoners —not including political prisoners—that put a lot of thieves back on the Mogadishu streets. The thieves soon went back to work, and there was a wave of break-ins in both our own and other embassies. I had supposed that my Soviet counterpart, Mr. Ilichev, was well protected at home, but he woke up one night to find a thief in his bedroom. Beyond thievery, Mogadishu driving was low speed but dangerous, and there were a number of traffic deaths, often at a crossroads we called Kamikaze Corner. And, after the Libyans came to town, we had to be seriously concerned about terrorism.

I decided that there were several things to be done about the situation. The first I hoped had been accomplished in my cable prohibiting further staff increases; morale would certainly tend to go down if the place was overstaffed—better to be lean and busy. But the security situation was difficult. Terrorism was not just a hypothetical question; it was a real threat. With John Hirsch's encouragement—indeed it may have been his idea—we began a regular series of American community meetings, involving spouses as well as employees, at which John and I discussed in frank terms the security situation as well as other main problems facing our embassy. We could not totally reassure people; I think most of them must have realized that any American in Mogadishu was an easy target for a trained assassin. Still, we could and did usefully talk things over and remind everyone to take elementary precautions.

Yet there was still more to be done. There was no doubt a need for me to act as the father figure in the American community, not just to show proper leadership but to try to set a happy tone in the life of this not-so-small community. I could not use official funds to entertain groups of Americans alone, but food and liquor were not costly, and I began inviting small groups of embassy Americans to my house for drinks and small things to eat on Thursday evenings at five-thirty, after the workweek had ended. The sun would already be low in the sky, falling toward the western ridge in the city just behind us. As the sun fell, its heat decreased, and the steady monsoon wind blew cooler. At six came sunset, and soon after that we could see the sky turning dark eastward over the ocean, until the line between sea and sky was invisible, and the bright stars began quickly to shine out in the heavens. Who would want to be anywhere else at such a moment? Too bad the feeling did not last.

It was important to me to be a participant as much as a leader in the American community. There was a group of Hash House Harriers in Mogadishu, as in many other places around the world (our daughter Elizabeth belonged to the Bangkok group at this same time): a loosely organized group of runners who went for weekly runs in the bush outside town. A "hare" would run ahead and leave small paper traces for "harriers" to follow. I tried to be a faithful harrier, and it was fun for all, except one evening when Gayle Plymale, the wife of our defense attaché, Charles Plymale, took a wrong turn and was held for some time at gunpoint by suspicious guards outside the oil refinery. There were a few times when I could make myself look usefully ridiculous. I still treasure a photograph of the American ambassador pulling his teammate along in a man-with-donkey race during a bazaar at the American school.

But inwardly, I thought there were limits to the role I should play as chief morale raiser. When my wife and I had been younger, we had served at some other difficult posts—Panama during the 1959 riots, Moscow during the 1962 Cuban missile crisis, Prague in the bleak 1970s after the Soviet invasion—and although we had ambassadors whom we respected and who provided good leadership, it seemed to me that my wife and I had basically taken care of our own morale. We had done this by getting interested in the country where we were living, by studying the history and customs of the place, and by getting out and meeting people and seeing things. Only once, before going to Moscow, had I had the chance to study a new country and its language before arriving there. I had gone to Panama, Prague, and Rome on short notice and had had to learn the country and the language after my arrival—and I had done so. I tried to encourage our people at Mogadishu to do the same.

Part of the Mogadishu morale problem was intractable. A certain number of Americans in Mogadishu simply did not like the thought of being immersed in Somali society and found their main amusement in watching videos at home. There was not much I could do about people who had spent their off hours staring at blue screens since they were children. Fortunately, not all the Americans were like that. In 1985 over three dozen former Peace Corps volunteers were working in Somalia, some as AID officers, others in UN and private agencies. Like almost every former Peace Corps volunteer that I ever met, they were hardworking, dedicated people. Some of them had an exceptional knowledge of Somalia and, to put it simply, loved the country. But there was more to the problem. For some years, half of the large tract of land that the Somali authorities had given us in the 1960s for a new embassy compound had been used for an American-managed, but international, golf and tennis club. There were a number of Somali members as well as Americans and some Europeans. While I was in Somalia, the club opened a fine, new outdoor swimming pool, which I tried to find time to visit once or twice a week, partly to encourage other Americans to do the same. But after several months, the number of Americans using the pool remained small. I discovered that many of our staff members, most but far from all of them white, continued to frequent a smaller, older pool located in a small compound where only Americans lived. They used that pool simply because there were no Somalis there. My initial reaction was that it was largely a question of white American attitudes toward blacks, but many of these Americans, ex–Peace Corps or not, had spent years in Africa and mixed easily with Africans. Perhaps Somalis were less likable?

I myself had not found this to be the case, but I was willing to admit to myself that for my American colleagues who had served elsewhere in Africa, the Somalis must seem different. Only a minority of Somalis were fluent in English. They were Muslims, and a few were Muslims of a puritanical sort, although at the other extreme there were also a few who were heavy drinkers and, by any standard, debauched. There was also, apart from Islam, a degree of Somali xenophobia, as well as a vindictiveness and ruthlessness that perhaps their harsh environment had bred into them over the centuries. The Somalis were a people of proverbs, and one proverb ran *Ninka aan aarsan waa nin ablaawe ah*, which is to say, "A man who does not take vengeance is a barbarous man." The British dean of Somali studies, I. M. Lewis, has described Somali attitudes toward the outside world as combining both traditional courtesy and "deeply-ingrained suspicion[,] . . . an aggressive self-confidence and, traditionally, open contempt for other people."[1] Somali scholars would perhaps not describe their own people in such a way, but neither was I aware that they had contested what Professor Lewis said.

1. I. M. Lewis, *Somali Culture, History, and Social Institutions* (London: London School of Economics and Political Science, 1981), pp. 39–40.

I do not mean to portray Somalis as a bad type of humans. While they could be vindictive, they had, and have, many virtues, including a highly developed sense of humor, which unquestionably has helped them confront adversity and disaster.[2] I always remember a day when Scerif and I were driving down the highway toward Merka and passed a small group of women waiting, as perhaps they had been doing for hours, on the other side of the road for a truck or jitney to take them to Mogadishu. It was a hot day, there was no shade, and our car raised dust as we passed—and they laughed and waved at us.

Nevertheless, Mogadishu was a place where kids came up to a foreigner with their hands out for *bakshish* and then threw stones at him as he walked away. There were a number of cases where Americans and Somalis became good personal friends, but all things considered, it was not a place where most Americans felt at ease. In a few cases, psychological problems that might have remained minor at another post grew critical at Mogadishu. During my tour in Somalia, three of our American staff members were medically evacuated for psychological reasons. An AID officer whom I liked and admired came down with a serious skin ailment that our doctor suspected had psychosomatic causes. He improved, but on his way to Washington on transfer, in Nairobi, he died.

Quite aside from the question of people in our own embassy, some other members of the foreign diplomatic corps in Mogadishu had decidedly anti-Somali attitudes. The Soviet ambassador, Ilichev, was a case in point, and while his attitude in good part reflected the bad state of Soviet-Somali relations, there were other ambassadors who simply disliked the place and people. As against these, though, there were objective, well-informed ambassadors like Florin and Fullerton, two Arab ambassadors I will not name here, and the distinguished ambassador of Kenya, John Siparo, who did much to improve Somalia's relations with Kenya.

Again, the question was what I could or should do to improve my staff's morale and thereby, one hoped, their performance. Even the Americans who took an interest in the place found, as I did, that information was hard to come by. Books on Somalia were few and far between. The only publishing house in Somalia belonged to the state; for this publishing house the West

2. See Charles L. Geshekter and Said Ahmed Warsama, "An Introduction to Humour and Jokes in Somali Culture," in *Voice and Power: The Culture of Language in North-East Africa*, ed. R. J. Hayward and I. M. Lewis (London: School of Oriental and African Studies, Univ. of London, 1996), pp. 141–53.

Germans had lately provided an ultramodern, air-conditioned printing plant (which would function just as long as the Germans manned it, and they were planning to leave at the end of 1986). But there was strict censorship in Somalia, and little of interest got published. The only good Somali novelist, Nuruddin Farah, had been in exile abroad for years, and Somali censorship did its best to keep his antiregime works out of the country. Most of the published works on Somalia were old and out of print, available only in libraries in London, Rome, or Washington. After several months I put together, after reading all I could find and with help from the Historian of the State Department, a five-page outline entitled "Somalia through the Ages," which listed, inter alia, early American contacts with Somalia; I distributed it to those interested, including Mohamed Jama Elmi, who was director general for Euro-American affairs in the foreign ministry. (See the Appendix for an updated version.) I used my outline as the basis for a talk I gave one day to an international women's group. I did not stir up much new interest among our staff members in the history or prehistory of Somalia, but at least I myself was learning interesting things, and in my inquiries I was meeting interesting people.

One of the most interesting of these was Steven Brandt, an archaeologist from the University of Georgia who subsequently joined the faculty of the University of Florida and who has spent much of his professional life working on the prehistoric archaeology of Somalia. Steve Brandt came to town with his colleague Henry Bunn from the University of Wisconsin, and one Friday the three of us, together with Hussein Suleiman Ahmed, who directed the small but valuable Mogadishu museum, went on a walking tour through Hamarweyn and Shingani, the oldest quarters of Mogadishu. The people there were different from the inhabitants of the other parts of town, most of whom had moved in from the countryside in recent years. In Hamarweyn, as I had noticed when I first arrived, the women dressed more conservatively, in black and with facial veils that one did not see elsewhere in Somalia. Many of these people had lighter skin. At home they spoke a different dialect that, Somali friends told me, could be hard for other Somalis to understand. The different skin color and the dialect presumably derived from the seafarers and merchants who had frequented this coast for millennia. At the little port of Brava, south of Mogadishu, the differences were still greater. Brava was a linguistic island, with a language close to the Swahili spoken hundreds of miles farther south on the coast of Kenya.

There was yet another unique place on the Somali coast, the village of Gandarsheikh, south of Mogadishu. On the sea edge was a ruined village with a stone fort that looked to be some centuries old and a two-room white-washed building of a type seen elsewhere in Somalia. One room served as a mosque. The other, which had four columns in the center, contained two tombs, covered with many draperies, that were said to be the tombs of a Muslim saint and his son. Inland, beyond a large palm grove, was the modern village. Its people were light skinned with nearly Caucasian features. I had heard two accounts of how the village had come to be; one had it that the founders were Arab traders, the other said Persian. My well-informed driver, Scerif, said there was also a third story, which was that long ago an English sailor "whose boat stopped working in the sea" had come ashore there, found an existing settlement, and joined it, becoming a Muslim and, eventually, the village headman. Years later an English vessel had stopped there and offered to take him off, but he had stayed with his new people and his new family, and it was his remains, together with those of his son, that were venerated in the white building. I liked that story, and that place.

There were many differences among Somalis, even if they all spoke the same basic language and professed the Islamic faith. One of the more interesting days that my wife, son Andrew, and I spent in Somalia was the day we saw the annual *Is-tun*, or stick fight, at Afgoi, the nearest Shebeli River town to Mogadishu. *Is-tun* was part of a pre-Islamic celebration of the *Dabshid*, or solar new year, somewhat like pre-Islamic observances persisting in Iran. Whether this celebration had been imported into Somalia by traders from present-day Iran, no one can tell, but the oldest tomb inscription ever found in Mogadishu, with a date corresponding to 1217 A.D., was that of a Persian from Naysabur.[3]

The ritualized stick fight at Afgoi took place between two large groups of men, altogether several hundreds, representing two major, longstanding divisions in the local population. When the custom began no one knows; the first recorded observance was in 1883.[4] In earlier times men had died in the fight, but now the whole affair was regulated by officialdom. Sticks were kept to a certain size, and there was a fire truck at the edge of the field ready to spray any fighters who got too exuberant. After we had been watching for some minutes, exuberance took hold, and the firemen turned on the hose—but something happened, and the stream of water died. Nevertheless, only minor injuries resulted.

3. Enrico Cerulli, *Somalia: Scritti vari editi ed inediti* (Roma: Istituto Poligrafico dello Stato, 1957), vol. 1, p. 2.

4. See the detailed account by Virginia Luling, "Festive Violence: The Stick-Fight of Afgoy-Geledi in Context," *Proceedings*, pp. 190–205.

I saw and greeted Siad Barre's minister of information, Mohamed Omar Jess, at the stick fight. Seeing a ranking Somali official there reminded me how the last shah of Iran had revived the solar new year ceremonies in Iran, furnishing his Islamic fundamentalist foes one more ground on which to attack him. But Omar Jess was at the fight simply as spectator, not sponsor. Most Somalis saw nothing of religion in the fight. The fundamentalists had other grounds, like women's rights, on which to attack the president.

It seemed to me that the Somali dog was still another example of intra-Somali differences. Most Somalis, like many if not most Arabs, think that dogs are unclean creatures. But there is a handsome race of Somali dogs, short haired, long eared, and medium sized, that at least until the young machine gunners hit Mogadishu streets in the 1990s lived in those streets, largely on occasional handouts from local inhabitants. They somewhat resemble the other domestic dogs of East Africa, and they must have a long history of living with, or near man. Italian guidebooks of the 1920s described a tribe of Somali hunter-gatherers who lived a hundred miles inland from Mogadishu and who trained and kept dog packs to hunt leopards. In Mogadishu, some Somalis did more than feed the local dogs; Scerif kept one as a pet, until his neighbors complained. I myself resisted the temptation to adopt one handsome animal that started following me home from my morning run.

That Friday when Hussein the museum director led Steve Brandt, Henry Bunn, and me on our walk through Hamarweyn, we came in time to the *Giami*, or Friday, mosque, the oldest mosque in the city. Hussein showed us at the base of the minaret the dedicatory inscription, which bore a date equating with August 14, 1238 A.D. The ground surface had risen appreciably, but no one knew how fast, in Hamarweyn, because of blowing sand and the deposit of refuse; as a result the mosque was half-underground. Inside, it was peaceful and cool, bright enough, the walls painted in pastels. The floor was covered with straw mats. Two older men were sleeping, and a younger one was sitting and reading the Koran. A good place for worship.

In 1980, in the little square outside this mosque, the late British archaeologist Neville Chittick had excavated an exploratory trench. His team dug down fifteen feet and found pottery dating probably from the twelfth century A.D., the century before the minaret inscription. Then the trench caved in. Chittick left Mogadishu without being able to resume the work. He still did not know how old Mogadishu was, but I did not suppose that Chittick's finds dated from the first years of the city. The great traveler Ibn Battuta visited Mogadishu in 1331 A.D. and wrote that it was a town of enormous size. Brandt told me that the experts were willing to leave open the possibility (discussed above) that Mogadishu was the "Sarapion" mentioned in the first-century *Periplus of the Erythraean Sea*. Hellenic pottery, pre-Christian, had been found on this coast.

Later, after I left Somalia, a new dig was begun in Hamarweyn, but it too was stopped, this time by the civil war. Hamarweyn, like the rest of Mogadishu, was badly damaged by the senseless strife of recent years; but it seems likely that there, still waiting to be found deep underground, lie very ancient remains.[5]

Eventually I had the opportunity to visit Steven Brandt's dig, a hundred miles inland near Baidoa, at a site called Buur Eibi. The landscape was extraordinary. From a vast, perfectly flat grassy plain rose a series of roundish, steep hills, almost little mountains, which were outcroppings of pinkish Precambrian granite, some of the oldest rock in Africa. The highest of these hills rose eleven hundred feet above the surrounding plain; this was Buur Eibi. It was a place of pilgrimage; just as some Somalis went on the *hajj* to Mecca, so others came here to walk up Buur Eibi, a custom perhaps dating to pre-Islamic times.

Brandt's dig was in a huge grotto on the side of Buur Eibi, several hundred yards beyond the small village and the village spring. The grotto was like a natural room, forty feet across, open to the plain on its outer side, where the rock ceiling was perhaps twenty feet high. It was the traditional meeting place for the village; Brandt supposed that it might have served as the village meeting place for many thousands of years. On the grotto's inner wall were faint prehistoric paintings. In 1935 the Italian archaeologist Paolo Graziosi saw these, dug a trench, and turned up prehistoric material. Professor Graziosi returned to do more work after World War II, but it was Steve Brandt who for two years now had been doing the systematic job that the site warranted. He had divided the earthen floor of the grotto into one-meter squares, and together with a small group of volunteers from Europe and America, he was carefully digging downward. In part of the area, the digging had gone down about five feet, which meant roughly ten thousand years, and the excavators had turned up many artifacts and a dozen ancient human skeletons.

5. Dr. Chittick described his dig in "Medieval Mogadishu," *Paideuma* 28 (1982). Ptolemy's *Guide to Geography*, from the second century A.D., indicates that Sarapion was the most important point along this coast; it is the only place he describes as both "station" and "emporium." But again, we still we do not know whether Mogadishu was once Sarapion.

During most of these hundred centuries, the Horn of Africa was dry country, as it is now, but there had been a wetter period ending in about 3000 B.C.—when, as has often been described, even the Sahara Desert was good grassland. As the Sahara turned to desert, some of its inhabitants probably trekked east into this region. In Somalia now, the only domestic cattle are *Bos indicus*, the humpbacked sort that does well in arid conditions. But farther north in Somalia, Steve Brandt and others had found prehistoric cave paintings of cattle without humps, cattle coming presumably from a milder climate. The cave painting in Buur Eibi was different; indeed, it was not all old. Brandt pointed out where next to a faint prehistoric design someone had painted "Lt. Gen. Mohamed Ali Samantar visited here." Whether the defense minister was a communist or not, I thought, he was a vandal.

Visits from experts like Steve Brandt were great moments for those of us in Mogadishu, Somalis and Westerners alike, who were interested in Somalia's past as well as its present. Professor I. M. Lewis came to town from London and gave a well-attended lecture at our international club. We met at lunch at the British embassy, and I found him critical of Western aid projects, which too often ignored the dynamics of Somali society. I agreed and said that I would like to see more aid to education—not to produce more Somali MBAs (and there was a Somali MBA program) but to produce more people with good primary and secondary educations and more skilled mechanics and artisans. Lewis agreed. I had a good impression of Dr. Lewis. He was restrained in his public criticisms of Siad Barre's regime, as were other foreign academic specialists on Somalia. As one American professor said to me frankly, it was difficult to be other than restrained if one wanted to keep getting Somali visas.

Twice I was fortunate to have former American ambassadors as my houseguests. Each of them had come to give lectures to Somali audiences, under the auspices of the U.S. Information Agency. The first, who came soon after I reached Mogadishu, was Mabel Smythe, who had been ambassador to Cameroon and was now a professor of African studies at Northwestern University. Here for the Somalis to see and listen to for the first time was an American ambassador who was a woman. There was another aspect to her as well. When she went to lecture at the Somali National University, she began by mentioning that the dress she was wearing came from Sierra Leone; if anyone disputed her right to wear it, she would want them to know that she had ancestors from that country. She gave a simple and eloquent lecture on change in society and then asked for comments. For at least a minute no one spoke, and then a polite, but also fierce and frank, battle of the sexes erupted between the younger men and women in the hall. There was no doubt that Somali women thought they had yet some way to go before reaching equality—and that many Somali men thought they had gone far enough. Some months later I had the opportunity, thanks to Ambassador Smythe, to lecture on Somalia to her students at Northwestern.

My other ambassadorial visitor was Fred Hadsel. He had been the ambassador at Mogadishu in 1969–71 and later ambassador to Ghana. I remembered Fred Hadsel well. I had been first secretary of our Rome embassy when he was in Somalia, and among my other responsibilities I followed Somali affairs and met with our man in Mogadishu whenever he came through Rome. One June day in 1970, he came by my office during a visit and asked a favor. He and his wife were planning their annual Fourth of July reception in Mogadishu and had decided it would be very American to offer their guests fresh cherries; after all, the young Washington was remembered for having cut down a cherry tree. But cherries were unknown in Somalia. Could I buy him a couple of cases? I went down to the open-air market at Ponte Milvio, purchased two cases of the best cherries, and got them to Hadsel in time for his flight home. Now, after a dozen years, I wondered if he still remembered this. He did; the party had been a great success. I confessed that the midgrade officer who bought the cherries in Rome never imagined then that he might one day himself give a Fourth of July reception at Mogadishu.

Another interesting visitor came in May 1986. This was Dr. Paul Johnston from the Peabody Museum in Salem, Massachusetts, sent by the U.S. Information Agency to lecture at our posts around the Indian Ocean. His lecture in Mogadishu was well attended by Somalis. Johnston had brought slides showing artifacts in his museum's collection that American sea captains had obtained on this coast in the early 1800s, and also excerpts from these captains' logs on their experiences calling at Somali ports. Somalis put considerable emphasis on tradition; a Somali minister recited for me one day at lunch a string of sixty ancestors. American contacts with Somalia did not go back that far, but they went back to the early decades of our republic, and it was useful to remind Somalis of that fact.

Tom Hull, who headed our U.S. Information Service office, was energetic in promoting cultural events, but the budget was modest. Sometimes we could organize our own events. Officers in AID had formed a country-and-western band, and one evening they put on a concert at our house. The crowd included several Somali ministers and their wives. Another pleasant occasion came when we managed to pay for 170 basic reference works, which I presented to the Somali National Library. This event cost us less than three thousand dollars but got major coverage, which I decided was deserved, since the library's total holdings amounted to only three thousand volumes. A large, new building for the library was completed while I was at Mogadishu, and Tom Hull began writing to American publishers to see what they would donate. We had obtained sizable such donations when I had served years earlier in Moscow; we had every hope of being able to secure thousands of volumes for Somalia.

Most other foreign embassies in Somalia also ran cultural programs, with varying success. The Egyptians for some years usefully provided Somalia with hundreds of Egyptian elementary- and secondary-school teachers, who taught Arabic and other subjects and who, until the Somali shilling was devalued in 1985, found it possible to send decent sums home to their families in Egypt. The French did their best to present French culture, but . . . I remember especially a classical guitar concert I attended, arranged by Tom Hull's French counterpart. The concert took place at the Hotel al-Curuuba, a large and not unhandsome establishment near our embassy that was said to feature a rat in every room. The concert attracted a good-sized audience, around 150 Somalis and Europeans. The hotel people had built a slightly raised platform in the hotel ballroom and had put a chair for the performer on this platform, together with a standing lamp with a big shade. The guitarist was a stocky, bearded, rather young Frenchman named, I recall, Sadanowsky. He mounted his platform and began his program. He was good. About five minutes into his first number, four Somalis walked out onto the floor behind him. They were talking audibly, apparently intent on starting some audio equipment that was sitting on a table. One of them reached down and pulled a wire, and the lamp by the guitarist went out. There was a little light from the back of the hall, and M. Sadanowsky continued to play. Someone turned on the ceiling lights, which made a worse effect. Someone turned off the ceiling lights. The wind was whistling loudly. I felt for the poor musician. Now the floor lamp went on again, then off again. And the perspiring M. Sadanowsky, continuing in a suite by Bach, smiled the inscrutable smile of a Polish-Frenchman playing classical guitar for the first and no doubt last time in Somalia, while the northeast monsoon wailed in the eaves.

There was one important sort of cultural undertaking for which the Somali authorities needed no additional foreign aid but on which they unfortunately did little: the preservation of texts of traditional poetry. The Somali language had been reduced to writing only in 1972, but over the centuries the Somali people had produced a remarkable number of accomplished poets. Just as in northern peasant societies that long lacked writing, like those of the Finns and Russians, so among the Somalis the significant poems had been handed down from generation to generation by men who committed thousands of lines to memory. Now, in the 1980s, the traditional ways were fading, and much of this poetry was being lost. Little was being done to transcribe and publish it. (The Somalis still maintained an oral culture in other ways. Almost every Somali seemed to have a small transistor radio, and the BBC Somali service had a large audience. Overseas Somalis often sent audio cassettes rather than letters home. Tom Hull, on a visit once to the Somali censorship board to spring loose a package it was holding that had been sent us by international mail, caught a rare glimpse of censors listing to cassettes they were pulling out of postal packages.)

I hoped, after I came to Mogadishu, for visits by members of Congress, even though many such visits abroad really are the junkets they are commonly called. My wife and I had seen at other posts—Rome above all—a number of senators and representatives and their spouses who were interested in little but seeing the sights, shopping, eating, and drinking. But we had also met members of Congress—above all, Sen. Lloyd Bentsen of Texas, a Democrat, and Sen. Charles Mathias of Maryland, Republican—whom we privately numbered among the most decent, hardworking, and impressive Americans we ever saw. I was pretty sure that any members visiting Mogadishu would be serious minded; if they had any sense, they would not come here for the pleasures of the place. In the event, just one member of Congress visited Somalia during my time there, and his visit was not useful but harmful. This was Howard Wolpe, an influential Democrat; he headed the African affairs subcommittee of the House Committee on Foreign Affairs.

I had never met Mr. Wolpe, but he was said to be pro-Ethiopian. Still, I could hardly believe that he had much affection for Mengistu's horrendous pro-Soviet regime in Addis Ababa. In any case, we were told that he was coming, and we were instructed to arrange appropriate appointments for him with Somali officials. Siad Barre flatly refused to see him. I finally convinced Jama Barre, the foreign minister, to receive him in order not to damage Somalia's standing in Washington. So Jama Barre saw him, and Wolpe made clear to the minister that he was as pro-Ethiopian and as anti-Somali (not just anti-Siad) as the stories said. After the Wolpe visit I decided that it was just as well that Somalia visits had such low priority on Capitol Hill.[6]

Much of the long coast of Somalia is accessible only by sea. I had always believed that a diplomat could not fully comprehend his or her country of assignment without traveling up, down, and through it. I had often urged foreign diplomats in Washington to get out beyond the Beltway and see Michigan and Oregon and Arkansas if they wanted to understand our people's view—or lack of view—of the world. Somalia was much the same but lacked roads. I had therefore leaped at the chance when, as mentioned before, Captain Wanzor of our oceanographic vessel USNS *Harkness* offered to take me and my German colleague, Martin Florin, along when his ship next headed north from Mogadishu on its long survey of Somali waters. The *Harkness*, which was operated by the navy's Military Sealift Command, was not one's usual idea of a naval vessel. Three thousand tons in displacement and four hundred feet long, it was painted white and had a top speed of a dozen knots. Wanzor and his officers and crew were not navy but civil service; there was also a navy unit, headed by Lt. Cdr. Robert Booker, that did the oceanographic work, and a navy helicopter and crew.

After four days' slow sailing northward, I came on deck at dawn and found that we were standing two miles off Ras Hafun, the easternmost point of Africa, a hundred miles south of Cape Guardafui, the Horn, where the north-running Indian Ocean coast of Somalia turns sharply west along the Gulf of Aden. Over the last four days, I had had long and useful talks with the German ambassador, whose views on aid programs were close to mine and who knew much more about Africa than I could ever hope to. But the main reason I had wanted to make this trip was Ras Hafun.

Ras Hafun is a large tableland that juts out into the Indian Ocean. I was looking now at its eastern, seaward side, reddish and yellow eroded cliffs of sandstone and limestone that were a good five hundred feet high. This tableland is about fifteen miles from east to west, ten miles north to south, and stands almost detached from the mainland. At the northwest end

---

6. David Korn, who was our chargé d'affaires in Ethiopia from 1982 to 1985, has described in his *Ethiopia, the United States, and the Soviet Union* (Carbondale: Southern Illinois Univ. Press, 1986, p. 64 ff.) how Wolpe visited Addis Ababa in 1983 and met Mengistu. Though Mengistu spoke harshly to him of the United States, Wolpe nevertheless insisted later that he was encouraged by the meeting and that Mengistu should not be viewed as a Marxist-Leninist (which Mengistu himself said he was) but as an African socialist, like Robert Mugabe of Zimbabwe or Julius Nyerere of Tanzania.

of Ras Hafun, a low sand spit points farther northwest, in the direction of the mainland. This sand spit almost, but not entirely, closes off from the sea a very shallow bay, several miles across, that lies between the tableland to the east and the mainland to the west. On the southwest side of the table-land, another sand spit goes due west all the way to the mainland, blocking off the south end of the shallow bay from the sea.

Soon after the First World War, the Italians realized that this shallow bay, which had a long, low beach along the mainland side, was a perfect place for a large salt works. In 1922 a Milan company began construction. In 1922 the site was attacked by two thousand Somalis who were still resisting Italian domination of northeastern Somalia; the attack ceased after an Italian gunboat was called in to shell the attackers. Construction resumed, using 3,500 Italian and 1,200 Somali workers, and was completed in 1929.[7] Soon the enterprise at Ras Hafun was exporting by sea over three hundred thousand tons of salt a year for industrial use. There was a resident staff of 150 Italians at the company town, which the Italians named Dante; it was a regular port of call for the passenger ships linking Italy with its Somali colony. But in 1941, during World War II, the British, who had lost British Somaliland to an Italian attack, sent north into Somalia from Kenya an expeditionary force that captured all of Italian East Africa and in the process destroyed the salt works. The works were never rebuilt.

I knew that the West German Agency for Technical Cooperation, GTZ, had done a study on Ras Hafun. More recently, an American consulting group had produced a similar study for an American business group that was interested in putting Ras Hafun back into the salt business but, from what I could gather, had not found the estimated fifty-four million dollars needed to finance the project. The prewar production capacity of Ras Hafun had been half a million tons of salt a year. If Somalia could export a half-million tons a year, it would be a major step toward resolving the country's awful trade gap—and the potential was even greater. According to the American study, a rebuilt Ras Hafun works could produce as much as four million tons of salt a year, and while this was a huge amount, overall world consumption was said to be 175 million tons.

After lunch that day on the *Harkness*, Kim Shepard, the lieutenant commander who piloted the ship's helicopter, led Martin Florin and me to his craft. We buckled ourselves in, side by side in seats along the right wall, facing the open cargo door on the left side, which promised a good view

7. *Guida d'Italia: Possedimenti e Colonie* (Milano: Touring Club Italiano, 1929), pp. 805–6.

Peter Bridges and German
ambassador Martin Florin
about to board helicopter on
USNS *Harkness*, off Ras Hafun,
Somalia, March 1985.

from the air. We took off and flew to shore, coming in low over the vast evaporating pans on the western edge of the shallow bay. Commander Shepard kindly flew the helicopter slightly heeled over to the left, so that we two passengers were looking down as well as out though the open door. It took a moment to reassure myself that I was buckled in and not about to tumble out. Then I saw that thousands of tons of salt were still sitting there, in neat, long mounds, bulldozed from the pans but never exported before the war had stopped operations. Next to the pans was the little village of Hordio. From here the Italians had built an aerial cableway that ran a dozen miles across the shallow bay—now we were flying along its long line of crumbled towers—to Dante, where the sand spit that closed off the south side of the bay joined the mainland. Now we could see the line of seven taller towers that ran from the ruins of Dante south into the sea for a mile, to a point where the water depth was thirty feet and the salt ships could be loaded. It had indeed been a large enterprise.

I cabled a report to Washington after my trip, hoping that it might stir some additional interest in the salt works. I was not surprised when no progress was made, either during my tour in Somalia or later, toward rebuilding the works of Ras Hafun. There were several reasons why this was so. One main reason was the unwillingness of foreign investors to sink capital into any business in a country with so rapacious a regime as that of Siad Barre. Tourism, for example, was logically another good possibility for Somalia, given its beautiful and still unspoiled coasts. Kenya, Somalia's neighbor to the south, had fine beach resorts. But the major hotel chains that came probing the Somali scene shied away as soon as they had sampled the business—more properly, antibusiness—climate there. A business visitor was likely to be harassed at the Mogadishu airport both on arrival and on departure. One American businessman was arrested as he was about to board a departing flight, on charges of smuggling currency, because he had his salary check from his employers in his pocket. Consul Costanzo had to press hard to get him released. It was common for such a visitor to find Somali officials greedy and demanding. The visitors would often fall ill, perhaps from eating a green salad in a restaurant or from questionable ice in a soft drink. The Hotel al-Curuuba, where foreigners often stayed, was, as mentioned earlier, full of rats. Siad Barre used to complain to me that our government was not doing what it could to attract American investors to Somalia. Well, we tried, but we had to talk straight with them. The president never seemed to realize that sizable foreign investment could not be attracted on false premises.

Salt was not the only reason for American interest in Ras Hafun. There was also potential military interest, which increased after Gen. Robert Kingston was succeeded as CENTCOM commander in chief by Gen. George Crist, a four-star marine officer. Crist soon came out to Somalia, both to call on Defense Minister Samantar and, without telling Samantar, to go take a look at Ras Hafun. General Crist was a short, wiry, and likable man, and he and I had a generally pleasant meeting with the still shorter but less wiry minister. Then we boarded the defense attaché office's twin-engine Beechcraft C-12, which I had come to find a practically indispensable piece of equipment if one was to get around Somalia without spending days on the road or at sea.[8]

From Mogadishu we flew north, refueling at Hargeisa without filing a definite flight plan, and then flew east five hundred miles to Ras Hafun. We flew over and around the great tableland, giving George Crist a good look at what some of his staff were suggesting might be built into a large American military base. Ras Hafun was a barren place, but the tableland was relatively flat on top and, protected by cliffs and the sea, would afford good security. The idea was to create there a major logistical base that could support operations farther east, presumably against Soviet forces. But I did not like the idea, and I said so, briefly to George Crist and in more detail later, after I had thought things over, in a cable to the State Department.

8. The only scheduled domestic air service in Somalia was provided by Somali Airlines' one remaining twin-engine Fokker F-27. I learned that this plane was in bad repair, and eventually I issued orders that no American was to fly on it. There had been a second F-27. Some months before my arrival, it was barely functioning, and one day its pilot refused to take it north from Mogadishu on a scheduled flight. He was told to take off or go to jail. He took off, and a few minutes later it crashed and killed all on board.

My concern had nothing to do with the difficulties involved in building a large military base in one of the most isolated places north of the equator. If the Italians could build the salt works, we could build a base. It was also true that once a base was built, we could hold it against anyone who wanted to take it by force, including the Somalis. But there was more to be said. If we sought Somali agreement to build a new base at Ras Hafun—and it was clear that we could not build one on the basis of existing U.S.-Somali agreements—there could be no question but that Siad Barre would insist on a major quid pro quo. He would want not just additional aid but, I had no doubt, massive additional military aid, which we did not want to give him. And while we might be able to build an impregnable military base far up the coast from Mogadishu, Siad could always hold the rest of our presence in Somalia hostage if we later came to disagree over what was going on at Ras Hafun. Beyond all this, I simply questioned the need for such an installation; I continued to believe that Somalia's strategic importance was less than some of our planners thought. This time, at least, Washington agreed. So, apparently, did General Crist, and the idea of the big fort on the far tableland was shelved for good.

I myself had still another, totally personal, interest in Ras Hafun, which left me tantalized by my two brief views of the place from the air. Ras Hafun had unquestionably been visited by the mariner who wrote *The Periplus of the Erythraean Sea* a century after Christ. The author said that south of "the precipitous headland which is the eastern end of the Barbarian mainland"— which must be Cape Guardafui—there lay a trading mart called Opone, where the local people traded spices, incense, tortoiseshell, and slaves for the products of the Roman Empire. The latter-day editor of the *Periplus* had added flatly that the name Opone "descended from the ancient Egyptian name for the region, Pun-t, and still survives in Ras Hafun."[9] Beyond this, Neville Chittick, the archaeologist, conducting a brief excavation in 1975 at the southwestern edge of the Ras Hafun tableland, had come on foundations apparently dating to Roman times.[10] Chittick never returned to Ras Hafun, and he died in England, aged only sixty, just before I reached Somalia. Neither has any later archaeologist worked there, nor is any likely to do so for a long time to come. I was tantalized, and remain tantalized, by the thought that there on the Somali coast may lie buried artifacts and ruins that could, someday, confirm the ancient accounts of the trade between two worlds.

9. Huntingford, ed., *Periplus*, p. 94.
10. Neville Chittick, "An Archaeological Reconnaissance in the Horn," *Azania* 11 (1976).

fourteen

Disasters and Arcadias

Aid—financial aid, food aid, military aid, development projects—was the main matter, indeed it sometimes seemed the only raison d'être, for our Mogadishu embassy. Looking back now, one may ask what, if any, good all this aid did. One important thing, at least: our food aid and other support for the refugees in Somalia saved hundreds of thousands of human lives. It seems probable that a number of these people later fell victims in Somalia's civil war; but human life is nevertheless worth saving, at any time, no matter what the future may bring.

I am inclined to believe that not just the recurring famines but the wars and strife that this part of East Africa has known for decades are linked somehow with overpopulation, whether the slogans have been socialist, nationalist, or tribal, and whether the war has been waged over ownership of the Ogaden or control over the city of Mogadishu. Perhaps it is a mystical thought, but one wonders if somehow all this death reflects an attempt by great Gaia to regain a lost balance between life and land. Certainly want has often promoted strife in Somalia. Riverine Somalis used to speak of three kinds of years: *laba-mooyaale*, *laba-maalisley*, and *laba-maylinley*, that is, two mortars, two milkings, or two spears. In the first, rainfall was so abundant that two mortars would be needed to grind all the grain; in the second, crops might fail, but grazing would be good enough that animals were milked twice daily. In the third kind of year, the spears came out, one for slaughtering the stock and the other for warfare and looting.[1]

---

1. Lee V. Cassanelli, "Society and Culture in the Riverine Culture of Southern Somalia," in *Somalia in Word and Image*, ed. Katheryne S. Loughran (Washington, D.C.: Foundation for Cross Cultural Understanding, 1986), p. 69.

Not many years ago in the Somali lands, whole families of nomads would die if the drought got bad enough, and the population was also reduced by interclan fights, which killed hundreds and sometimes thousands of people a year. These deaths helped provide a balance between humans and their fragile environment. For a long time the developed world knew little, and cared little, about life and death in the Somali grasslands, even when deaths reached massive proportions. Reporting out of the Ogaden is still scarce today. But, as I had written in my diary after discussing refugees with Lou Cohen and Frank Pavich that day in 1985, the world will no longer sit passively and watch mass death from famine once it hears what is going on. Yet even when the media do report on death in Somalia, what is not said is that the old, rough, cruel balancing act of nature is no more. Food aid and modern medicine have helped human and animal populations to grow to a point where vegetation vanishes and there is no possibility of overall economic progress. Someday the Somali population explosion will slow and halt, as it has done elsewhere in the world. But the foreseeable future looks grim, and the recent Somali civil war did not help restore the balance of nature but devastated the country further.

On a less philosophical level, many of us were worried in 1984–86 about the loans that the United States and others in the international community had made to Somalia. It did not seem possible that Somalia would ever repay them; nor was this surprising, given the parlous state of Somali finances. There had been at least one major Somali default that worried us not at all—on billions of rubles' worth of Soviet loans. But default on American loans could have serious consequences. A month after I signed with Finance Minister Mohamed Sheikh Osman a new agreement lending Somalia twenty-five million dollars to buy seventy thousand tons of American grain, Somalia came close to falling a year in arrears on a payment to the United States of just six hundred thousand dollars on an older loan we had made. If it had in fact done so, this would have triggered the Brooke Amendment, legislation authored by the former senator from Massachusetts, which required cutting off all further assistance from the United States government until the arrears were paid up. The crisis was in the end avoided—Somali debts were rescheduled, and the pressure came off. Still, that left the question of whether it made sense to continue to provide loans that would in all likelihood would never be repaid—and that never have been. The candid answer was that loans could be defended on Capitol Hill more easily than frank, flat-out grants of aid.

We did, however, also make sizable grants not requiring repayment. The largest of these came under our worldwide Economic Support Funds program. The ESF grants to Somalia represented civilian and not military assistance, but they were in effect the payoff for the access Somalia granted us to the old Soviet-built military and naval facilities in Somalia. The largest single block of ESF money, thirty-nine million dollars, went to rebuild the port facilities at Kismayu in the south. My first visit to Kismayu had, as noted earlier, come in February 1985. My second and last visit as ambassador came in January 1986, when I took part in a ribbon-cutting ceremony marking the actual beginning of work on the quay. Our navy had organized itself in good time, considering that all the materials and most of the workers had to be imported. The Somali minister of public works, Abdiqassim Salad Hassan, was slated to be the ribbon cutter on the Somali side, and he kindly invited my wife, son Andrew, and me to drive to Kismayu with him and his wife in their Land Rover. It was an interesting three-hundred-mile trip. The newly paved part of the road, which was most of the route beyond Merka, had been completed by an Italian contractor with funding from the European Community. It was the shoddiest, worst job of paving that I had ever seen. For most of the way, a very thin asphalt layer had been put down over what looked like sand. There were already potholes; I feared it would not take the big banana trucks long to tear it up. It was, however, still in passable condition when, just five years later, Siad Barre and his entourage fled down that highway on his final departure from Mogadishu.

There was little to boast about in southern Somalia's infrastructure. Beyond the wretched job on the road, the long and almost unused Kismayu airport runway, and the disintegrating quay (which we were finally going to do something about), there was the Kismayu city water system. This had been built by the United States in the 1960s, at the same time we built the quay. In contrast to the quay, it had been well built, and for some time it supplied the city with safe, filtered water from the nearby Juba River. But the terms of the project did not call for us to maintain it; we turned both the system and the responsibility for maintenance over to the Somali authorities when the system was completed and functioning. Eventually, as I explained to my wife as we were getting ready for dinner at the Hotel Waamo, which was also American built, the filtration equipment had broken down, and the city's water supply thereafter came untreated from the Juba. There was some concern that the Juba water might harbor the blood fluke that causes schistosomiasis. "Nice of you to tell me," said my wife. "I took a shower just before

Peter Bridges speaking at inauguration of Kismayu port rehabilitation, Somalia, January 1986; seated with canes, Minister of Public Works Abdiqassim Salad Hassan (with hat) and President Mohamed Siad Barre.

Peter Bridges shaking hands with President Mohamed Siad Barre at inauguration of Kismayu port rehabilitation, Somalia, January 1986; visible in middle (applauding, with hat) is Minister of Public Works Abdiqassim Salad Hassan.

you came in." (When we went to dinner we found that Mohamed Siad Barre had unexpectedly come to Kismayu for the ribbon cutting the next day. Andrew Bridges, aged sixteen, found himself seated at dinner next to the president of the Somali Democratic Republic. Andrew seemed less than awed by the experience.)

In November 1985 the World Bank held another meeting in Paris of the Consultative Group on Somalia. In contrast to the meeting soon after I had arrived at Mogadishu, I decided this time that I would attend myself, taking Lou Cohen along; our delegation was chaired by Larry Saiers, the able number-two in the AID/Washington Africa bureau. When it came time for each aid donor to report what it intended to do for Somalia in 1986, we found that altogether the country would be receiving all the project aid that it could reasonably absorb, but it would be short of cash to import oil and to meet its financial obligations. Well, that was not surprising. What was striking at the meeting was the reticence of the representatives of the Kuwait Fund and the Saudi Fund, who unlike other participants had absolutely no new financial assistance to announce, although we had made it clear to the Somalis months earlier that we could not offer additional financing and that they should turn to their fellow Arab League members for help. We knew, however, that the Saudis in particular had turned much cooler toward Siad Barre's regime. One possible reason was reports that Siad Barre had diverted to private pockets, perhaps his own, as much as twenty million dollars of Saudi money intended for Somali purchases of oil. In addition, an Arab ambassador had told me of a rumor that the Somalis had received a tanker load of oil from Saudi Arabia and had then resold it to South Africa, on which the rest of the world was trying to enforce an oil embargo. And members of the Saudi royal family might well be displeased by the fact that Siad Barre kept in prison a number of friends of theirs, including Omar Arteh, the former foreign minister.

The Paris meeting was also significant for the suddenly negative attitude that, as mentioned earlier, the Germans, and to a lesser extent the French and other Europeans, took on the question of the proposed high dam at Bardera on the Juba River. The German representative pulled out of his pocket a list of over twenty questions that he said had to be answered before any further consideration could be given to financing the dam. Martin Florin had recently finished his tour of duty as German ambassador to Somalia. When we had first discussed Bardera, he had suggested that perhaps the prospect of major famines in the future argued for building the dam.

But before he left his post, Florin had told me that he had finally decided that the dam made no economic sense and that he planned to go over the project with his colleagues when he reached Bonn. Apparently he had gotten their attention. We ourselves could not legally move forward on dam financing at this point; we were bound to wait on the completion of two studies, one on Juba valley soils and the other, just getting under way, on the environmental and social consequences of a high dam at Bardera. But, I had just learned, AID/Washington people were, for reasons I did not understand, taking a more positive approach toward the idea of a dam. Now, though, this newly negative European attitude made it seem unlikely that an international financing package could be put together. The Somali delegation in Paris was headed by the finance minister, Mohamed Sheikh Osman, and the minister for Juba Valley development, Ahmed Habib Ahmed. If they reported truthfully to Siad Barre on what transpired at the Paris meeting—and I knew of other occasions when Somali representatives had been afraid to do so—the president may have seen this as the end to his great dream. It was just that.

These Paris meetings were chaired by the World Bank, but the International Monetary Fund played an important role, and the two institutions worked together in Mogadishu and at their Washington headquarters on overall programs for Somali economic and financial reform. The bank understandably viewed animal husbandry and agriculture as Somalia's best hopes for the future, and the bank's core programs were in this area, as were our own. Our embassy and those of the other donor nations worked closely together, and although the senior UN representative in Somalia did not play the donor-coordinating role he should have, the World Bank's able and amiable resident representative in Somalia, an Englishman named Brian Falconer, did much to bring us together.

The IMF too was ably represented in Somalia by Salvatore Schiavo-Campo, an American. He and the fund fought a hard battle for financial stabilization in Somalia. Throughout my time in Somalia, the IMF was trying to enforce the requirements of the standby agreements that Somalia had first concluded with the IMF in 1981. Their basic aims were to increase government revenues, restrain government spending, and free up exchange rates and foreign trade. By 1985 the Somalis had been brought to agree to a freer, more realistic exchange rate for the Somali shilling. Eventually in 1987, the year after I had left Mogadishu, Siad Barre decided that the IMF-imposed measures had not resolved the country's problems while impinging on his cronies' and his clan's own financial interests. He gave up on the IMF and returned to controlled prices and fixed exchange rates. The following year he was forced by a new economic downturn to come to terms again with the IMF. The year after that, 1989, saw the beginning of the slide toward national chaos in which such matters as financial reform became simply irrelevant.

While we strongly supported the IMF's program, I personally was worried over the effect of some of its provisions. Not the freeing up of foreign trade—this could only help the economy, while, I hoped, cutting down on opportunities for Siad Barre's family and friends to rake in money from their control of export monopolies. Freeing up exchange rates was a more complicated problem. Even if most Somalis remained very poor in material goods, the country had been living beyond its means. The more realistic exchange rates of 1985–86 led to a reduction of imports, which the country basically could not afford. But there was more to the situation than that. The materials of a decently built new house in Mogadishu, for example, beyond the local rock of the walls, had to be almost entirely imported from abroad—plumbing, electrical wiring, floor tiles, even the wood and cement. The prices of imports went up, and people stopped building houses. Our Somali employees reminisced about the good old days when even a clerk in the American embassy could afford to build himself a little house. Outside our embassy, in the many ministries, staffs were being cut back, again in response to the IMF's demands for fiscal discipline. All this built resentment in the people.

When the Yugoslav chargé d'affaires came to pay a farewell call on me—the poor fellow was being transferred to Tehran after long, difficult years in Mogadishu—he expressed his concern over "the IMF approach" in Somalia. He found me willing to listen. To begin with, he did not think that either the Europeans or Americans who managed the IMF understood this country very well. A number of Somalis spoke a cultivated English or Italian; a number of them studied abroad in Europe or America (or India—the Indian ambassador had recently told me there were perhaps three thousand Somali students in India). But, said the Yugoslav, I think they still have the mentality of the nomad. I do not say this pejoratively, and I am not saying that this is the Mysterious East. I am just saying that after seven years here, I am continually finding that my Somali friends and I are not on the same wavelength. And what is true for me is more true for IMF. But some of the things the IMF is bringing about would be troublesome even in Yugoslavia.

Don't be sure, for example, that the dismissal of all these ministry employees will work the way it is supposed to. As you know, the government is encouraging them to be farmers and giving them plots of land near Afgoi. But who ever leaves a city voluntarily to go back to the countryside? There could be an eruption. Siad could say "To hell with the IMF," and he might well get popular support.

My caller and I had agreed that neither of us would need to report home on a friendly conversation. I told him that I did not disagree with him, but neither did I see how the IMF could do things much differently. Somalia might be one of the poorest countries, but it was linked inextricably with the rest of the world, and the rest of the world could not ignore the fact that it acted like a profligate. I went on to tell him frankly, as I later recorded in my diary, that

> I had reached two conclusions. The first was that we were fortunate to serve in Somalia now, because a decade from now was likely to be much worse. My second conclusion represented a change in my thinking since I had arrived in Africa. Before that, several years before that, I had decided that the so-called developing world was really a deteriorating world. Its problems were not entirely the fault of the people of that world, but they were huge, growing, and probably beyond resolution. And I had decided that this looming tragedy was going to imperil what there was of civilization and progress elsewhere, mainly North America and Europe and the industrialized parts of Asia and Oceania. Now I saw things differently. Africa could become a seething poor hopeless mass— but it need not, probably would not, affect the comfortable lives of people sitting heedless in Dortmund and Denver.

Notwithstanding what my Yugoslav colleague had said about the different mentality of Somalis, the longer I lived and worked in Somalia the more confident I became that I did understand this people. In many ways I came to like them, and I made a few close and trusted friends. But no reasonable person could abide the Somali regime. Siad Barre and his ministers were as suspicious as they were rapacious.

There were also a number of ministers, a Somali friend warned me, who simply had little understanding of their country's economic problems; an internal jockeying for power was going on that did not augur well for the chances of ministers, or Siad himself, achieving a better informed or more objective view of the situation. I knew from my meetings with Foreign Minister Jama Barre that he, for one, was a minister with little understanding of economic problems. On November 24, 1985, several weeks after the World Bank meeting in Paris, I dictated to Kathy Astala a letter addressed to the foreign minister. I showed the letter to John Hirsch and Lou Cohen, who liked it, and I sent it to Jama Barre, noting in the letter that I was sending copies also to other Somali ministers concerned with economic and developmental questions. Later I cabled the text to Washington, which as far as I can recall (although I do not seem to have made a note at the time) sent back a positive reaction. Rereading this letter now, more than a dozen years later, I would not rephrase what I said:

I would first make the point that while my Government understands that Somalia's problems are not entirely of its own making, we know that there are certain steps that Somalia can take, now, to improve its situation. The aid which my Government furnishes . . . is given in the expectation that the Somali authorities will take all possible steps to improve the country's economy and finances. . . .

In the past, concern has been expressed on the Somali side about the possibility of "donor fatigue." I see no sign of donor fatigue, at least on the part of my Government, but . . . money is short in the developed countries, and governments and parliaments are taking an increasingly hard look at budgets for foreign assistance. They are also taking an increasingly hard look at results. . . . Fortunately, in the recent past my Embassy has been able to point to at least some positive trends in Somali economic affairs.

I come now to the question of Somalia's relationship with the International Monetary Fund. . . . [T]he nub of Somalia's current differences with the IMF is the question of exchange rates[;] . . . the changes . . . have made the cost of imported goods much higher. I doubt that many Somalis, seeing the high cost they must pay now for imported cloth to make trousers, or a transistor radio, or foreign cigarettes, would agree that a year or two ago the cost of these goods was too low. And yet it was, in terms of what this country earns abroad. . . . I am not convinced, and I doubt that either the IMF or other donors are convinced, that Somalia is doing all it can to improve its foreign trade position. State agencies continue to be an obstacle to export development in several lines, and foreign donors will view this in a most negative way as long as it continues.

I also doubt that Somalia is doing all it can to find new foreign markets. . . . [I]t is unfortunate that the remarkable Somali trading heritage is not focused more effectively on the search for new opportunities abroad. Nor, as I have tried to make clear in the past to my Somali friends, has Somalia done enough to attract foreign business which can be useful in Somali development. . . .

I cannot fail to point out also the question of domestic finances. My own Government, to be sure, is suffering a grave financial deficit. So is yours. My understanding is that in 1985, Somali governmental expenditures have increased while governmental revenues declined. And this too weighs heavily in the question of economic health and donor confidence.

These questions may touch also on the question of national sovereignty. I think the Somali people are second to none in national pride, and they and their Government are naturally sensitive to the question of outsiders trying to dictate to them. I cannot speak for other governments, but my own Government has the highest respect for Somalia's national sovereignty. . . . However, as friends we owe you our best advice, and as donors we owe not only you but ourselves the duty of judging whether our aid is used effectively.

A couple of ministers later said to me privately that my letter had been useful. I had not addressed it to the man who reigned supreme, but probably every recipient had sent him the text. And it had absolutely no effect on his government's policies or practices. I had not expected much result, but I had felt a deep need to send the letter.

It was true that, as the Yugoslav chargé d'affaires had mentioned to me, many Somalis studied abroad. Even if I thought that the United States should do more to educate Somalis, the fact was that we had done a lot. In addition to having practically created the teachers' college at Lafoole, AID had since 1978 been providing to Somalis both short-term training and long-term scholarships at American universities. Lou Cohen told me one day that he and his energetic wife, Barbara, thought it might be fun to give a reception at their house for all these Somalis who had studied in the United States. What did I think of the idea? I said I thought it was a fine idea and only wished I had thought of it myself. I would be happy to attend and to make a few remarks to their guests.

When Scerif drove me over to the Cohens' house for their reception, pretty much on time, I found Lou and Barbara Cohen, several AID Americans, and not a single Somali guest, not even any AID Somali employees, though I knew that most of them had been invited. What was going on? Maybe you didn't notice, Lou said, that there are several NSS [National Security Service] types down at the corner who are stopping all the Somali guests, even our own employees.

Why? No clue. Come on, Scerif, I said. We walked down to the corner, where three thin men in civilian clothes were standing. Does any of you speak English? Italiano? No. All right, Scerif, ask them in Somali what they're up to. The best answer I could get was that they were acting on orders. Whose orders? Couldn't say. No Somalis reached the Cohens' house that evening.

The next day I learned from a reliable source that a certain minister, hearing about the planned reception, had gone to Siad Barre and told him that Cohen was planning to organize an American political movement among Somalis and was about to call an initial organizational meeting. Stop it, said Siad—and they stopped it.

It had now been some time since I had threatened the possibility of cutting off aid over Libyan terrorism. I went to see the foreign minister. I said (not telling him what I had heard about the report to Siad by another minister) that in view of the fact that the police had prevented Somali guests from attending a reception intended to celebrate the cooperation between our two countries, I was considering holding up all our aid programs until I got a satisfactory explanation. I then went back to the embassy and reported to Washington what I had done—and Washington, as in the case of my warning on the Libyans, did not demur.

Two evenings later, the president of the republic invited the American ambassador and all his embassy section heads to a friendly dinner in the garden of Villa Somalia. The president was very sorry about the incident, which was entirely due to the stupidity of some subordinate who had acted without authorization. Of course I accepted his explanation. But none of us forgot for a minute what had happened.[2]

2. Four years later in Mogadishu, a somewhat similar event occurred. The Italian ambassador invited to his embassy's national-day reception the signers of the recent "manifesto" calling for major reforms in Somalia. The police prevented them from attending. Ambassador Sica told the number-two in the foreign ministry that if he did not receive an official apology, he might have to report to Rome that his usefulness in Somalia had come to an end. Sica, pp. 44–45.

Needless to say, not all Somalis were like that. In early 1986 I came to know, and to like, the man who had been the prime minister of Somalia in 1969 when Siad Barre staged his coup. This was a tall gentleman from the north, an Isaq named Mohamed Ibrahim Egal, recently released from prison, where he had spent most of the time since 1969—all of it, in fact, except for a few months. At one point in the 1970s, Siad Barre had released Egal from prison and sent him as ambassador to India. But, Egal told me, he was soon called back from New Delhi on consultation and sent back to prison. Why, Egal was not sure, but he had been told that Siad's Soviet advisers had "whispered in his ear" that Egal was plotting against him in New Delhi.

Siad Barre had a way of sometimes coming to terms with real or potential rivals. After again releasing Egal from jail, in 1986 Siad Barre named him head of a new Somali chamber of commerce. Egal bought a word processor and told me that in his spare time he was writing small pieces about Somali life and ways. I expressed interest, and he gave me copies. Two of his essays, on a Somali Arcadia, I liked very much.[3]

Mohamed Ibrahim Egal wrote that in the old days, Somali pastoral society had been Arcadian, almost idyllic. It had been "what the ecologists in America and the Green movement in Europe are yearning for and missing in their affluent lives." Somalia had never been a wet land, he wrote, but except in times of drought there had been grass enough for the animals. Egal thought that Somali pastoralism had been the ideal form of human life. I could not imagine that life in the Somali lands had ever been quite as idyllic as he said. But from what I knew, he was perfectly accurate in his description of how an explosion in human and animal populations was wreaking havoc:

The people of my own age group have seen in their lifetime the gradual devastation of our pasture lands by overgrazing and soil erosion. It was the fashion those days of my youth to send the children to the interior during the summer months, so that they could drink the health-giving fresh camel's milk. I remember I used to join our *Rer* [a group of several families] in a plain called Aroori only a few miles outside the township of Burco. . . . The plain was very green and it was awesome to

3. Later I found in the Lyndon Baines Johnson Library in Austin an Egal letter that I liked equally well. On April 4, 1968, after visiting the United States, Egal wrote President Johnson that he had found in America "a people who remain uncorrupted by power, who learnt to wear greatness with humility and who found pleasure in service without the rewards of acclaim or praise." I wondered what he would say if ever he returned to Washington.

watch the distant herds of camels and sheep with their image distorted by mirages. We played hide and seek among the tall lush grasses. Today the plain is a frightening desolation and an augury of what is to come.

If I needed any confirmation of Egal's disturbing words, it came in the form of a four-person mission sent to Somalia under the auspices of the Missouri Botanical Garden in St. Louis. They had come to collect succulent plants; the Horn of Africa had been arid country, with some intermittent wetter periods, for tens of thousands of years, and a number of unique species had developed here. One of the mission members was a native of Greece named John Lavranos. He was now an insurance broker in Johannesburg, but by avocation he was a botanist, and he had been visiting Somalia as a botanist for a quarter-century. On his visits Lavranos not only collected plants but put down metal markers that enabled him on succeeding visits to measure the loss of soil. He had a grim tale to tell of how the land had been denuded of vegetation and the soil washed or blown away in many areas of central and northern Somalia. He left me a paper he had written as early as 1970 warning that "in the arid regions of Somalia, pasture destruction and desertification are ever present in every possible phase and their extent is frightening."

Lavranos and I fell into a discussion of goats. I said that in Italy I had hiked through much of the central Apennines. As Lavranos must know better than I, since I thought the situation was much the same in Greece, the Apennines had once been heavily forested mountains. While it was men who had cut the trees, it was goats that had prevented reforestation by eating seedlings and indeed anything green. I thought that goats must be the chief, though not the only, destroyer of vegetation in Somalia. Lavranos agreed. He added that in both Italy and Greece it had taken a dictator to control the goat problem. Both Mussolini and Metaxas had put a lid on the number of goats allowed each village, and the villagers were taxed for any excess. Siad Barre was as much a dictator as the other two had been, but while hard on his compatriots, he had unfortunately done nothing about goats.

Siad Barre had, on the other hand, done something about wildlife. His regime had passed legislation that absolutely banned hunting. It was an ugly sham. Throughout my tour of duty in Somalia, I heard credible tales of invitations to Saudi princes and other notables from Arabian Peninsula states, who in exchange for largess of one sort or another were permitted to come shoot whatever they could find in the Somali hinterland. The tales were credible because I knew a foreign ambassador in Somalia who was permitted to do the same. Well, I was not antihunting, provided a species was not already too scarce. But there was a worse aspect to Siad's two-faced approach.

A European who I believed thoroughly reliable told John Hirsch and me in 1985 that there had been a horrendous slaughter of elephants in southern Somalia during the previous several years. It was hard to estimate what the herd sizes had been, since the animals had sometimes roamed southward over the Kenyan border, but our source thought that perhaps twenty-five thousand elephants had been killed in Somalia, all for the sake of ivory, and all under official auspices. The ivory obtained was officially described as having been brought in by refugees fleeing from Ethiopia; this was done because there was a Somali law permitting the refugees duty-free entry for their possessions, including ivory. But, our source emphasized, the ivory came not from Ethiopian but from Somali elephants. He himself had hiked along one of the long, straight swaths through the forest near the Kenyan border that had been cut in earlier years by seismic exploration crews working for oil companies. The trail, he said, was littered with the carcasses of hundreds and hundreds of elephants, tusks all gone. It was the Somali police that had killed them, with automatic weapons.

Could this really be true? Bill Fullerton, my British counterpart, told me that he had been informed that there was a store of fifty tons of elephant ivory in a government warehouse in Mogadishu, which was being sold off gradually in order not to depress prices. (World ivory prices were then— before the international agreement to halt trade in ivory—at least $150 a pound, making the value of the warehoused ivory at least $15 million.) We could not be sure that elephant herds in the south of the country had ever numbered as many as twenty-five thousand animals, but one of our drivers told me that in the 1970s he had once seen a herd of about four hundred elephants cross the main road between Mogadishu and Kismayu.

We reported all this to Washington. We did not think that remonstrations to the Somali authorities over the killing of wildlife would do any good, but we suggested that it might be worthwhile to brief writers and private organizations on what we had heard. I do not know whether anyone in Washington did so. In October 1990 *Rolling Stone* published an article by Christopher Dickey on elephant slaughter, carried out not by officials in Somalia but by ethnic Somalis in Kenya. Dickey quoted Richard Leakey, then head of the Kenya Wildlife Service, as saying that 98 percent of the elephant poachers in Kenya were of Somali origin. George Adamson, the widower of Joy Adamson, author of *Born Free*, had reportedly called the Somalis the most destructive people on earth, saying that they had turned their own country into a desert and would do the same in Kenya. That was perhaps an exaggerated criticism of a whole people. In any case, I was sorry that nothing was said in print about the slaughter of the elephants carried out, I had no doubt, at the express orders of Mohamed Siad Barre.

Enough animal life remained in Somalia to make for an interesting scene. One of our AID contractors and his wife lived near the edge of Mogadishu; one day the wife answered a knock on her back door and found that a baboon had come to call. As for birds, my wife and I were not experienced bird-watchers, but in Somalia and during one visit to Kenya we added well over a hundred species to our life list. Once on a run at dawn, when I stopped to stretch my tendons, I got hit on the bald spot atop my head. At first I thought some child must have thrown a rock at me, as had happened once before, but then I looked up and saw hovering a big, black kite, *Milvus migrans*, which had been unable to resist a shiny target. There were still a few hippos along the lower Shebeli, where, even when the river stopped flowing in the dry seasons, there would be pools and marshes. At night the hippos came out of the water to eat Somali farmers' crops, and the Somalis killed some of them; in turn the hippos, which could be fast on their feet, occasionally killed a farmer. There was a fascinating bat cave I had walked through, near the beach where we went swimming. And offshore, there were sharks. Still, wildlife numbers had declined sharply from the 1930s, when an Italian guidebook reported that even in the arid northeast of the country game was abundant: dik-diks, gazelles, antelopes, kudus, oryxs, gerenuks, wild asses, boars, rabbits, wildcats, lions, leopards, cheetahs, and other species.[4]

Sometime in 1986 I found that my new Soviet colleague—the florid Mr. Ilichev had been replaced by a more personable ambassador who was not Russian but Uzbek, Bakhadyr Abdurazakov—frequented the Lido beach at dawn as I did, me running and him walking. What would you do, he asked me one day, if you saw someone being attacked by a shark? It was a natural question. The Lido beach had been free of sharks until a few years earlier—my predecessors had swum there—but then Mogadishu's new slaughterhouse had been built nearby, and the offal tossed into the sea attracted many sharks. Yet many Somalis still waded there or even swam out

4. *Guida dell'Africa Orientale Italiana*, p. 617.

some yards. I told Ambassador Abdurazakov that I could not answer the question; I did not know what I would do. Several weeks later, he answered his question for himself. One morning a shark attacked a wading boy and killed him, and the Soviet ambassador stood and watched, feeling helpless to step in—just, I decided, as I would have felt myself.

My wife and youngest son and I still remind each other about our swim one lovely day at the town of Brava, on our way south to Kismayu. We had stopped there with our friends the minister of public works and his wife, who suggested we take a swim while they did errands. They assured us that there were no sharks. The water was clear and cool. After a few minutes we began to see pieces of camel—hooves, a head, other hunks—float by. Someone had slaughtered an animal and tossed the remains in the sea, and there we were cavorting in the waves along with other kinds of shark bait. We went back to the sand in quick time. Later, when I mentioned our Brava swim to my Italian colleague Mario Manca, he offered to lend me a book one of his sons had given him for Christmas. It had been published in South Africa, and it was well illustrated with color photographs. Its title was *Shark Attacks in the Indian Ocean.*

fifteen

To the Horn and Home Again

In December 1985 my wife and youngest son, a dozen friends, and I camped for three days on a white beach sixty miles south of Mogadishu. We were far from any other people, far, it seemed, from the many problems of Somalia. Our Italian friends Gianluigi and Luciana Mutto, whose banana plantation was some miles away, had erected on the beach a big tarpaulin that made a kind of pavilion and kept us all, white and black skinned, from dying of sunburn. We swam and fished and hunted shells and sand dollars under the immense bright sky of day, and at night under the brilliant stars we ate and drank and sang.

At other times it was less easy to forget that one was living in a police state, though it was the Somalis and not the foreign diplomats who suffered under it. I had lived in two northern police states, Czechoslovakia and the Soviet Union, and the thought came to me that at least the Somali police state was less efficient than those. But again, that was little solace to the Somali citizens. The same month as our pleasant camp on the beach, the military police sent press gangs through Mogadishu to round up young men (and some not so young) for military service. Thierry Terrier, the number-two in the French embassy, claimed to have heard on good authority that fifteen youths had been shot down while trying to flee these press gangs. After a day of this, the streets and cafés were free of the usual crowds of idle young men. So the MPs waited a couple of days, and when the young men reappeared, they pounced again. This continued for several weeks.

Like the northern Communist states, Siad Barre ran a legislature that was a farce, the People's Assembly. I went, as did most ambassadors, to one session. It began with a listing by the assembly's president, Mohamed Ibrahim Ahmed, of all the junketing that assembly members had done over the

year—trips to meetings in Bucharest, Inverness, Baghdad, Dakar, Lome—
which, I calculated, must have cost this poor country well over a hundred
thousand dollars—and it wasn't even a real parliament. Most of the diplomatic corps had decided to attend the session because Siad Barre was to
speak. In the end he didn't come, and I left.

The Somali regime also, like the Soviets on November 7 in Moscow,
ran a big annual parade in Mogadishu to mark their equivalent of the Bol-
shevik October Revolution. The Somali parade was held on October 21,
the anniversary of the coup that brought Mohamed Siad Barre to power. In
general I like parades, and this was a pretty good one. Each part of the city
produced a group of marchers and of dancers dressed in traditional cos-
tume, doing fairly intricate steps to drumbeats. After that came military
units and groups of civilians, all of them doing the goose step. I estimated
the number of goose-steppers at about ten thousand people, which was
even more, I thought, than I had seen on a memorable November 7 in
Moscow when my wife and I had watched, from John Steinbeck's room in
the National Hotel, the Soviet military parade in Red Square.

The Somali marchers included units from almost every Somali organization: ministries, university departments, trade unions, cooperatives, firemen, police, militia, and finally the military. After the military units came
the military vehicles: American-made trucks pulling some Chinese-made and
some American-made howitzers; a few aging Fiat and Panhard armored
cars; jeeps carrying 106-mm recoilless rifles (we had finally sent the Somalis
some jeeps that worked); a number of other American trucks towing Soviet-
made missiles with visible rust marks; and finally, twenty old M-47 tanks,
long in the hands of the Italian army and recently rehabilitated and sent
here. I could imagine Ambassador Abdurazakov suggesting to Moscow that
his counterpart in Addis Ababa tell Mengistu he didn't need to worry about
another Somali invasion.

The irritating part of the scene, as far as I was concerned, came from
the bright-colored, uniform clothes being worn by all the thousands of
civilian marchers. A Somali friend had told me a few days earlier that the
state clothing factory had labored for months to produce these uniforms,
which, my friend said, would go on the rag heap right after the parade; no
Somali would think of wearing that parade rig a second time. Yet Siad Barre
had importuned me to provide uniforms and boots for his army, saying that
the "poor fellows" were half naked, he had no money to buy anything, and
his friends didn't want to help. We had decided to help. Many soldiers in

that parade were wearing new American boots and new uniforms made from fabric we had air-shipped in over the last several months. In those same months, Siad Barre's clothing factory had found time and cloth to make all these soon-to-be-discarded uniforms for all these goose-stepping students and officials. I had been tricked, and while it was probably not for the first time, this was a painfully visible trick.

I have mentioned earlier Abdillahi Ahmed Addou, who was minister of the presidency for much of my tour in Mogadishu and who, as such, helped me as best he could in my dealings with the president. Addou had served earlier for ten years as Somali ambassador in Washington, and he returned there as ambassador while I was still in Mogadishu. During his first tour in Washington, his purchase of a house on Foxhall Road for his daughter had reportedly been the second-largest residential real-estate sale in the District of Columbia that year. There was no proof of wrongdoing, but the ambassador had done well for a nomad's son on a Somali official salary. Addou's elegant and attractive wife, Asha, also owned a string of villas in Mogadishu, and she built two large ones near the compound of our Office of Military Cooperation. She tried very hard to get me to rent one for our embassy. She wanted, she said, six thousand dollars a month for either of them, payable in dollars not shillings, please (which would be in contravention of Somali currency regulations). I told her we did not need any large, new villas. Then I heard that she was threatening to rent them to the Libyan embassy; she commented to an American that no doubt the Libyans would find it advantageous to locate near our military compound. That was pure blackmail. I told her husband that if she rented those villas to the Libyans, the Somali government would soon be sorry. In the end, after I had left Mogadishu, she rented one villa to Conoco's new resident manager, Raymond Marchand, a fearless Frenchman who continued to live there, protected by a company of private guards, even after our embassy was evacuated in the chaos of 1991.

Even if we did not need any elegant new villas, we needed at a minimum, as I have explained earlier, new offices. The next piece of concrete that fell through the chancery ceiling might well kill me or a colleague. Aside from that, our embassy was too spread out. Beyond the chancery, the U.S. Information Service offices were in an almost equally shabby building nearby, while both AID and the Office of Military Cooperation were in compounds miles away, which did not make my coordinating efforts easier. Fortunately, Congress had appropriated funds for new construction, and we held a groundbreaking ceremony at the new site on November 19, 1985.

Peter Bridges, Somali finance minister Mohamed Sheikh Osman, USAID director Louis Cohen, and Somali official at unloading of U.S. flour, Mogadishu, March 1986.

The land that the Somalis had given us for an embassy in the 1960s was far more than we would ever need, and the half that had been converted to an international golf and tennis club would remain that. (This pleased my wife, who sometimes liked to wander over the golf course in the middle of the day, when it was little used, with her *Birds of East Africa* and binoculars.)

The half of the compound that we were going to build on held the shells of a half-built chancery building and an equally incomplete ambassadorial residence. After the groundbreaking, the American architect who had won the new State Department contract came to Mogadishu, and we walked over the compound together. I was delighted when he agreed with me that the residence shell ought to be blown up. For one thing, the style was what might be called 1960s American Ugly. But more important from my point of view was the need for our ambassador, and at least some other embassy officers with representational responsibilities, to continue to live in the city itself, not out in this rather isolated compound toward the edge of town. Besides, though I could not argue this with Washington, I enjoyed my view of the great ocean and being able to run on the beach at dawn; nothing could replace that. After my departure, it was decided after all to build a new residence for ambassadors and housing for other staff in the compound. This may have saved lives that day in 1991 when the marine helicopters landed there to evacuate our people. But as I hope I have already made clear, that was not a future I foresaw in 1986.

In the spring of 1986, I told the Department of State that I was going to end my mission in Somalia. I was also going to leave the employ of our government. I had served Mr. Reagan faithfully, but in my view he was doing no better by our country in his second term than he had in his first. I was not quite fifty-four years old, and I thought I was still young enough to find new things to do. Meanwhile, though, I was going off to northeast Somalia with my British colleague Bill Fullerton and his Brooklyn-born wife, Arlene. It being spring, my wife was again working on tax returns in Rome. "I'm sorry you can't come along," I told her.

"Remembering a couple of your trips in earlier years," she said, "I'm not sorry—but be careful."

Fullerton and I had been talking about this trip for some time. In comparing notes one day, we had found that no one in either of our embassies had been to the northeast since Lou Cohen had visited there briefly in 1983, the year before I reached Somalia. There were some modest aid projects there, mostly British; both AID and the Soviets had been involved with aid projects in the area in earlier years. It was a large region, lightly populated and always arid. Information was scanty, but it appeared that the rains of 1985 that broke the drought in the rest of Somalia had not hit the northeast; as of spring 1986, there had apparently been almost no rain in the region for several years. We were under frequent pressure from Somali officials to do more for the northeast, but we wondered what the real needs were.

Besides, on this trip, which we supposed might take a week or more, perhaps we could also have some fun. Some might not call it that. The fun would be to make our way, by whatever means we could find, all the way out to Cape Guardafui and stand at the very tip of the Horn of Africa, as perhaps no ambassador had ever done before—none we had ever heard of, anyway.[1]

I mentioned our plans to Minister of Interior Ahmed Suleiman Abdallah. This was a man who I knew had been responsible, in his earlier post as head of the National Security Service, for a lot of harsh prison sentences and a great many executions. But he also made sense when he talked about foreign aid. I had heard him speak frankly and sharply at the inauguration of a new AID project. He had warned against projects that brought into Somalia technology that the Somalis were not ready to handle, as well as projects whose main aim seemed to be to employ foreign consultants at high salaries. Ahmed Suleiman said that he was glad we were going to the northeast, his own clan territory; he was a Dolbahante. He was not going to give me some exaggerated account of what the region needed; we could judge that

1. Fullerton wrote me subsequently of further such jaunts he made after he had left Somalia and was serving as governor of the Falkland Islands and South Georgia. Later he was British ambassador to Kuwait and to Morocco.

for ourselves. What he would give us was his helicopter, which was up at Bosaso on the Gulf of Aden. Thanks, I said; that would be very useful.

Getting to northeast Somalia was not difficult, at least for us two ambassadors. On March 9, 1986, the Beechcraft of our defense attaché office, piloted by our naval attaché, Capt. Richard Sim, and our air attaché, Maj. Ross Collinsworth, flew Bill and Arlene Fullerton and me to Erigavo, a town inland from Somalia's north coast on the Gulf of Aden. While I was authorized to use the plane for official business, and though it was, as noted earlier, practically indispensable for long in-country trips, I tried to use the plane only on occasions when it would in any case be flying. Today we had as a fellow traveler the visiting desk officer for Somalia from the Defense Intelligence Agency in Washington, making his first trip to the country. Want to go on to the Horn with us? Thank you, sir; I guess not.

Bill Fullerton had meanwhile sent to the north from Mogadishu two Land Rovers with drivers for use after we landed. When we reached Erigavo, we found one Land Rover; the other vehicle had broken an axle on the way north. Ambassador Fullerton quickly enlisted the help of a young German named Manfred Steidel, who headed the aid project at Erigavo, which was sponsored by ActionAid, a private British organization. He provided us a four-wheel-drive Toyota and said that he and his pregnant Somali wife, Habiba, would come along with Bill, Arlene, and me.

Erigavo was a poor but not small town of perhaps forty thousand inhabitants, located in dry country at six thousand feet above sea level. Erigavo had a town generator to provide electricity, but it was broken down. There was a radiotelephone link with Mogadishu; sometimes one could get through. We were briefed by Steidel and his Somali coworkers on ActionAid's projects, mainly the construction of small schools, and then we left Erigavo, happily enough. In the next several days we made our way east toward the Horn. Not far from Erigavo we came to Medishe, a long, narrow valley that contained a strongly flowing stream, irrigated gardens, and some huge and noble trees, resembling sycamores, that I thought must constitute the remnant of an ancient valley forest.[2] The great Sayid, Mohamed Abdallah Hassan, had been living in this green valley in 1920 when British warplanes, a thing he had never seen before, appeared in the air. We met a sheikh from Kulmie, the village at the lower end of the valley, who said that the people had just stood

2. My later inquiries resulted in a letter from Nigel Ede, an Oxfam specialist at Erigavo, identifying them as two kinds of fig, *Ficus salicifolia* and *Ficus granifolius*, known, he said, as *daray* in Somali.

and watched the planes; then the bombs had fallen and killed one of the Sayid's wives. He showed us her large stone tomb on the hillside. The Sayid had later ridden south a hundred miles to his sturdy stone fortress at Taleh, built for him by masons from Yemen. There, as mentioned earlier, he was bombed again by British planes and fled into the Ogaden, where he died.

Our next visit was to a place I had long wanted to see, the only coniferous forest in all of Somalia—indeed, the only forest of any sort, other than the fast-disappearing woods along the Juba River in the south. This forest lay at about seven thousand feet above sea level, on the mountain ridges that rose sharply from the hot, arid coast of the Gulf of Aden. My German friend Martin Florin had told me of coming here two years ago to spend Christmas in a British-era forester's house in the forest. Florin had said that he could almost imagine himself in northern Europe. Could it really be so? Whatever it had once been, the situation was clearly changing, and for the worse, in all this region. It had changed for the worse in the area of high plains that we traversed east of Erigavo. There we met village elders who, with Habiba translating, told us that when they were children—and they looked ancient, but I realized they were probably no older than I—these high plains had been covered with vegetation that was shoulder high. Now it was scanty and at best a foot high.

We were therefore pleased, when we drove up to the high ridges, to find that there really was a forest there, a big-tree forest. The trees were *Juniperus procera*, the African pencil cedar, sturdy conifers up to eighty feet high.[3] The cedars could grow on these ridges because they received up to thirty inches of rain a year. We walked to the north side of the forest and found ourselves on the edge of a cliff two or three thousand feet high; below us, an increasingly arid landscape stretched down to the hot, hazy shore of the Gulf of Aden, six or seven thousand feet below us but not more than fifteen miles away. There were many dead trees in the forest, no young ones, and no ground cover at all. There were animal turds everywhere. Grazing should not have been permitted in such a precious place as this, but it was. Worse, as we learned from the forest supervisor—a certain Hussein, who had a teaching certificate but admitted he knew nothing about forestry—the Ciidanka Asluubta, the prison guard service, had opened a

3. This species reaches over a hundred feet elsewhere in East African mountains. The cedars of the Somali forest have sometimes mistakenly been identified with the cedar of Lebanon, for example in John A. Hunt, *A General Survey of the Somaliland Protectorate, 1944–1950* (London: Crown Agents for the Colonies, 1951), p. 108.

sawmill that fed on these trees. Only on the dead ones, said Hussein. I decided that they would all be dead before many more years passed. Did it matter that a forest died in Somalia, where so much of the land had always been arid, where so many human beings died? Certainly it mattered. It mattered because in this land, which would never be industrialized, people must depend on the land, and the land was being ruined. In places like this, when the vegetation went, the rainfall dropped; from what I knew, this was already happening.

Nor was this simply the fruit of national independence. Overgrazing, with all its evils, had begun under the British before the present century began. By 1951 in British Somaliland, which had an area of about 110,000 square miles, there were at least four million sheep and goats and 1.2 million camels; in contrast, at roughly the same time in Sudan, at least nine times larger, there were relatively fewer grazing animals, 8.8 million sheep and goats and just 1.1 million camels.[4] Once, before overgrazing, there had been no dearth of vegetation; there had been so much vegetation that in British Somaliland there were elephants, big and small antelopes, gazelles, and many other game species. There had been so many lions that even in 1951 a British expert, noting that a pride of five lions had been shot at Erigavo in 1947, could write, "There is no danger of extermination of the lion, and for the sake of the stock-herders as many as possible should be poisoned."[5]

On our way toward the Horn from the sad forest, we saw few wild animals, none of more than modest size: one gerenuk, an occasional small Pelzeln's gazelle, some tiny dik-diks. Elephants and lions were only vague memories and place-names. We drove down the escarpment from the cool heights to the hot coast, stopping to look at the incense trees, which seemed to grow out of the rock itself. We saw many burial mounds, one of them the tomb of Sheikh Isaak (or Isaq), the eponymous Arab progenitor of the Isaq people. Soon we came to the village of Mait. Off the village, six dhows were moored in quiet water. At the edge of the village were two huge dhamas trees, and under the trees were many villagers asleep in the afternoon heat, covered with pink shawls protecting them from flies. We had entered a new Somali world, a seashore world unlike that of the inland nomads, who abhorred the sea, fish, and people who ate fish. We found a place in the village to buy lunch and drank Pepsi Cola bottled in Abu Dhabi. The villagers told

4. C. F. Hemming, "The Vegetation of the Northern Region of the Somali Republic," *Proceedings of the Linnean Society of London* 177:2 (July 1966), p. 193.
   5. Hunt, p. 117.

us that from Mait it was four days by dhow to Aden, nine to Abu Dhabi, and no more than that—sometimes—to Bombay. Bill Fullerton and I looked at each other. Shall we take a dhow? We both thought we would like to. Arlene Fullerton was more doubtful.

From Mait we drove east along the beach and coastal plain. There was no road, but sometimes there was a track. Along the way we saw collections of dead tree trunks, some two feet thick—mountain cedars, I thought, which must have washed down from vanished stands of trees farther inland. Progress was slow. The Toyota kept getting stuck, and the Land Rover, with me at the wheel, would have to tow it out of the soft sand. After five hours and a hundred miles, we came to Las Qoray, a seaside town of two thousand people with an extinct fish cannery that the Soviets had built in 1964 and operated until their break with Somalia in 1978. There was still, incredibly, a fishery payroll of 120 Somalis—what aid program would pay for that?— and a manager who said that the fishing boats had broken down three months after the Russians left. Sand had drifted over the dock; the manager murmured in English, "We really must clear it away." The Romanian embassy in Mogadishu had indicated, he said, that that nation might help refurbish the plant. But from what I knew of Romania's own financial straits, and my talks with the Romanian ambassador, it was clear that nothing would be done. There were still old clippings from *Pravda* on a bulletin board. I slept in a room whose former Soviet inhabitant, no doubt a little bored at times, had decorated a wall with a fresco of two frigates fighting under sail. One of them flew the Russian imperial flag.

We kept driving east along the Gulf of Aden. At Bosaso, then a town of perhaps ten or fifteen thousand people, I found that the mayor had studied for eight years in Prague; we tried our rusty Czech on each other. A little red freighter was standing offshore, and 2,500 tons of Italian rice and cooking oil were being discharged into lighters and brought in close to shore. The lighters were stopping in four feet of water, the crewmen off-loading the sacks of rice and cans of oil onto the shoulders of a couple of hundred men who carried them to land. This was the first I had seen in person of what the new Italian aid program was bringing. Not just rice and oil: there were sixty big, brand-new Fiat trucks on the shore, and from here the Italians were going to build a road inland at a huge cost. But that was not enough for the governor of the Bari Region, Abshir Jama Omar, who approached, and reproached, Bill Fullerton and me separately on what we had not done for his region. The commitments of

Mr. Cohen, he told me, must be carried out! But I knew that Lou had not made any commitments.

Bosaso was also where we were supposed to pick up the interior minister's helicopter to fly east to the Horn. We learned that the helicopter was not here; it was broken down, somewhere in the south of Somalia. What to do? The governor told us that the police had talked to an American pilot who had landed in Bosaso on a charter flight; the pilot would be happy to fly us east as far as Alula. We suspected that the police had leaned on the pilot, who turned out to be a pleasant, bearded man named Les La Bar, from the state of Washington; in any case, La Bar said he would be happy to take us eastward. The next morning he did so, together with his paid passenger, a British geophysicist working on a seismic survey for an oil company.[6]

A memorable flight it was. We flew down the coast at three thousand feet, and there ahead of us was a great mass of rock a thousand feet high that looked to us, coming from the west as we were, like the head and upper body of an elephant. Its Arabic name was Ras Filuk, meaning Elephant Cape; it was without doubt "the headland Elephas" described in that ancient gazetteer, the *Periplus*. Just for fun, our pilot flew us on to Cape Guardafui, and there below us was the rocky Horn of Africa, with the lighthouse the Italians had built right on the point of land. We turned back and landed west of Alula at a little fish cannery that had been built by our AID in the 1960s and was now being renovated, with British aid funds, by a New Zealander then resident in Cyprus, Peter Bromiley.[7] We had good luck there: Bromiley had a small plane and a pilot, who agreed to come for us at 11 A.M. the next morning at Alula to take us back to Bosaso. We flew the several miles from the cannery to Alula, where the police chief and district commissioner greeted us. They had been notified by radio from Bosaso that we were coming and that we wanted vehicles to get to Cape Guardafui. They seemed doubtful about the whole thing but readily handed over their two aging Land Rovers, with drivers. Alula was a not unattractive small port, where dhows were still being built from the wood of the dhamas, a native tree that a Swedish aid team had

6. A decade later Bosaso, which escaped the worst of the Somali civil war, had become a city of over a hundred thousand people, administered by my friend Mohamed Abshir Musse, the former National Police chief, and prospering on trade with Saudi Arabia and the Gulf. See the articles on Bosaso by Stephen Buckley in the *Washington Post*, March 3, 1996, and by Ann M. Simmons in the *Los Angeles Times*, July 9, 1997.

7. Bromiley, who later became an American citizen, had been building and renovating similar installations in Somalia off and on for twenty years, since 1965.

Peter Bridges at
the Horn of Africa,
April 1986.

found to have a high tannin content that helped protect hulls against marine worms.

We started east in the Land Rovers, not knowing how hard it would prove to traverse, on the earth's surface, the forty miles that we had flown from Alula to the Horn and back again. In just over an hour we came to the village of Bereda, where we met with the mayor under a great, spreading dhamas tree. The way east from here, he said, was impassable by any vehicle —but he would provide a boat. Hurrah! My notes go on:

Ferried 2 at a time out to 25-foot diesel open fishing boat. 5 of us + District Commissioner + NSS man, 1 soldier (soldier, with rifle, went all the way with us), 1 policeman, 2 villagers, 3 crew. Lv Bereda—some swell from NE—me on L [left side] got wet (3 of us elegant on cushions & rubber foam mattresses from mayor's house, which got quite wet with spray). Headlands come down near sea. Most of way, a bright green sea—sand bottom, deeper than it looked—clear water. Several times big turtles shot by—several schools of porpoises (always 11 or 12 of them?)—big dark masses that were schools of little fish—also smaller groups of 2-footers. At times sea birds swimming, floating, diving at fish —do we want to develop fishing on this unspoiled coast? Couple of times a big body—first thought it was a ray, but realized these were huge sea turtles which moved faster than I thought. Incense trees growing in clefts on cliffs.

Passed around our Del Monte dried fruit; they gave us hot sweet tea & fresh rolls. At Olloch [village] we went to within 10 yards of rock ledges at land's edge & dropped 2 villagers each with bundles of pos-sessions—first man dropped from side into water over his head, but held bundle high out of water & walked into shallows.

At c. 1420 arrived at Damo village—dozen huts. Arlene discovered later only 9 inhabitants including kid who fled military service. Got boat almost up to ledges, then we waded a few feet in.

1500: started up sandy incline, going around to R of cliffs on L which came to sea edge, & on top of which is I think Cape lighthouse. Arlene & Habiba stopped (A. sick with diarrhea)—in 1/2 hour got up to what I thought was the ridge & near lighthouse—but saw it in far distance. Group: me, WF, Manfred, D.C. (who'd never been here be-fore), 2 villagers, our soldier, & other (NSS?).

Lighthouse from distance looked like had white fence by door—was 2 white buildings. Got to lighthouse c. 1630—stone over door: 1930 Ann. VIII[8]—metal plaque marking 1st two Italian steamship cap-tains who sailed past in Indian Ocean trade—second was Nino Bixio *(deposto la spada per il timone)*.[9]

Light not working—no generator, no fuel—but village people still paid to go "tend" it. Picked up 3 pyramid-shaped marble pieces for MJB, Arlene & Habiba—Walked toward point, sat down sweaty. De-hydrated but the tenders gave us tea (hot, sweet), thank God. Left at 1700.

Hurt my right thigh joint. Way back was hard—came glissading down sandy slope (past goats eating last of vegetation) at 1800-plus. Found Arlene & Habiba. Shark dead on sand, about 8' long, some fish drying. Out to our boat 1-by-1 in a rowboat made basically from 1 log—balance difficult because no keel—sliver of moon descending in West, just about dark as we left at 1847. Moon went quickly down be-hind mountain ahead to L as we chugged W at c. 8 knots. Stars bright but not perfectly brilliant, probably because Arabian sand brought by NE monsoon. Sat on roof of engine housing but got too chill so squinched down next to Arlene & Bill on mayor's mattresses just for-ward of engine, backs to warm bulkhead. The steersman sings some not very melodic song. In the water, star reflections & phosphores-cence in the little waves moving out from our hull—little greenish sparks.

8. 1930 was the eighth year of the Fascist regime in Italy.

9. Bixio was Garibaldi's lieutenant in the struggle for Italian reunification and had "laid down the sword for the rudder."

Arrived Bereda at 2050—flashlights and gasoline lanterns on the beach—boat came in within 10 feet of beach, so off shoes & a bit of wading. Walked to mayor's house—served us pasta with pieces of kid on top—us 5 & D.C. shared dish & used right hand but difficult make a lump of pasta with only R hand so I cheated[10]—dessert canned pineapple—then tea (had served us orange juice to start)—was I thirsty!—from the hike. Mayor talked re island W of Socotra, Abd el Kuri, where their relatives lived. Villagers used to take animals there to graze but could no longer. Bill answered for us: S. Yemen was practically in hands of Russians; he would speak to Soviet ambassador.

At eleven P.M. we were back safe in Alula. The governor had been calling frantically by radio from Bosaso to ask our whereabouts. We had been out of touch with Alula since morning, and the governor was beginning to wonder how he could ever explain to the Minister of Interior the disappearance of two foreign ambassadors. Well, we were back, and we had been to the very Horn of Africa.

The next morning we had several hours free before our plane was due, so we five travelers went off to the beach, together with our soldier with his white, visored cap and AK-47. Just beyond the town was the mouth of a sizable stream. A strong tide, too strong to swim against, was sweeping cold, clear, green seawater up the stream. I let it carry me for fifty yards, waded to the sandy edge, and suddenly saw a very long creature—shark, porpoise, manatee?—go sliding upstream past me. I decided it was time to take to the dry sand, where Arlene, Habiba, and our friendly soldier were playing a game of *tammam*. In *tammam*, twenty-five little holes were made in the sand, and the progress from one hole to another of the pieces—small stones—depended on how several cowrie shells landed after being thrown in the air. I was not a gamesman, and I sat back to enjoy the general scene. Upstream were what looked like mangroves. The stream, I thought, might well be one of the two "laurel groves" that the author of the *Periplus* had described in this area. I could imagine some Roman mariner swimming in this stream.

The sea here was exceptional for the upwelling of cold water from the depths, a phenomenon that produced all the schools of fish we had seen. This was why both AID and the Russians had built canneries on this coast.

10. I am left-handed. With the usual Somali rice dish, I could just manage to roll a little ball with my right hand, as was polite, and eat it. Pasta, however, was impossible, so I cheated and used my left fingers too.

But it was an extremely isolated coast. At the cannery that Peter Bromiley the New Zealander was rebuilding, we had seen his old amphibious landing craft come in bringing a new truck and bulldozer from Mombasa, which was a full fifteen hundred miles from here. I hoped that the cannery would succeed, although it had not when first built. I hoped that it would not fall prey to greedy Somali officials. But if such enterprises were to succeed, they would, I had no doubt, have to be run by foreigners for many years to come. The old Soviet cannery at Las Qoray, its dock drifted over with sand that "we really must clear away," was not a sight that I would ever forget.

The plane came and took us back to Bosaso, where our Toyota and Land Rover were waiting, and we left on the hundred-mile trip southeast to Scusciuban, at first along the rough but passable track that the Italians were, at tremendous expense, going to make into a proper highway. Why? I counted the vehicles we passed in the first twenty-five miles from Bosaso to a place called Carin: a total of two private trucks plus several of the new Fiat trucks from Italy. Marco Panella, who had shamed the Italian parliament into putting up all the aid money, would himself be shamed if he came here—but I doubted he would ever come here.

At Carin we stopped to visit a young Frenchman who was running a date palm project headquartered in an old British army building with the year "1944" above the door. Date palms were an ancient business in this region. There had been a million trees, the governor had told us at Bosaso, but 15 percent of them had died "for lack of water"—which we had thought probably meant lack of care. We judged, from what we saw and the Frenchman told us, that the reduction was actually much greater. The cause had not been disease or lack of demand; it had been a combination of mismanagement under Siad's earlier "scientific socialism" and his continuing interest in subordinating good management to raking off the profits from any economic activity.

The Frenchman gave us tea and watermelon, and in late afternoon we drove out across the great, dry Daror plain, which no European had seen until 1881. It had not rained here for two years. We were driving eastward across a striking landscape, mountains far off to the north and, nearer, barren buttes. Soon a great thunderstorm came up, and it swept over us and washed down all the country. The night came on us quickly as our two vehicles tore along side by side, doing fifty miles an hour across the flat, red, rain-soaked land, a dim line of mountains on our left. Soon we came to the village of Scusciuban, another of the Sayid's old fortresses, where we were to spend the final night of our trip. From Carin, where we had had tea with the young Frenchman, to Scusciuban it was 110 miles, and I had kept on counting trucks. After Carin we had passed just one private truck and two new Fiat ones. I did not think that was quite enough traffic to justify Italy's spending a quarter of a billion dollars—could it really be so?—on the new highway.

It was Friday night, and we had been traveling since the previous Sunday. We were dirty, and I had not changed clothes; everything I had brought with me had been soaked our first day out when a jerry can tipped over. The minister of interior had sent word north that the British and American ambassadors were his guests and were to be accommodated in the official guest houses. That was decent of him, but the guest houses were awful, and when we saw a small, clean hotel in Bosaso, we envied its guests. Scusciuban's guest house was the worst of all, with no fresh water except a trickle going into the toilet, but we still had a bottle of whisky, so we sat and drank that and turned on my little Sony radio. The Voice of America explained that Reagan was insisting on a hundred million dollars for the Contras in Nicaragua; some American commercial station came in clearly and reported that the Dow Jones average was up twenty points in early trading. We laughed. It would be difficult to call one's broker from Scusciuban.

We found, the next day outside Scusciuban, one modest aid project that had succeeded. The American Friends Service Committee, which was still working in this region, had in the 1960s built a kilometer-long canal to bring water from the sizable springs outside the town to fields that could be irrigated. The local people were keeping the canal in good repair and producing sizable harvests. We also visited a warehouse where ten women sat sorting incense. There were ten categories, we were told, and a total of 350 tons—more than I had imagined—was being shipped annually to Berbera for export.

In the afternoon, Dick Sim and Ross Collinsworth picked us up on schedule in the C-12, at the long gravel strip near Scusciuban that the British had built in World War II. We flew to Ras Hafun so that I could take one last look at that great tableland, and then we headed south to Mogadishu, flying at twenty-eight thousand feet past big thunderheads. It was March, still the time of *tanganbili*, but it had rained on the Daror and, God willing, the good *gu* rains would come soon to central Somalia. I said goodbye to the Fullertons, found Kathy Astala at our embassy, and dictated a report on our trip. AID was working on a new Partners for Development project, which was to help fund some small new aid projects run by private agencies in the northeast. This, I told Washington, was the only way to go; the northeast was "an area of extinct or moribund aid projects; nothing requiring more than the simplest maintenance will continue after the end of foreign funding and upkeep."

Then I went home and put on my coffee table the pyramidal piece of pink marble that I had picked up at the Horn. I remembered that when Edward Whymper climbed the Matterhorn in 1865, he found that the very tip of it was a little piece whose shape resembled that of the whole mountain. This piece looked like the Horn of Africa. When I was five, my father once went to Africa, and I asked him to bring me home a little piece of the Pyramids. But he was apparently distracted by business and a near-fatal case of dysentery. Dear Gov, I thought to myself, you never brought me a piece of the Pyramids, but I stole the Horn of Africa.

sixteen

Departure, Return, Destruction

It is an April evening. I am standing on the roof terrace of my house in Somalia, looking out over Mogadishu and the Indian Ocean. We had a good rain today, the first of the year in Mogadishu, breaking the long dry season and the sultry *tanganbili*. I had become confident that it would rain when, the last two days at dawn, I saw rainstorms out at sea. I wonder if it has rained again in the northeast. Although we saw one grand thunderstorm there, we also saw places that had missed the rain, places where there had still been no rain for two long years.

It is cooler this evening, and the air smells fresh. The red bougainvillea flowers on the wall are brighter, washed clean. Behind me, inland, to the west, the sky is black above the horizon where our storm is still continuing. There are just a few signs of red; the sun is quickly going down.

On the roof of the house next to mine sit two black kites. They take off and soar across my neighborhood, beating their graceful wings. A pied crow is sitting on the wall of the embassy of Djibouti, across the lane. One sacred ibis flies over me bound for his haunts in the Shebeli Valley. Until three weeks ago the ibises came over in Vs of twenty and thirty birds, flying to the coast and out to sea at dawn and flying back to the river at night. Now it has rained in the Shebeli, and there are more things to eat there.

In the sandy lane below me, some skinny teenagers are walking home from soccer on the beach. A six-year-old in a faded green dress trips and sprawls in the sand. Her smaller brother toddles on, heedless.

Little waves are breaking slowly over the reef at the Lido beach. Farther out, four freighters are lying at anchor off the port. One is Yugoslav—I saw the name through my binoculars—and it has been there several days, probably waiting on a new destination. Far, far out at sea, a hundred miles out, new thunderheads are building. The thought comes to me that like that ship, I too am waiting on a new destination. I have resigned my commission—enough of diplomacy. I did try to be diplomatic in the formal letter of resignation that I sent to President Reagan on April 18. I wrote him that "I have served the United States Government for thirty years under seven presidents, and I believe the time has come for me to leave the federal service. I am very grateful to you for entrusting to me the embassy at Mogadishu. I am also grateful for the leeway which has been given me in conducting our relations here, which I trust it is considered I put to good use."

April 1986 was a busy month. A team of Foreign Service inspectors descended on us for one of the inspections carried out on a fairly regular basis at each American embassy. I was within two months of leaving government service, yet I naturally hoped their report would be positive. All in all it was, and certainly very positive about me. John Hirsch and some other officers also came out well. But the report also found that our embassy's ability to carry out its responsibilities had been undermined by "the sending of inexperienced, undermotivated or problem-plagued personnel to this isolated, maximum hardship post." That was partly true. But it was also true that most of the Americans in the Mogadishu embassy had worked hard, long, and skillfully at what our government wanted us to do in Somalia. And I knew that I myself could have done much more to bring them together, encourage them, help them do their jobs better. In any case, that was now the past. In the future, in five more years, though we could not know it then, there would be no post at all.

Just before I left Mogadishu, in May 1986, I sent a final telegram to the State Department, a cable that was widely distributed in that department and in other agencies. It was pessimistic and frank; I feared that Africa might be facing a hopeless future, "not least because the Africans have come to depend on the donor countries for their salvation—and the donor countries offer food aid which must someday fall short, and project aid which does not reverse this general progression toward disaster. In Somalia . . . the government comes begging to the aid trough and we fill it. We have led them to a new dependence, not to independence." I still thought, I said, that we should consider redirecting our entire aid program, to give much more aid to education. The aid money we put into Somalia could give every child in Somalia an adequate education—and in fields where trained people were lacking. I told Washington that in retrospect I was sorry that I had not pushed the Somali leadership harder on behalf of political prisoners; what I had done, I had done without instructions from Washington. I hoped, I said, that I was right in thinking that we were finally getting into a position of consistent support for human rights in every country: in Ethiopia and in Somalia; in Communist Poland and in NATO Turkey; in Russia, China, and South Korea; in South Africa and Liberia and Zaire.

I went back to Washington and turned in my papers in June 1986. The director general of the Foreign Service, George Vest, kindly had me in for tea; he gave me two flags, one of them the Stars and Stripes, the other the blue flag of an ambassador. I was happy to be home, and I looked forward to a new life outside government. But I had not had a long tour in Somalia, and I was sorry that I would never have another chance to see that poor, sunny country and its proud people.

Somewhat more than two years later, on a night in November 1988, I found myself southbound from Cairo on a new Airbus that the Europeans were trying to lease or sell to bankrupt Somali Airlines. The plane was being flown by the chief pilot of Airbus Industrie, a lean and amiable Frenchman, and by the equally lean and amiable chief pilot of Somali Airlines, whom I had met and flown with on past occasions. They invited me to come to the cockpit. The plane was on automatic control, and I sat in the pilot's seat. It was very quiet there in the front of the plane. We were floating down the Red Sea at thirty-five thousand feet on a cloudless night with a full moon. Arabia was dim on the left and all of Africa was on the right, and we were bound for the Land of Punt.

I was bound there because I had joined a major oil company in Houston, and I was accompanying my boss to Somalia, where he would sign a new exploration contract with the Somali government. In a number of companies, including ours, the geophysicists were now better equipped to analyze data, and in the wake of large new oil finds in Yemen, they were taking a new look at prospects in Somalia, where over sixty dry holes had been drilled in earlier years. In 1985 I had visited two of these dry holes myself at Afgoi on the Shebeli River, a World Bank project that at first seemed to have good prospects.

As we flew toward Mogadishu in 1988, I was concerned that my participation in this trip should help and not hurt my new company. We were to meet with Mohamed Siad Barre, who was still in power, despite my predictions when I was ambassador—and despite the serious injuries he had suffered in a highway accident just after I left. U.S. aid levels had dropped considerably in the two years since I had left Somalia, and Siad Barre was perfectly capable of blaming me for that. When we arrived in Mogadishu, however, the president sent word that he was pleased I had come; and Mohamed Ali Samantar, now serving as prime minister, called me his friend. Why not? The Somali leaders clearly hoped that oil revenues might in the end make things right for Somalia. Perhaps, someday, they can at least help to do so. But by the time I returned briefly to Mogadishu in 1988, things were turning more and more wrong. Two well-known scholars in America had already warned, the previous year, that a potentially catastrophic civil war was brewing in Somalia.[1] The Isaq revolt in the north had intensified, and Siad was increasingly using force against the Isaqs. Most of Hargeisa's population of several hundred thousand had fled into the countryside. More and more, Siad was turning inward for support, to his own Marehan clan and military entourage; he had tried recently, without success, to gain other clans' recognition of one of his sons as his eventual successor. In the new government that he had named in January 1988, Marehans were ministers or deputies in all ministries where money was to be made.

We signed our contract and began preparations to drill our first exploration well up near Ras Hafun—oil companies and embassies were staying in Somalia as long as they could. As noted earlier, one oil company manager stayed on, in the elegant villa that Asha Addou had tried to blackmail me into renting, even after our own and other companies suspended operations and all the embassies were evacuated.[2] Eventually the teenaged "technicals" with big guns made the situation hazardous for any resident of the capital and impossible for any foreigner. It was no clan but simply savagery that won the day.

The years from 1992 to 1994 brought a remarkable series of efforts by the United States, and then by the United Nations, to save Somali lives and prevent Somalia's civil war from destroying a state that had existed for more than three decades. These efforts saved many human lives. They failed to save the Somali state. My deputy in Somalia, John Hirsch, and Robert Oakley, who had been my predecessor as ambassador there, played key roles in these efforts, which occurred during the Bush and Clinton administrations, and they later provided an objective and detailed account in their *Somalia*

1. David D. Laitin and Said S. Samatar, *Somalia: Nation in Search of a State* (Boulder, Colo.: Westview Press, 1987), p. 161.
2. Still later, this villa was to become Bob Oakley's base when he returned to Mogadishu as George Bush's special envoy.

and Operation Restore Hope.[3] John Bolton, who had been assistant secretary of state for international organization affairs during the Bush administration, furnished, in *Foreign Affairs*, an equally valuable, sharply critical account of our "Wrong Turn in Somalia."[4] Let me provide here a few more details of what happened.

By 1989 it was clear that Siad Barre had been unsuccessful in putting down the revolt of the Isaq clans in the north, despite his brutal methods, which had killed thousands of unarmed civilians and caused the United States to end arms deliveries to Somalia that year. He was also losing the allegiance of other clans. When he arrested his defense minister, Aden Abdullahi Nur, whom I had known and admired when he was vice minister, Aden Nur's Ogadeni clansmen rose up in the south. In June of 1989 Siad Barre executed the leaders of demonstrations against his regime that took place in Mogadishu. The leaders were from the Hawiye group of clans, the largest group in and around Mogadishu. The Hawiye had stayed neutral in the civil strife, but now they turned against Siad Barre, and the fighting spread to Mogadishu. In May 1990 over a hundred brave Somali leaders signed a manifesto that called on Siad Barre to reform or step down. He did neither.

A new American ambassador, Jim Bishop, arrived in Mogadishu in September 1990, together with his wife and youngest daughter. Bishop had, as described above, been the deputy assistant secretary of state, responsible for East Africa, when I first went to Mogadishu; recently he had served as ambassador to another country falling into chaos, Liberia. Within ten days of their arrival in Mogadishu, Bishop's wife and daughter were terrorized by a group of Somali brigands. There was still an oversized embassy community, 147 persons. Bishop's predecessor, Frank Crigler, had recommended sharp staff reductions a year earlier, but Washington agencies had resisted, arguing that they needed to maintain staff levels to meet unspecified contingencies and hold out for a better day in Somalia. By 1990 it was finally clear to all that aid projects could no longer function, and they were abandoned. David Rawson, who served as American chargé d'affaires in Somalia for a year before Crigler's arrival, has written in his *The Somali State and Foreign Aid* that other countries' aid agencies as well as our own, however determined

---

3. Published in Washington, D.C., by the United States Institute of Peace Press, 1995.

4. *Foreign Affairs* 73:1 (January–February 1994). Other recent works on Somalia vary in reliability. For example, one can read that Oakley left his post as ambassador in 1982, expelled by Siad Barre for having raised the question of political prisoners. In fact, as I have written, he left in 1984 not because he raised the question of political prisoners—I was the one who did that—but because he was wanted for a new job in Washington.

to do good—or at least to disburse assistance allocations—never could quite understand that their agendas were not that of Mohamed Siad Barre:[5] "The central aim of Siyaad's government was to retain power through the crafty exercise of central authority, not to rationalize the economy or to reconcile social divisions."[6]

Finally, in November 1990 the American official staff was reduced, and dependents were sent home. In January 1991 the situation in the capital had become impossible, and Ambassador Bishop, our remaining embassy staff, a number of other foreign aid workers, and the chiefs of ten other foreign diplomatic missions and their staffs—including the Russian—were evacuated in two large marine helicopters from our new embassy compound. Three weeks later, Mohamed Siad Barre himself finally fled Mogadishu, southbound, with a column of followers.

Most Mogadishu residents stayed, willingly or unwillingly. Just before the American evacuation, my driver and friend Scerif handed over his life savings in U.S. dollars to an officer of our embassy, who Scerif supposed would carry the money with him safely out of Somalia. Instead, the officer locked Scerif's dollars in an embassy safe. Not long after the last helicopter had taken off from the compound, Somalis blew open all the safes there, and that was the end of Scerif's savings. Other Somali employees of ours fared worse. Bishop had asked Washington to order an airlift out into the relative safety of the countryside of employees and their families who had gathered in the embassy compound. Washington turned him down. After the last Americans had flown away, a number of these Somali employees and their relatives were murdered in the compound.[7]

In the northwest, the Isaqs declared an independent Somaliland Republic, which no other government has recognized, and began to seek a better future, as did the inhabitants of the northeast regions. But in Mogadishu, two leaders from the Hawiye group of clans, Ali Mahdi Mohamed of the Abgal subclan and Mohamed Farah Aydid of the Habr Gedr, soon emerged as rival "warlords," and carnage mounted. I had, parenthetically, a slight acquaintance with Ali Mahdi, whom I knew as a prosperous businessman; I had last seen him when I dined in 1986 at his small hotel, together

5. David Rawson, *The Somali State and Foreign Aid* (Washington, D.C.: Foreign Service Institute, U.S. Department of State, 1993).

6. Ibid., p. 121.

7. See James K. Bishop, "Escape from Mogadishu, 1991," in *Embassies under Siege*, ed. Joseph G. Sullivan (Washington, D.C.: Brassey's, 1995), pp. 149–66.

with a Somali minister. It is still difficult for me to comprehend how five years later he began to play the role he did.

In the months after Siad Barre fled from Mogadishu, the situation in the ex-capital grew increasingly tense as the two warlords prepared for war against each other. A bloody battle for control of the city began in November 1991. Early in 1992 the United Nations, under its new secretary-general, Boutros Boutros-Ghali, began to consider multilateral action in Somalia. In April the UN Security Council authorized a limited humanitarian operation including fifty unarmed observers. By midyear, hundreds of thousands of Somalis were dead or dying from starvation, disease, and plain murder.

In August, as I was told at the time by a reliable source, George Bush decided that continued American inaction in the Somali crisis could injure his chances for reelection as president that November; his Democratic challenger, Bill Clinton, was including our lack of action in his list of Bush's sins in foreign policy. Bush ordered an immediate U.S. military airlift of food and medicines to Somalia—so immediate that it began before our embassy in Nairobi had obtained the necessary permission to use Kenyan airfields.

The United Nations had carried on many peacekeeping operations around the world since the 1940s, with the consent of the parties principally involved. Somalia was presenting a different challenge. UN operations in other parts had aimed to keep peace between sovereign states—Israel and the Arab nations, India and Pakistan, for example—once fighting stopped. In the case of Somalia, the fighting had not stopped, and it was not a conflict between countries; it was civil war. The question was therefore one of peacemaking before peacekeeping and of international involvement in the internal affairs of what was still recognized as a sovereign country. There was a recent precedent for such interference, as John Bolton pointed out in *Foreign Affairs:* in 1991 the Security Council, condemning Iraq's attacks on its Kurdish population, for the first time had found that a government's repression of its own people could constitute a threat to international peace and security.

By late 1992 the Security Council had decided, with American support, to send troops to Somalia, beginning with a battalion from Pakistan, which arrived in October. Toward the end of the Bush administration, the United States proposed to the UN the deployment in Somalia of thirty thousand troops from member states, including the United States. This Operation Restore Hope would not have a mandate to make peace, but the troops would be prepared to use force to achieve their objective, which would be to stabilize the situation so that humanitarian foreign aid could flow into Somalia. The Security Council agreed. The first American troop contingent landed at Mogadishu in December 1992, a month before Clinton's inauguration as president, as part of the new international force known as UNITAF.

Clinton entered office in January 1993 after an election campaign in which he had called for an American policy of "assertive multilateralism." It was clear that he wanted to see the United Nations active in peacemaking as well as traditional peacekeeping, in Somalia now and presumably elsewhere later. In March, the Security Council passed a resolution, urged by Washington, that called on the UN special representative for Somalia to take on added responsibilities "for the consolidation, expansion, and maintenance of a secure environment throughout Somalia." The remaining months of 1993 showed that Clinton and the UN had taken on a task they were unable to handle, although UNITAF forces in Somalia reached a total of over thirty-eight thousand, two-thirds of them Americans and the rest from a total of nineteen countries.

In June, forces under Aydid's control killed two dozen members of the Pakistani contingent in Mogadishu. The Security Council authorized the arrest of those responsible, without naming Aydid specifically. Jonathan Howe, a retired American admiral who was serving as the UN special representative, declared loudly that Aydid was a war criminal who would be brought to justice and offered a twenty-five-thousand-dollar reward for Aydid's capture. But Aydid was never caught. On July 12, American helicopter gunships fired down into Aydid's command center in Mogadishu. Aydid was unharmed, but the Somalis later said that the attack had killed seventy people, many of them tribal elders—and it was the elders, most people thought, who could negotiate peace, if anyone could. It reminded me of the time in 1984 when, with Lebanon in turmoil, the battleship USS *New Jersey* stood off Beirut and fired sixteen-inch shells into the hills, perhaps hitting some Syrian missile sites but certainly killing a number of innocent Lebanese civilians.

Somali sentiment turned strongly against the foreign troop presence in Mogadishu. Habr Gedr clansmen who had not been supporting Aydid now turned to him. In October 1993 at least eighteen Americans were killed in a Mogadishu firefight, and a dead American marine was dragged naked through the streets. This was perhaps not just the doing of Somalis: the Saudi terrorist Osama bin Laden recently told an American interviewer that he sent a contingent of his men into Mogadishu at the end of 1992.

One of these boasted to the interviewer that he had slit the throats of three American soldiers in Somalia.[8]

In any case, the televised pictures from Mogadishu were not ones that American television watchers, or the U.S. Congress, wanted to accept. Moreover, Hirsch and Oakley note bluntly, as the situation in Mogadishu worsened "the Clinton Administration provided little explanation to the public or Congress."[9] In the end, Clinton pulled back from "assertive multi-lateralism," a policy that, as John Bolton has written, died an early death in Somalia. The last American troops left Somalia in March 1994, and the remaining UN contingents followed in the ensuing months. The civil war continued, and although it did not again reach the horror levels of 1992, there has been no lasting resolution to the quarrels of Somali clans, and today the country remains divided, with a shattered infrastructure and no central government. In 1992 I. M. Lewis opined that Somalia's best chance lay in reestablishing the authority of the traditional clan elders.[10] The elders, it seems, agreed. More than one agreement on national reconciliation has been negotiated between Somali groups—and has then been broken.

As in Lebanon a decade earlier, American actions in Somalia ultimately caused our friend and ally Italy serious disillusionment with American leadership. Italian defense minister Fabio Fabbri complained that the United States did not know how to calibrate the use of force in Somalia. It used too little force in the beginning, when there were thirty thousand American troops in the country, and later it used too much in trying to get rid of Aydid, with the result that a humanitarian mission turned into urban warfare.[11] The Italians were themselves far from blameless, inter alia conducting separate negotiations with Aydid, which weakened UN effectiveness. After four Italians were killed in July 1993, the commander of the Italian contingent, Gen. Bruno Loi, publicly disagreed with UN policy and announced that he would take orders only from Rome. Somalia caused fierce domestic debate, as well as criticism of the United States and the United Nations, inside Italy.[12] Subsequently, the media in Italy and in Canada revealed that troops from both countries had been guilty of atrocities against Somali civilians.

8. John Miller, "Greetings, America, My Name Is Osama bin Laden," *Esquire*, February 1999.

9. Hirsch and Oakley, p. 158.

10. Ioan Lewis, "In the Land of the Living Dead," *London Sunday Times*, August 30, 1992.

11. Fabbri was quoted in "Dropping the Ball?" *Time*, May 2, 1994.

12. See Angelo Del Boca, *La trappola somala* (Roma: Laterza, 1994).

Peter Bridges, SIDAM director Ibrahim M. Abyan, and USIS director Thomas Hull, at the ambassador's residence, Mogadishu, February 1985.

Operation Restore Hope did not live up to its name. The Somali debacle and Clinton's change of heart left the United States and the international community as a whole no closer than they had been to devising effective ways to restore peace to countries that, like Somalia, had blown apart.

The question remains whether the United Nations might have brought about a peaceful Somalia by sending a still greater force to disarm completely the warring Somali factions. This would have required a kind of determined American leadership that neither Bush nor Clinton provided. Such a force, as Hirsch and Oakley have written, "would almost certainly have become embroiled in a series of local clashes, both small scale and with large militias."[13] Yet such an effort might well have succeeded, if at the cost of more deaths among both peacemakers and Somalis, and it might have led to more success in efforts to prevent the disintegration of states elsewhere in Africa.

It would be difficult to exaggerate the dimensions of the Somali tragedy —the numbers of humans dead, the amount of property and infrastructure destroyed, the hatred engendered. I have no idea how many Somali friends and acquaintances of mine have lost their lives. I do know of one, a brave and honest man named Ibrahim Mohamed Abyan, who was murdered early in

13. Hirsch and Oakley, p. 104.

the civil war. Abyan headed SIDAM, the Somali Institute for Development Administration and Management, which received funding from the World Bank. Abyan would come sometimes for lunch or dinner at my house, most often with others, and our conversations on these occasions tended to be polite and general. But sometimes in the morning I would walk over to see Abyan at SIDAM, and he would tell me how (as I have mentioned above on page 135) he and his small group of fellow Darods were planning secretly for a better and democratic future once Mohamed Siad Barre left the scene. Whether the president eventually found out what Abyan was up to and had him killed, I do not know. He may have been an incidental victim of the violence. I will always remember him as one of the best of his nation.

seventeen

What Comes Next?

I have never returned to Somalia since the civil war erupted. Perhaps I never shall. But my last time there did not conclude my acquaintanceship, indeed my friendship, with Somalia or with Africa. In succeeding years I got to know well, and to like well, a country on the other side of the continent from Somalia, the Republic of Cameroon. I joined the African Studies Association, took part in its annual meetings, and found money from several oil companies to publish the proceedings of the first International Congress of Somali Studies, which had been held some years earlier. I wrote a little about Africa, warning in one article in 1987 what others have repeated more recently, that the specter of population explosion in Africa was being replaced by the specter of mass deaths from AIDS.[1] Very little that I saw in, or learned about, Africa made me more optimistic than I had been when I first went to Mogadishu in late 1984.

One can easily get into deep philosophical waters, if not deep polemics, talking and thinking about Africa. Americans, and Europeans, sometimes beat their breasts over Africa, lamenting that the industrialized world did not provide more, or more effective, aid to the sub-Saharan countries over the last half-century. Scholars, like Jared Diamond in his recent *Guns, Germs, and Steel*,[2] are still seeking better answers to the fundamental question of why Africans remain far behind the industrialized world in wealth and power decades after throwing off colonial domination. We would all like to know how we went wrong in Africa—if we did—as well as how the Africans have gone wrong—if they have—and what can be done in the future to create a better and more balanced world, both North and South.

1. "AIDS Now Worst Threat to Africa," *Los Angeles Times*, August 30, 1987.
2. Published in New York by W. W. Norton, 1997.

I think few people doubt today that in the decades after World War II a lot of money that was thrown at Africa—not just the Horn of Africa but most of the continent—under the guise of developmental aid resulted in absolutely no development. John Updike's bitter and funny 1978 novel *The Coup* contains much truth about the contest between the Capitalist West and the Communist East to see who could pour more aid into Africa for essentially political reasons. If I am not mistaken, it was Henry Kissinger who once said that Angola had become the main focal point of our confrontation with the Soviet Union—and saying it was so to some extent made it so.

The Europeans made as many mistakes as the Americans in aid to Africa; I have mentioned an example or two. Also, the Chinese made as many mistakes as the Soviet Union did. By the time I reached Somalia, the Chinese had become disillusioned with the Somali ability to carry through with Chinese-sponsored development projects, for instance the large rice project on the Juba River. But China had also been disappointed in its aid projects elsewhere in Africa, such as the Tanzara railroad, which Tanzania and Zambia proved unable to maintain properly.

Today—this is written in 1999—the African economic and political scene is mixed. The State Department likes to emphasize that in the last decade most sub-Saharan countries (forty out of forty-eight, according to the Department) have begun a process of democratization. That is well and good, but at the same time a number of sub-Saharan countries, including some of the forty, have come apart. Countries like Angola, Congo, Liberia, Sierra Leone, and Sudan have suffered such turmoil that they have won places on the only list where Somalia stands in first place: the list of failed states.

On the economic side, countries (like Cameroon) that a decade ago had bright hopes for the future have suffered terribly from low world commodity prices, for they have little to sell, at least for now, except basic commodities like petroleum, cocoa, coffee, palm oil, and tea. Nor, to take Cameroon again as an example, has it been possible to create nearly enough new jobs to employ the masses of young people coming into the workforce. This may change. In 1996 annual output growth reached 4.3 percent in sub-Saharan Africa, surpassing the population growth rate for the first time in a decade. Although African growth in 1998 was down to 3.7 percent, this was still the highest growth rate for any world region.[3] Many governments in sub-Saharan Africa have carried out economic reforms, liberalizing prices,

3. "African Policy Outlook 1999," Africa Policy Information Center, Washington, D.C., available on the Internet at http://www.africapolicy.org/docs99/afpo99.htm.

privatizing state companies, and reducing trade barriers and government expenditures. As two World Bank authors have pointed out, it is only in countries with good economic policies that aid can spur growth; the raw correlation between aid and growth is near zero.[4] But if the ultimate effect of such reforms is to improve economies and living standards, the early effect may be to increase unemployment and unrest—as happened in Siad Barre's Somalia.

Much of what has been happening in sub-Saharan Africa has happened without direct reference to the United States of America. Many American voters still believe that the United States spends enormous amounts on foreign aid, and few politicians or journalists try to correct this totally wrong belief. U.S. aid to developing countries is at a fifty-year low. The United States provides, as official development assistance, just eight hundredths of 1 percent (0.08 percent) of its gross national product. This is less than a quarter of the average contribution of industrialized countries.[5] And only about a tenth of U.S. assistance goes to sub-Saharan Africa. American giving to multilateral bodies, like the International Development Association of the World Bank, which lends to Africa on concessional terms, has also dropped. Perhaps the best thing that can be said about current American developmental assistance is that we, and the world, have learned some lessons. Above all, we have finally learned that, in general, small is beautiful—or, better said, more likely to succeed. The days of building big dams and of grandiose projects that functioned only as long as there were foreign technicians to run them are over.

I would still like to see the United States spend a greater part of its aid budget on African education, but in sub-Saharan countries we have helped produce what are now sizable cadres of educated people. We have learned to build on traditional African ways of farming, rather than trying to teach Africans totally alien ways. We have finally heeded what Bishop Colombo was trying to tell the aid providers in Somalia over a decade ago—provide sturdy equipment that villagers can use and repair—and what the Chinese, among Somalia's aid donors, may have been the first to realize: design things

4. See "Making Aid Work," *The Economist*, November 14, 1998.

5. News release from the Development Assistance Committee, Organization for Economic Cooperation and Development, July 19, 1998. In 1946–48, when the United States was concentrating on the reconstruction of Europe, our foreign aid was in relative terms twenty-five times higher, 2.1 percent of GNP. See David A. Baldwin, *Foreign Aid and American Foreign Policy* (New York: Frederick A. Praeger, 1966), p. 26.

like hospitals only after you have studied how people move, act, and work. Not least, the United States has learned to focus on African women. I have known impressive women both in Somalia and in Cameroon, and I think Madeleine Albright was exaggerating little if at all when she said, speaking of the empowerment of African women, "This is how social progress is made and how peace and prosperity are built."[6]

While the level of American developmental aid has dropped, the American effort in humanitarian relief to Africa has been greater in recent years than it was a decade ago. It seems that America will continue to provide its share, or more than its share, to save Africans from the recurring famines brought by drought, overpopulation, and the strife that, as I have suggested earlier, may itself result from economic hard times. But saving human life can be much easier than ensuring human development and prosperity. In Somalia, as in many other parts of Africa, many people will continue to live in misery for many years. I will not see this change much in my lifetime.

Whether there is any chance of the Somalis again achieving national unity is another question. Some parts of the country may not need national unity to achieve a degree of prosperity. As noted, this has been the case in the northeast of Somalia. But without a new central authority, there may be no way to contain tribal fighting—which went on to some extent even when there was, under Siad Barre, not just a central authority but a police state. Without a central Somali authority, Somali warlords have been drawn into the conflict between neighboring Ethiopia and Eritrea. Furthermore, without peace and order established by a central authority, it will be difficult at best for Somalia to attract much foreign aid and foreign investment. And even if foreign aid and investment should someday again flow into Somalia, we would face again the problem that I posed in my farewell cable to the State Department in 1986, that of foreign money leading the Somalis to a new dependence, not to independence.

Meanwhile, in November 1998, a decade after the Isaq clans of the northwest declared the constitution of a Somaliland Republic, five regions in the northeast announced the creation of a Puntland State of Somalia, with its capital the town of Garoe. This is not a tiny grouping; Puntland's organizers claim a population of 2.4 million. They say they are open to the possibility of overall Somali reconciliation and reunification, but the formation of this second semi-state would not seem to aid such a process.

6. Address by Secretary of State Albright at George Mason University, March 19, 1998. Text as released by the Department of State.

There is another serious problem in Africa alongside those of democratization, inadequate aid and investment, and civil war. This is the problem of international borders. The boundaries of Somalia established by the colonial powers—for European, not Somali reasons—left a number of Somalis outside the new republic in 1960, but at least inside the country almost all the population was Somali in language and culture. Elsewhere in Africa, the European-established borders that are still in force cut across ethnic and linguistic lines, and across what are in geographic terms natural economic units. At a minimum, such borders impede progress. Decades ago, the Organization of African Unity decided that the newly independent African republics should live within their present boundaries, since the alternative was war. The OAS decision was wise, and it was widely supported. But time proved that differences would out. Recent strife in Africa has to some extent been contained within borders, but the recent horrific events in Rwanda and what was Zaire make clear that such borders may not stand.

In Africa, as elsewhere, the basic nature of conflict is sometimes masked by a political or ideological coating. That has not been the case in the civil wars in Liberia or Sierra Leone, but it happened in our own country as we neared civil war in 1860, and it has happened more recently in, for example, Angola. For years we insisted that by supporting the UNITA rebels in Angola we were fighting a good ideological fight against the Soviet-supported government in Luanda. Now the East-West confrontation is over in Angola, we have long since recognized the central government, and UNITA is still fighting. Indeed, the situation in Angola grew so dreadful in 1999 that the United Nations decided to abandon its efforts at bringing the country back together, after an expenditure of $1.5 billion and the deaths of a number of staff members. Conflicts like that in Angola are basically ethnic, not ideological, conflicts—and their number rises. If civil wars or international wars in Africa lessen further the number of functioning states, the prospects for a better African future turn worse.

We do not need to be utterly pessimistic about Somalia, or about Africa. If we do not see again a centralized Somali republic, we may see sometime a looser kind of Somali federation, but one with enough authority to promote development and prevent a return to bloody strife. I see reason to hope that before my grandchildren have reached my present age, the African population will have stopped growing—principally, I hope, because of decreased fertility rates and not because of AIDS and other plagues. We will perhaps by then have reduced the economic differences between North

Mary Jane and Peter Bridges
and their first grandchild,
Amanda Bridges, Colorado 1990.

and South. We will have learned to reduce pollution around the world even as economies grow and to ensure that this growth is sustainable and not ravaging. We will, in short, have answered Andrew Marvell's complaint of three centuries ago that of all creatures it is only man, superfluously spread, that builds such unproportioned dwellings. Unfortunately, much more strife will meet us, and not just in Somalia, along the road to that happier future. We must expect in coming decades more years of two spears than of two milkings. I have recounted in chapter 15 how in 1986 we drove across the great Daror plain in northeastern Somalia into a blue-black thunderstorm. There had been no rain on the Daror for two years, and we hoped for a downpour. But all we knew was that the way ahead was dark; we did not know whether we would eventually come into a country freshened by good rain—or one deceived and more desperate after wind and a few drops. So it was, and is, in Africa.

Hadal oday been ma aha. What an old man says is no lie.

appendix

Somalia through the Ages

This is an updated and expanded version of the summary mentioned on page 154, which I prepared in Mogadishu for members of the American community and others. I benefited considerably from a memorandum on the course of U.S.-Somali relations (Historical Research Memorandum No. 1448) that the Office of the Historian in the State Department prepared at my request in June 1985. This appendix does not pretend to be authoritative. Islamic dates are rendered in Western equivalents.

Presumably, very early humans lived in what is now Somalia, as they did in nearby Ethiopia and Kenya. No remains of such humans have, however, been found yet in Somalia. The 1980s excavations by Dr. Steven Brandt of the village meeting-place at Buur Eibi reached a stratum of human occupation of about ten thousand years ago. Cave paintings in northern Somalia go back some thousands of years.

ca. 1478 B.C. Reliefs from the reign of Queen Hatshepsut of Egypt show expeditions to the Land of Punt, perhaps Ras Hafun in northeastern Somalia.

ca. A.D. 100 *The Periplus of the Erythraean Sea*, a gazetteer of the Red Sea and Indian Ocean, probably written by a Roman citizen of Greek origin, describes the Somali coast in some detail.

2d century Ptolemy, writing his *Guide to Geography* in Alexandria, describes the Somali coast in further detail, including the *statio* and *emporium* of Sarapion, which may have been Mogadishu.

ca. 700 Suleiman and Said of Muscat are said to have risen against the Caliph and to have then fled to "Zinj," perhaps the Somali coast.

ca. 920 The seven brothers of El Hasa, probably Arabs fleeing from the Arabian Peninsula, are said to have founded (or refounded?) Mogadishu and Brava.

10th or 11th century Sheikh Ismail Jabarti, traditional founder of the Darod clan-family, arrives from Arabia in northeastern Somalia.

ca. 12th century Sheikh Isaq, traditional founder of the Isaq clan-family, arrives from Arabia; buried near Mait on the Gulf of Aden.

217

1154   Al-Idrisi, Arab geographer at the court of Roger II of Sicily, mentions the city of Merka.

1217   Inscription on the tomb at Mogadishu of Abu Abdallah, a Persian from Naysabur.

1238   Date of inscription at the base of the minaret of the Friday Mosque in the Hamarweyn quarter of Mogadishu.

13th century   First written mention of a Somali group (the Hawiye, described as living near Merka) in an Arab source.

1332   Ibn Battuta, native of Tangier and great traveler, visits what he describes as the large and flourishing city of Mogadishu.

1427   An envoy from Mogadishu visits China. Three years later, a Chinese fleet visits Mogadishu and other sites on the East African coast. Several mentions of the city appear in Chinese records.

1499   Vasco da Gama, sent by the king of Portugal to open a sea route to India, passes the "large town" of Mogadishu but does not land.

1507   Tristao da Cunha, with four hundred Portuguese, attacks and burns the town of Brava.

1506–43   Ahmed Gran, Somali Muslim leader who attacks the Ethiopian empire.

1533   Stefano da Gama, son of Vasco da Gama, is the first European to come ashore at Mogadishu in perhaps a thousand years.

1798   Commander Blankett of the Royal Navy visits Mogadishu, which has "remarkable mosques, many fishing boats, and numbers of inhabitants."

1811   Captain Smee of the Royal Navy visits Mogadishu, a "not very considerable town" with four mosques and from 150 to 200 houses.

1822   The British conclude a treaty with Sultan Sayid of Muscat, who controls the Somali coast, to put down the Indian Ocean slave trade.

1828   The brig *Ann* of Salem, Massachusetts, Capt. Charles Millet, makes the first call by an American vessel at Somali ports, Merka and Brava.

1833   American negotiator Edmund Roberts signs Treaty of Amity and Commerce with Sultan Sayid of Muscat. The treaty is ratified by the United States in 1834.

1837   Richard Palmer Waters of Salem, the first American consul in East Africa, arrives in Zanzibar, Sultan Sayid's alternate capital.

1843   Sultan Sayid appoints a resident governor for Mogadishu.

1855   British explorer Richard Burton lands at Zeila from Aden, then travels inland to Harar. On his second trip to Somalia, Burton and companions are attacked at Berbera and abandon plans to travel south.

1865   A German, Baron von der Decken, steams up the Juba River in his vessel, *Welf,* and is killed near Bardera.

1869–70   Egypt occupies coastal points in northern Somalia.

1875   Col. Charles Chaille-Long, Maryland native in the service of the khedive of Egypt, leads expedition that occupies port of Kismayu and liberates more than five hundred slaves.

1884–86   The British reach agreements with northern Somali clans, leading to formation of the British Somaliland Protectorate.

1889   Leaders from Obbia and Alula accept an Italian protectorate; subsequently the influential Filonardi trading company is formed; in 1905, Italy formally establishes a colony.

1892   American explorer William Astor Chanler leads scientific expedition into unexplored regions between Tana (in present-day Kenya) and Juba (in present-day Somalia) Rivers.

1894–95   Philadelphia physician, sportsman, and biologist A. Donaldson Smith leads expedition across Somalia and southern Ethiopia, collecting previously unreported species of birds, reptiles, and insects.

1897   The British agree to give up to Ethiopia a British claim to sixty-seven thousand square miles of the Haud and Ogaden grasslands inhabited by Somali nomads.

1899   Sayid Mohamed Abdallah Hassan, known to the British as the "Mad Mullah," declares a holy war against the British and Ethiopians; never defeated, he dies in the Ogaden in 1920.

1925   The British cede Jubaland, in what is now southern Somalia, to the Italians. Italy sends a military expedition to the northeast to consolidate control; Somali armed resistance continues until 1927.

1934   An incident at Walwal between Ethiopian and Italian troops is seized upon by Mussolini as the pretext for the Italian invasion of Ethiopia, whose conquest is completed in 1936.

1940   Italy enters World War II and occupies British Somaliland.

1941   British forces from Kenya occupy Italian Somalia and retake British Somaliland, then occupy Italian-held Ethiopia.

1943   Formation of the Somali Youth Club, the first Somali political organization, in Mogadishu.

1948   The British hand over control of the Ogaden to Ethiopia.

1950   Italy receives a ten-year trusteeship mandate from the United Nations to prepare its former colony for independence.

1954   The United States and Italy sign Technical Cooperation Agreement for Somalia, creating $1.2 million development fund.

1957   The United States opens a consulate at Mogadishu, later raised to consulate general.

1960   The Italian Trust Territory and British Somaliland become independent and form a united democratic republic. The American consulate general at Mogadishu becomes an embassy.

1962   Prime Minister Abdirashid Ali Shermarke visits Washington and is rebuffed by John Kennedy on military aid. In 1963 Shermarke visits Moscow, where Nikita Khrushchev offers weapons, training, and advisers.

1968   Prime Minister Mohamed Ibrahim Egal meets with President Lyndon Johnson in Washington.

1969   Assassination of President Shermarke, overthrow of Egal's government, and formation of a revolutionary government headed by armed forces commander Mohamed Siad Barre. U.S. Peace Corps volunteers are asked to leave Somalia; several American embassy officers are expelled on fabricated espionage charges.

1970   The United States cuts off assistance to Somalia, as required by legislation, because Somali-flag vessels had traded with North Vietnam.

1970s   "Scientific socialism" and a heavy Soviet presence in Somalia. In 1974 Somalia becomes first black African state to sign a treaty of peace and friendship with Moscow.

1974   Ethiopian emperor Haile Selassie is overthrown by radical officers headed by Mengistu Haile Mariam.

1977–78 The Somalis invade Ethiopia and are defeated by Soviet-led Ethiopian and Cuban forces. Siad Barre expels all Soviet advisers and turns to the United States for help. Hundreds of thousands of ethnic Somali refugees stream out of Ethiopia into Somalia.

1980   The United States and Somalia agree on U.S. access to military and naval facilities in Somalia in return for military and economic aid.

1982   Ethiopian troops and Somali dissidents trained in Ethiopia launch attacks along Somali border, occupying two salients of Somali territory.

1984–85 Major drought and famine in the Horn of Africa.

1988   After several years of small-scale actions against Siad Barre by Isaq clans in northern Somalia, the conflict escalates toward civil war.

1989   The United States halts weapons deliveries as a result of Siad Barre's brutal actions against the Isaqs.

1990   Manifesto signed by 144 Somali leaders calls for Siad Barre to reform or step down. Fighting spreads to Mogadishu.

1991   Staffs of the American and other foreign embassies and foreign aid workers are evacuated from Mogadishu on January 5. Siad Barre flees Mogadishu on January 27. The Isaqs declare a separate Somaliland Republic on May 17. Business leader Ali Mahdi and Gen. Mohamed Farah Aydid, leaders of Hawiye clan groups, emerge as rival "warlords" in Mogadishu.

1992   The United Nations Security Council on April 24 authorizes a UN operation in Somalia (UNOSOM I) to include fifty unarmed observers. In August the United States begins a food airlift (Operation Provide Relief) after strife produces mass starvation. In December the UN

Security Council endorses the U.S. plan for Operation Restore Hope, involving major military operations to protect relief efforts. U.S. Marines land in Mogadishu December 8, followed by ten thousand troops of other nations as part of UN-authorized UNITAF.

1993　Somali groups sign an agreement, subsequently breached, on a cease-fire and national reconciliation. On March 26 the UN Security Council replaces UNITAF with a new peacekeeping force, UNOSOM II, to provide security in Somalia and promote political rebirth. Increasing American casualties raise congressional concerns. In June UN special representative (and retired U.S. admiral) Jonathan Howe calls for Aydid's arrest. In July U.S. helicopter gunships reportedly kill dozens of Somali elders; pro-Aydid and antiforeign sentiment increases.

1994　Withdrawal of the last U.S. forces. The UN Security Council decides that all UNOSOM II forces will be withdrawn by March 1995.

1995　Mohamed Siad Barre dies in exile in Nigeria on January 2.

1995–99　Life and death continue in Somalia, with a minimal foreign presence. No central government exists at Mogadishu, and strife continues despite new efforts toward reconciliation. In the north, the Somaliland Republic, initially administered by Mohamed Ibrahim Egal, continues in existence, unrecognized by other governments. In the northeast, administered by Mohamed Abshir Musse, trade with the Gulf states revives and brings a degree of prosperity. Later, in November 1998, northeastern regions declare themselves the Puntland State of Somalia.

bibliography

Manuscript Collections

Presidential Papers, Lyndon Baines Johnson. Lyndon Baines Johnson Library, Austin, Texas.

William A. Wilson Papers. Georgetown University Library, Washington, D.C.

Books and Articles

Abdalla, Raqiya Haji Dualeh. *Sisters in Affliction*. London: Zed Press, 1982.

Achtner, Wolfgang. "The Italian Connection: How Rome Helped Ruin Somalia." *Washington Post*, January 24, 1993.

Albright, Madeleine K. "U.S. Policy toward Africa." Address at George Mason University, March 19, 1998. Washington, D.C.: Office of the Spokesman, U.S. Department of State [1998].

Amalrik, Andrei. *Involuntary Journey to Siberia*. Trans. Manya Harari and Max Hayward. New York: Harcourt Brace Jovanovich, 1970.

———. *Will the Soviet Union Survive until 1984?* Ed. Hilary Sternberg. New York: Penguin, 1980.

Baldwin, David A. *Foreign Aid and American Foreign Policy*. New York: Frederick A. Praeger, 1966.

Barnes, Virginia Lee, and Janice Boddy. *Aman: The Story of a Somali Girl*. New York: Pantheon, 1994.

Benson, Jackson J. *The True Adventures of John Steinbeck, Writer*. New York: Penguin, 1990.

Bishop, James K. "Escape from Mogadishu, 1991." *Embassies under Siege*. Ed. Joseph G. Sullivan. Washington, D.C.: Brassey's, 1995.

Boffa, Giuseppe. *Memorie dal Comunismo*. Milano: Ponte alle Grazie srl, 1998.

Bolton, John. "Wrong Turn in Somalia." *Foreign Affairs* 73:1 (January–February 1994).

Bridges, Peter. "AIDS Now Worst Threat to Africa." *Los Angeles Times*, August 30, 1987.

223

———. "America's Hazy View of the World at Large." *Los Angeles Times*, March 29, 1987.

———. "Disentangling the U.S. Foreign-Affairs Mess." *Christian Science Monitor*, November 3, 1987.

———. "Ethiopia, Somalia: More Famine and Fighting at a Horn of Unplenty." *Los Angeles Times*, April 3, 1988.

———. "May Days in Siberia." *Tales of the Foreign Service*, ed. Ralph Hilton. Columbia, S.C.: University of South Carolina Press, 1978.

———. "On the Isthmus: A Young American at the Panama Embassy, 1959–61." *Diplomacy and Statecraft* 9:2 (July 1998).

———, Joel Barlow, pseud. "On Managing American Diplomacy." *Foreign Service Journal* 58.2 (February 1981).

———. "Prince Albert and King Lothar." *The Virginia Quarterly Review* 73:3 (Summer 1997).

———. "Safirka: The Envoy in Somalia." *Michigan Quarterly Review* 37:1 (Winter 1998).

———. "Triumphant Failure." *Dartmouth Alumni Magazine* (October 1980).

———. "U.S. Foreign Service Suffers from Politics." *Los Angeles Times*, November 30, 1986.

Brzezinski, Zbigniew. *Power and Principle*. New York: Farrar, Straus, Giroux, 1983.

Buckley, Stephen. "Boosaaso: A Somali City Thrives without Aid." *Washington Post*, March 3, 1996.

Burton, Richard F. *First Footsteps in East Africa*. 1894. Reprint; New York: Dover, 1987.

Cassanelli, Lee V. "Society and Culture in the Riverine Culture of Southern Somalia." *Somalia in Word and Image*. Ed. Katheryne S. Loughran. Washington, D.C.: Foundation for Cross Cultural Understanding, 1986.

Cerulli, Enrico. *Somalia: Scritti vari editi ed inediti*. Roma: Istituto Poligrafico dello Stato, 1957.

Chanler, William Astor. *Through Jungle and Desert: Travels in Eastern Africa*. New York: Macmillan, 1896.

Chittick, Neville. "An Archaeological Reconnaissance in the Horn." *Azania* 11 (1976).

———. "Medieval Mogadishu." *Paideuma* 28 (1982).

Commission on the Organization of the Government for the Conduct of Foreign Policy. 8 vols. [Murphy Commission report.] Washington, D.C.: U.S. Government Printing Office, 1975–76.

Del Boca, Angelo. *La trappola somala*. Roma: Laterza, 1994.

Diamond, Jared. *Guns, Germs, and Steel*. New York: W. W. Norton, 1997.

Dickey, Christopher. "A Land Called Slaughter." *Rolling Stone*, October 4, 1990.

Dinesen, Isak. "The Dreamers." *Seven Gothic Tales*. New York: Vintage, 1972.

Dobrynin, Anatoly. *In Confidence*. New York: Times Books, 1995.

Elmi, Abdullahi Sheikh. "Khat Consumption in Somalia." *Proceedings of the First International Congress of Somali Studies.* Ed. Hussein M. Adam and Charles L. Geshekter. Atlanta: Scholars Press, 1992.

Erlich, Alexander, and Christian R. Sonne. "The Soviet Union: Economic Activity." *Africa and the Communist World.* Ed. Zbigniew Brzezinski. Stanford, Calif.: Stanford University Press, 1967.

"Flooding Spreads across East Africa." BBC News bulletin, 16:40 GMT, December 10, 1997.

Gabriel, Erhard F., Martin Florin, and Peter Conze. *Afrika Transparent.* Baden-Baden: Nomos Verlagsgesellschaft, 1990.

Geshekter, Charles L., and Said Ahmed Warsama. "An Introduction to Humour and Jokes in Somali Culture." *Voice and Power: The Culture of Language in North-East Africa.* Ed. R. J. Hayward and I. M. Lewis. London: School of Oriental and African Studies, University of London, 1996.

Ginzburg, Evgenia Semionovna. *Viaggio nella vertigine.* Trans. Aldino Betti. Milano: Arnoldo Mondadori Editore, 1967.

Guida dell'Africa Orientale Italiana. Milano: Consociazione Turistica Italiana, 1938.

Guida d'Italia: Possedimenti e Colonie. Milano: Touring Club Italiano, 1929.

Hemming, C. F. "The Vegetation of the Northern Region of the Somaliland Republic." *Proceedings of the Linnean Society of London* 177:2 (July 1966).

"Highlights in U.S.-Somali Relations." *Historical Research Memorandum No. 1448.* Washington, D.C.: Office of the Historian, U.S. Department of State, June 1985.

Hirsch, John L., and Robert B. Oakley. *Somalia and Operation Restore Hope.* Washington, D.C.: United States Institute of Peace Press, 1995.

Hunt, John A. *A General Survey of the Somaliland Protectorate, 1944–1950.* London: Crown Agents for the Colonies, 1951.

Huntingford, G. W. B., ed. *The Periplus of the Erythraean Sea.* London: The Hakluyt Society, 1980.

James, George. "Somalia's Overthrown Dictator, Mohamed Siad Barre, Is Dead." *New York Times,* January 3, 1995.

Korn, David. *Ethiopia, the United States, and the Soviet Union.* Carbondale: Southern Illinois University Press, 1986.

Laitin, David D., and Said S. Samatar. *Somalia: Nation in Search of a State.* Boulder, Colo.: Westview Press, 1987.

Lamberti, Marcello. "Proverbs in Somali Society and Literature." *Proceedings of the First International Congress of Somali Studies.* Ed. Hussein M. Adam and Charles L. Geshekter. Atlanta: Scholars Press, 1992.

Lewis, Ioan [I. M.]. "In the Land of the Living Dead." *London Sunday Times,* August 30, 1992.

———. *Somali Culture, History and Social Institutions.* London: London School of Economics and Political Science, 1981.

Lewis, William H. *Beyond Constructive Engagement*. New York: Paragon House, 1986.

Licata, Glauco. "E finalmente tutti si sentirono somali." *Corriere della Sera*, June 11, 1985.

Luling, Virginia. "Festive Violence: The Stick-Fight of Afgoy-Geledi in Context." *Proceedings of the First International Congress of Somali Studies*. Ed. Hussein M. Adam and Charles L. Geshekter. Atlanta: Scholars Press, 1992.

"Making Aid Work." *The Economist*, November 14, 1998.

Matatu, Godfrey. "South Africa's Hand in Somalia." *The Observer*, April 28, 1985.

Meade, Robert C., Jr. *Red Brigades: The Story of Italian Terrorism*. New York: St. Martin's, 1990.

Metz, Helen Chaplin, ed. *Somalia: A Country Study*. Washington, D.C.: Federal Research Division, Library of Congress, 1993.

Miller, John. "Greetings, America, My Name Is Osama bin Laden." *Esquire*, February 1999.

Orlova, Raisa. *Memoirs*. Trans. Samuel Cioran. New York: Random House, 1983.

Pallabazzer, Rodolfo, and Abdulkadir A. Gabow. "Wind Resources of Somalia." *Solar Energy* 46:5 (1991).

Potholm, Christian P. *Four African Political Systems*. Englewood Cliffs, N.J.: Prentice-Hall, 1970.

Rawson, David. *The Somali State and Foreign Aid*. Washington, D.C.: Foreign Service Institute, U.S. Department of State, 1993.

Samatar, Abdi Ismail. *The State and Rural Transformation in Northern Somalia, 1884–1986*. Madison: University of Wisconsin Press, 1989.

Sheik-Abdi, Abdi. *Divine Madness*. London: Zed Books, 1993.

Sheikh, Mohamed Aden. *Arrivederci a Mogadiscio*. Roma: Edizioni Associate, 1991.

Shultz, George P. *Turmoil and Triumph*. New York: Scribner's, 1993.

Sica, Mario. *Operazione Somalia*. Venezia: Marsili Editori, 1994.

Simmons, Ann M. "A Somali Alternative to Chaos." *Los Angeles Times*, July 9, 1997.

Simpson, Christopher. *National Security Directives of the Reagan and Bush Administrations*. Boulder, Colo.: Westview Press, 1995.

Smith, A. Donaldson. *Through Unknown African Countries: The First Expedition from Somaliland to Lake Lamu*. London: Edward A. Arnold, 1897.

Spain, James W. *In Those Days: A Diplomat Remembers*. Kent, Ohio: Kent State University Press, 1998.

Tenderini, Mirella, and Michael Shandrick. *The Duke of the Abruzzi*. Seattle: The Mountaineers, 1997.

Tyler, W. T. *The Lion and the Jackal*. New York: Linden Press/Simon and Schuster, 1988.

USIA/USIS Newswire No. 99, February 24, 1988. Washington, D.C.: Office of Public Liaison, United States Information Agency.

Vance, Cyrus. *Hard Choices*. New York: Simon and Schuster, 1983.

Internet Sources

"Africa Policy Outlook 1999." Africa Policy Information Center, Washington, D.C.
http://www.africapolicy.org/docs99/afp099.htm

News Release, Development Assistance Committee, Organization for Economic
Cooperation and Development, Paris, June 18, 1998. http://www.oecd.org/dac

Soviet and East German Official Messages, 1977–78. National Security Archive,
Gelman Library, George Washington University, Washington, D.C. http://
www.seas.gwu.edu/nsarchive/CWIHP/BULLETINS/68-9a9.htm

index